# Garfield makes it big

BY: JIM DAVIS

BALLANTINE BOOKS · NEW YORK

Published in the United States by Ballantine Books, a division of Random House, Inc., New York, and simultaneously in Canada by Random House of Canada Limited, Toronto.

Library of Congress Catalog Card Number: 84-91658
ISBN 0-345-31928-1

Manufactured in the United States of America

First Edition: March 1985

30 29 28

# NEWS FLASH!
# Jim Davis a Fraud!

The Big Cheese, The Head Honcho, The Chief Muckamuck...

Teddy bear Pooky recently revealed that Jim Davis did not create the Garfield comic strip. Garfield himself writes and draws the world–famous cartoon. Garfield has been sitting at a drawing board for the last six years as Davis has gained notoriety through national television and print. Davis was not available for comment, but Garfield was. "The way I figured it, who would ever believe a cat could do a comic strip. So, I hired this down–and–out, hack cartoonist to take the credit for it. Sure ... he looked good and said all the right things, but it's time the truth was known."

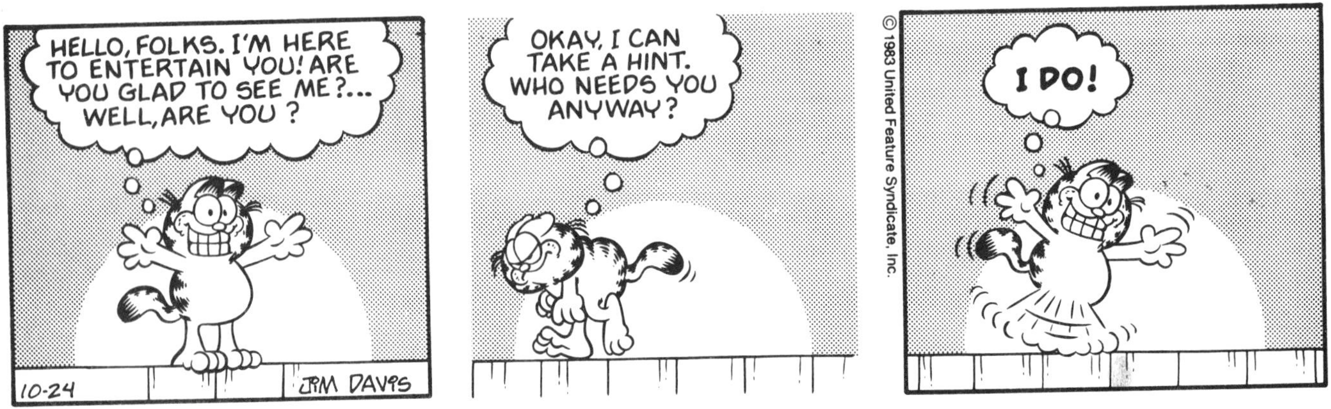
HELLO, FOLKS. I'M HERE TO ENTERTAIN YOU! ARE YOU GLAD TO SEE ME?... WELL, ARE YOU ?
10-24
JIM DAVIS
OKAY, I CAN TAKE A HINT. WHO NEEDS YOU ANYWAY?
© 1983 United Feature Syndicate, Inc.
I DO!

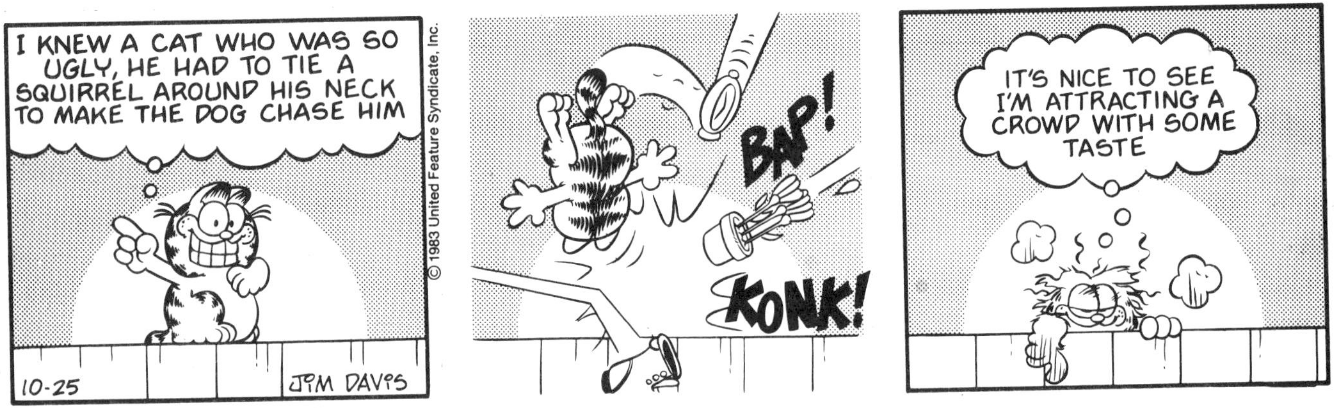
I KNEW A CAT WHO WAS SO UGLY, HE HAD TO TIE A SQUIRREL AROUND HIS NECK TO MAKE THE DOG CHASE HIM
10-25
JIM DAVIS
© 1983 United Feature Syndicate, Inc.
BAP!
KONK!
IT'S NICE TO SEE I'M ATTRACTING A CROWD WITH SOME TASTE

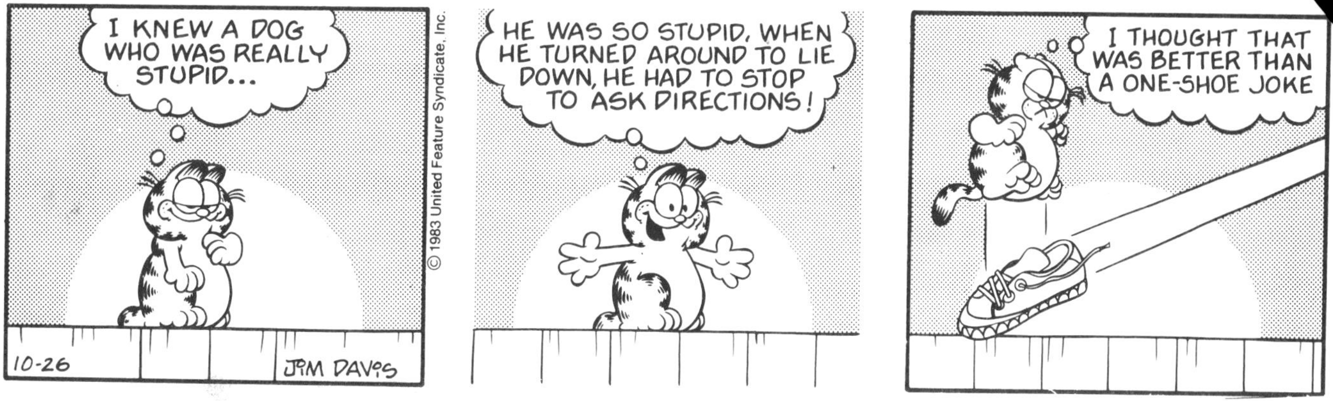
I KNEW A DOG WHO WAS REALLY STUPID...
10-26
JIM DAVIS
© 1983 United Feature Syndicate, Inc.
HE WAS SO STUPID, WHEN HE TURNED AROUND TO LIE DOWN, HE HAD TO STOP TO ASK DIRECTIONS!
I THOUGHT THAT WAS BETTER THAN A ONE-SHOE JOKE

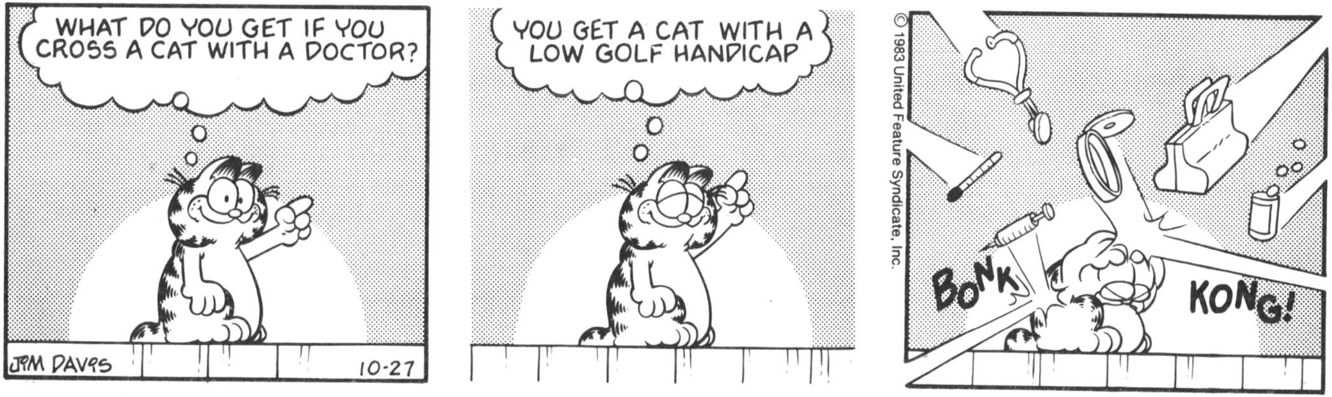
WHAT DO YOU GET IF YOU CROSS A CAT WITH A DOCTOR?
JIM DAVIS
10-27
YOU GET A CAT WITH A LOW GOLF HANDICAP
© 1983 United Feature Syndicate, Inc.
BONK
KONG!

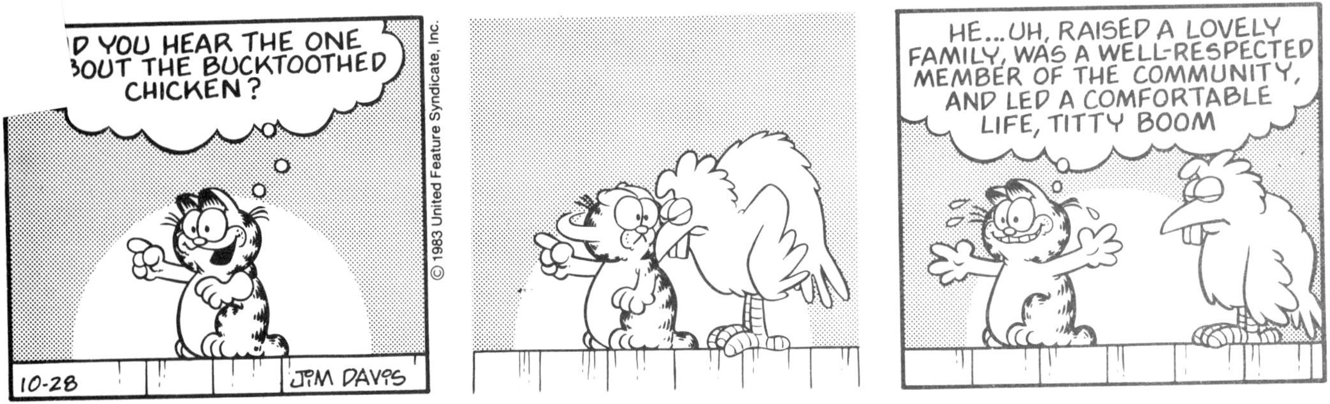
D YOU HEAR THE ONE
BOUT THE BUCKTOOTHED
CHICKEN?
10-28
JIM DAVIS
© 1983 United Feature Syndicate, Inc.
HE...UH, RAISED A LOVELY FAMILY, WAS A WELL-RESPECTED MEMBER OF THE COMMUNITY, AND LED A COMFORTABLE LIFE, TITTY BOOM

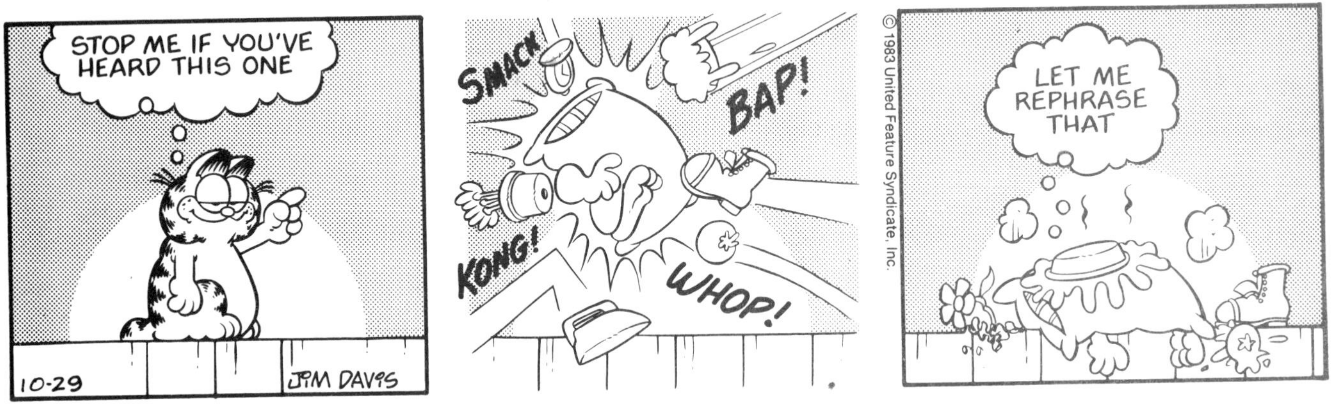
STOP ME IF YOU'VE HEARD THIS ONE
10-29
JIM DAVIS
SMACK
BAP!
KONG!
WHOP!
© 1983 United Feature Syndicate, Inc.
LET ME REPHRASE THAT

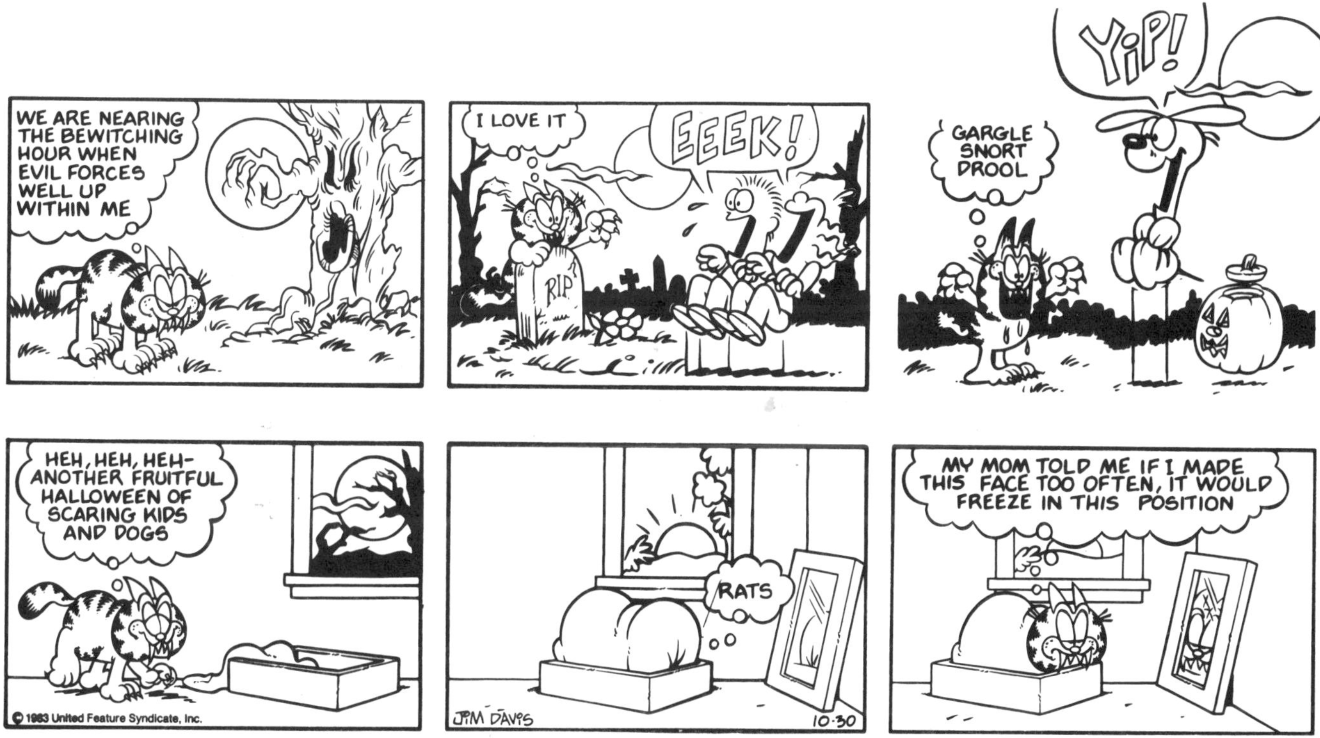
WE ARE NEARING THE BEWITCHING HOUR WHEN EVIL FORCES WELL UP WITHIN ME
I LOVE IT
EEEK!
GARGLE SNORT DROOL
YIP!
HEH, HEH, HEH- ANOTHER FRUITFUL HALLOWEEN OF SCARING KIDS AND DOGS
RATS
MY MOM TOLD ME IF I MADE THIS FACE TOO OFTEN, IT WOULD FREEZE IN THIS POSITION
© 1983 United Feature Syndicate, Inc.
JIM DAVIS
10-30

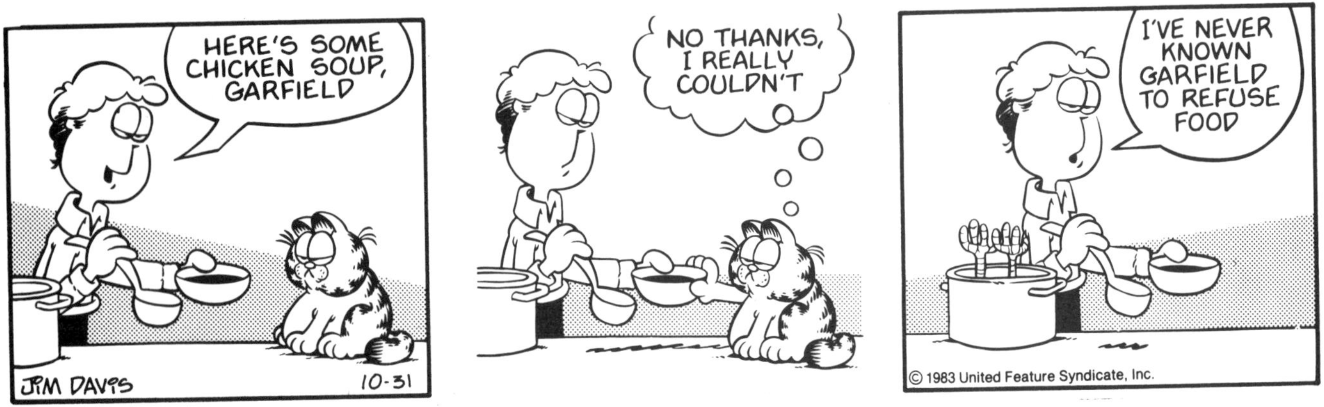
HERE'S SOME CHICKEN SOUP, GARFIELD
JIM DAVIS
10-31
NO THANKS, I REALLY COULDN'T
I'VE NEVER KNOWN GARFIELD TO REFUSE FOOD
© 1983 United Feature Syndicate, Inc.

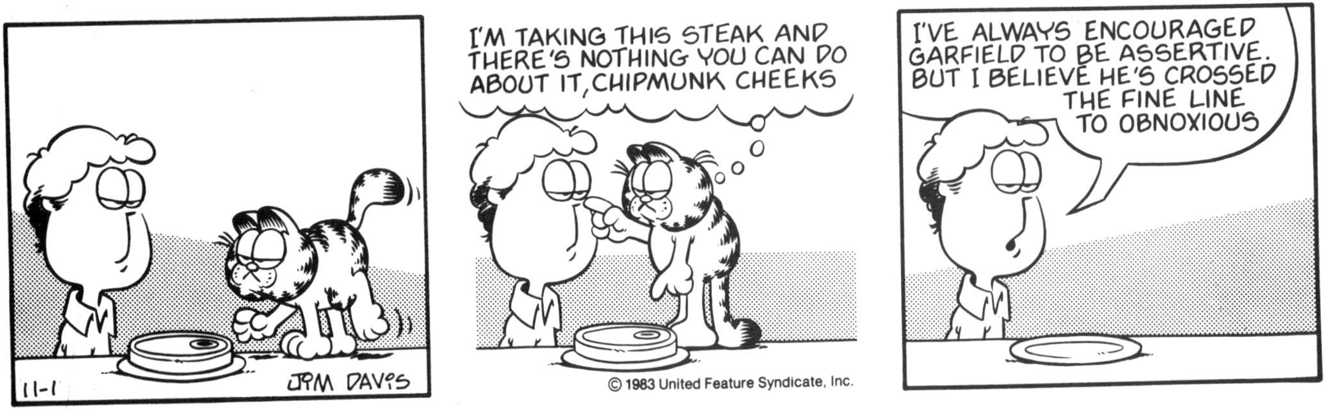
11-1
JIM DAVIS
I'M TAKING THIS STEAK AND THERE'S NOTHING YOU CAN DO ABOUT IT, CHIPMUNK CHEEKS
© 1983 United Feature Syndicate, Inc.
I'VE ALWAYS ENCOURAGED GARFIELD TO BE ASSERTIVE. BUT I BELIEVE HE'S CROSSED THE FINE LINE TO OBNOXIOUS

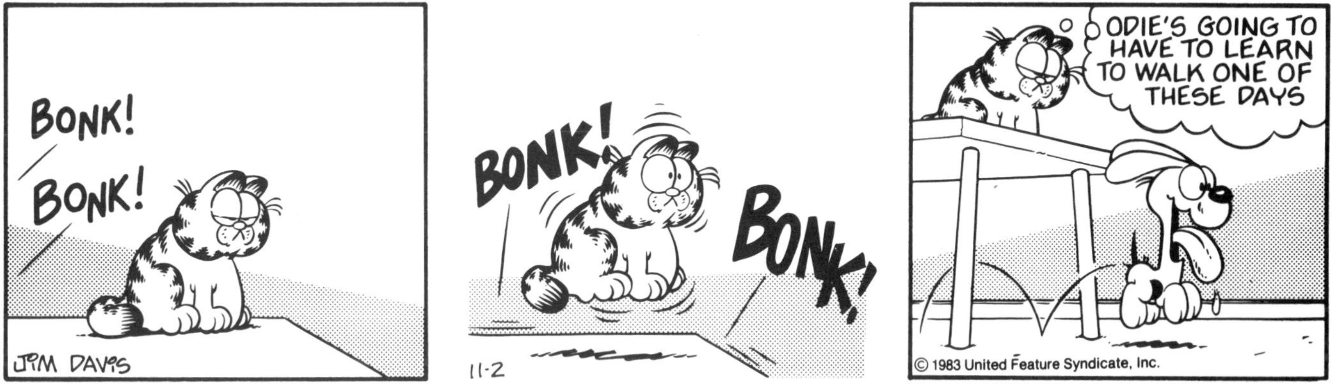
BONK!
BONK!
JIM DAVIS
BONK!
BONK!
11-2
ODIE'S GOING TO HAVE TO LEARN TO WALK ONE OF THESE DAYS
© 1983 United Feature Syndicate, Inc.

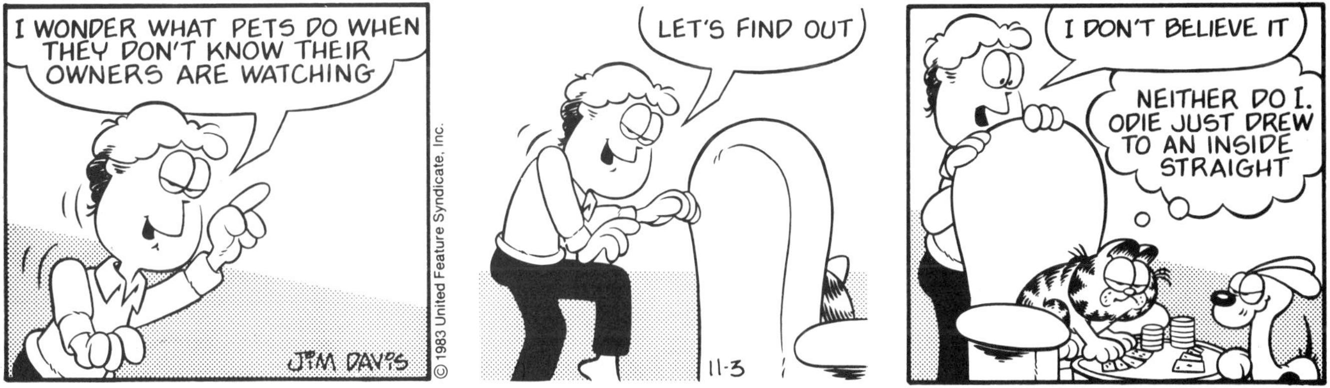
I WONDER WHAT PETS DO WHEN THEY DON'T KNOW THEIR OWNERS ARE WATCHING
JIM DAVIS
© 1983 United Feature Syndicate, Inc.
LET'S FIND OUT
11-3
I DON'T BELIEVE IT
NEITHER DO I. ODIE JUST DREW TO AN INSIDE STRAIGHT

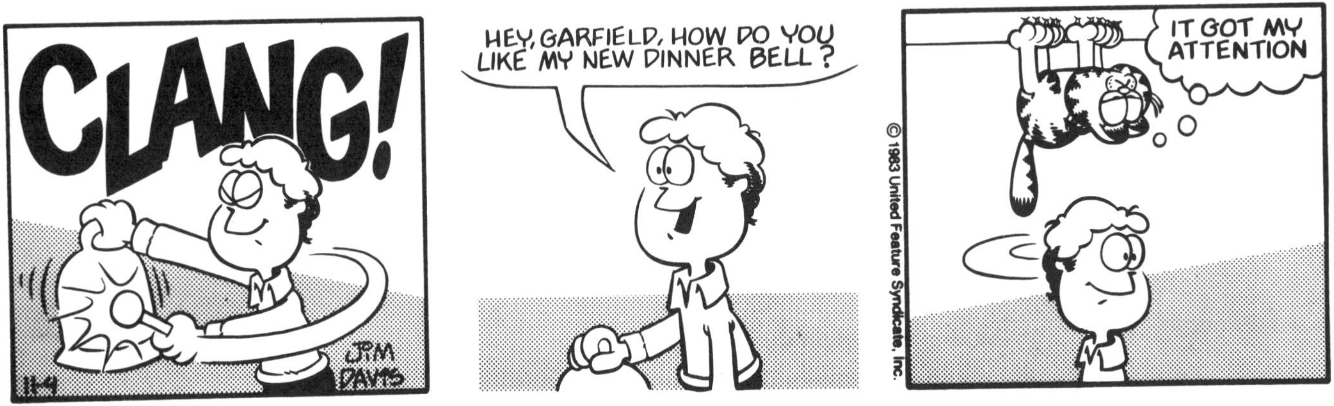
CLANG!
11-4
JIM DAVIS
HEY, GARFIELD, HOW DO YOU LIKE MY NEW DINNER BELL?
© 1983 United Feature Syndicate, Inc.
IT GOT MY ATTENTION

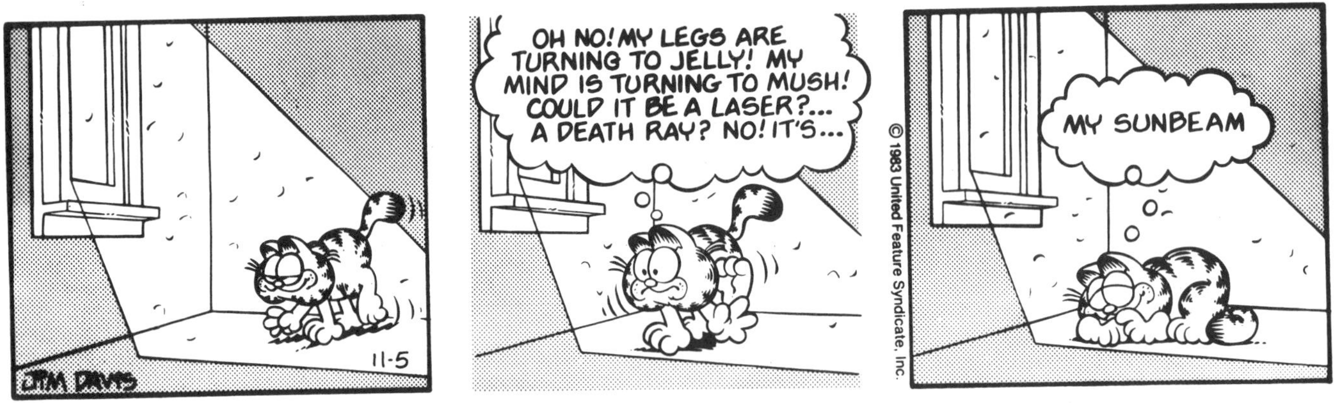
11-5
JIM DAVIS
OH NO! MY LEGS ARE TURNING TO JELLY! MY MIND IS TURNING TO MUSH! COULD IT BE A LASER?... A DEATH RAY? NO! IT'S...
© 1983 United Feature Syndicate, Inc.
MY SUNBEAM

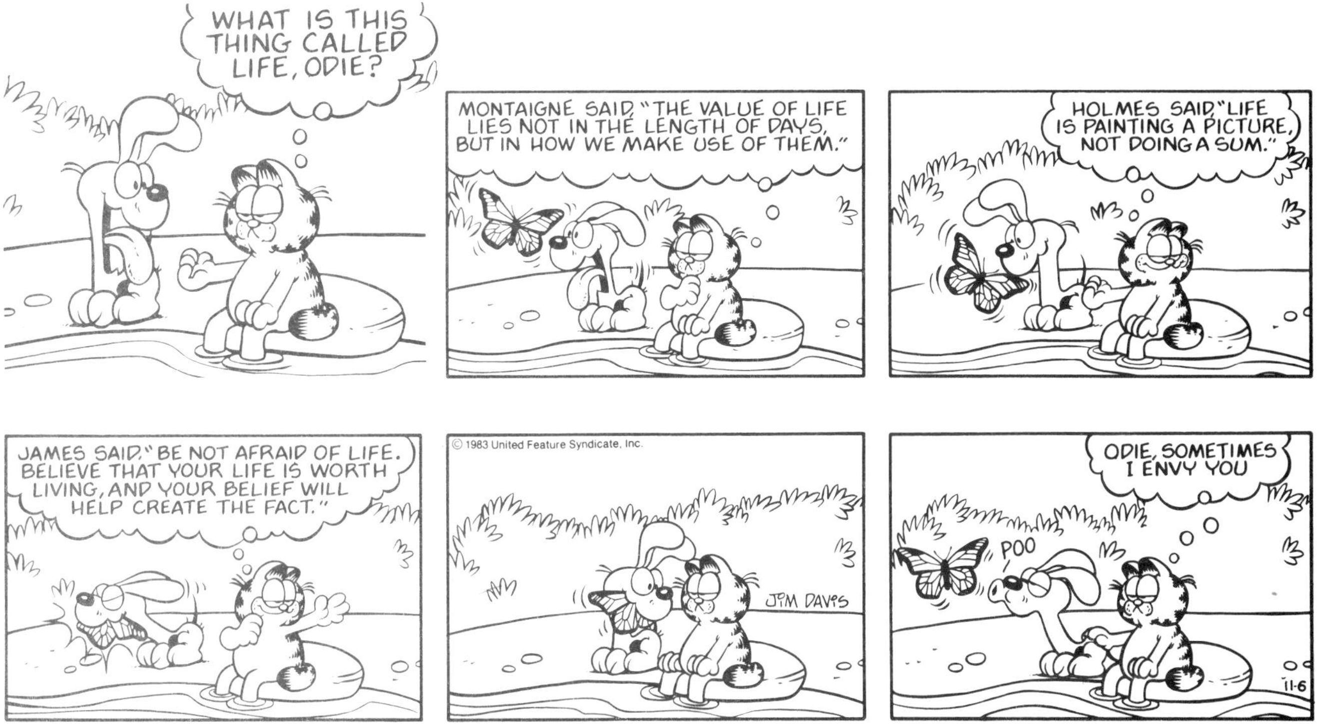
WHAT IS THIS THING CALLED LIFE, ODIE?
MONTAIGNE SAID, "THE VALUE OF LIFE LIES NOT IN THE LENGTH OF DAYS, BUT IN HOW WE MAKE USE OF THEM."
HOLMES SAID, "LIFE IS PAINTING A PICTURE, NOT DOING A SUM."
JAMES SAID, "BE NOT AFRAID OF LIFE. BELIEVE THAT YOUR LIFE IS WORTH LIVING, AND YOUR BELIEF WILL HELP CREATE THE FACT."
© 1983 United Feature Syndicate, Inc.
JIM DAVIS
POO
ODIE, SOMETIMES I ENVY YOU
11-6

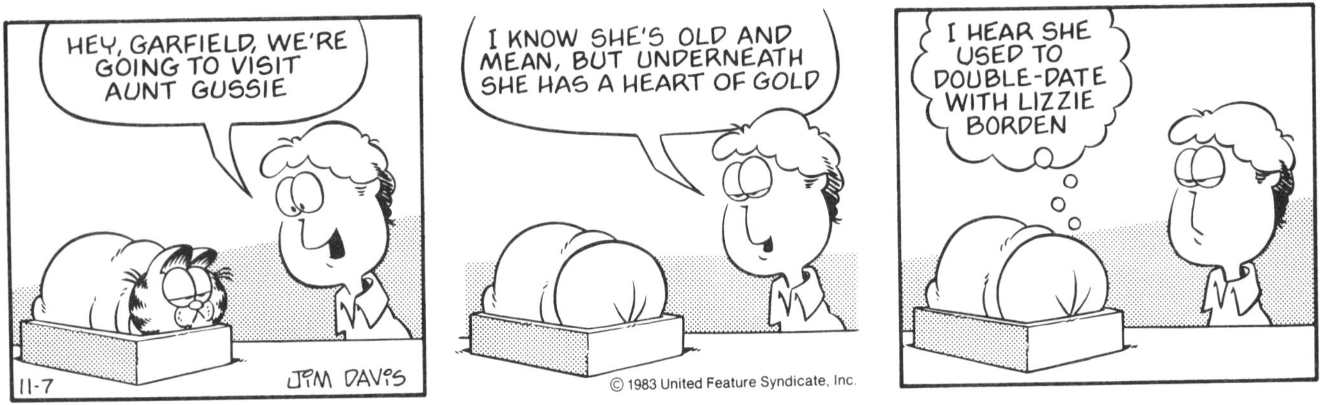
HEY, GARFIELD, WE'RE GOING TO VISIT AUNT GUSSIE
I KNOW SHE'S OLD AND MEAN, BUT UNDERNEATH SHE HAS A HEART OF GOLD
I HEAR SHE USED TO DOUBLE-DATE WITH LIZZIE BORDEN
11-7
JIM DAVIS
© 1983 United Feature Syndicate, Inc.

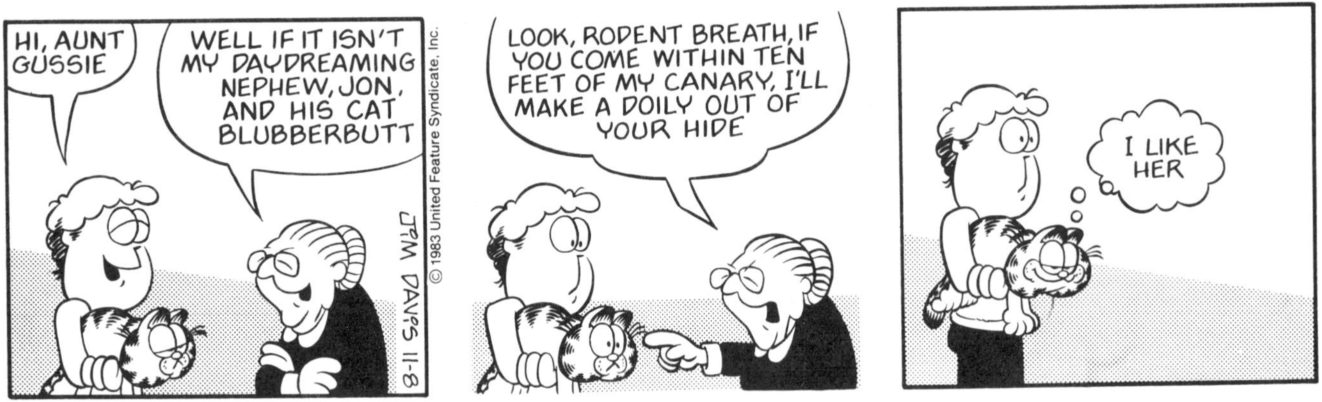
HI, AUNT GUSSIE
WELL IF IT ISN'T MY DAYDREAMING NEPHEW, JON, AND HIS CAT BLUBBERBUTT
LOOK, RODENT BREATH, IF YOU COME WITHIN TEN FEET OF MY CANARY, I'LL MAKE A DOILY OUT OF YOUR HIDE
I LIKE HER
JIM DAVIS 11-8
© 1983 United Feature Syndicate, Inc.

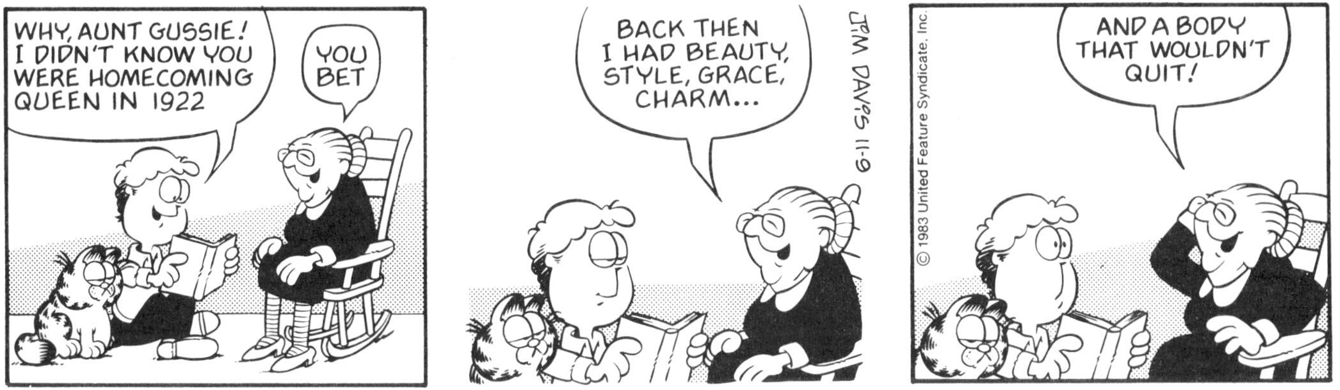
WHY, AUNT GUSSIE! I DIDN'T KNOW YOU WERE HOMECOMING QUEEN IN 1922
YOU BET
BACK THEN I HAD BEAUTY, STYLE, GRACE, CHARM...
JIM DAVIS 11-9
© 1983 United Feature Syndicate, Inc.
AND A BODY THAT WOULDN'T QUIT!

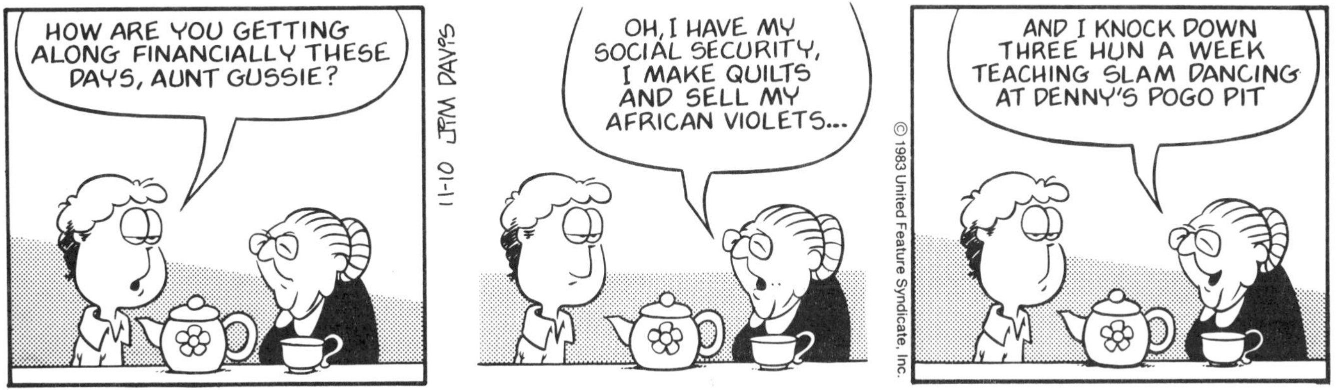
HOW ARE YOU GETTING ALONG FINANCIALLY THESE DAYS, AUNT GUSSIE?
JIM DAVIS 11-10
OH, I HAVE MY SOCIAL SECURITY, I MAKE QUILTS AND SELL MY AFRICAN VIOLETS...
© 1983 United Feature Syndicate, Inc.
AND I KNOCK DOWN THREE HUN A WEEK TEACHING SLAM DANCING AT DENNY'S POGO PIT

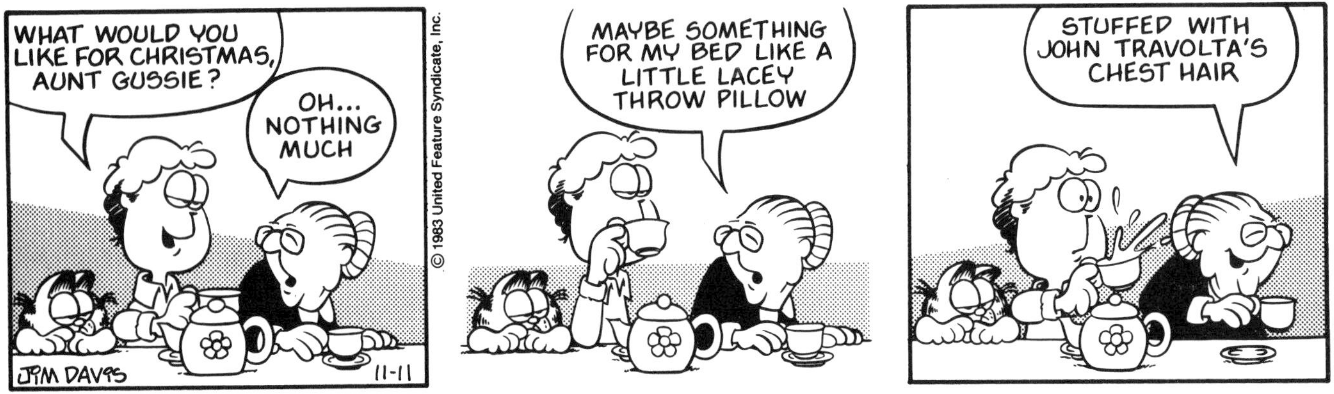
WHAT WOULD YOU LIKE FOR CHRISTMAS, AUNT GUSSIE?
OH... NOTHING MUCH
JIM DAVIS
11-11
© 1983 United Feature Syndicate, Inc.
MAYBE SOMETHING FOR MY BED LIKE A LITTLE LACEY THROW PILLOW
STUFFED WITH JOHN TRAVOLTA'S CHEST HAIR

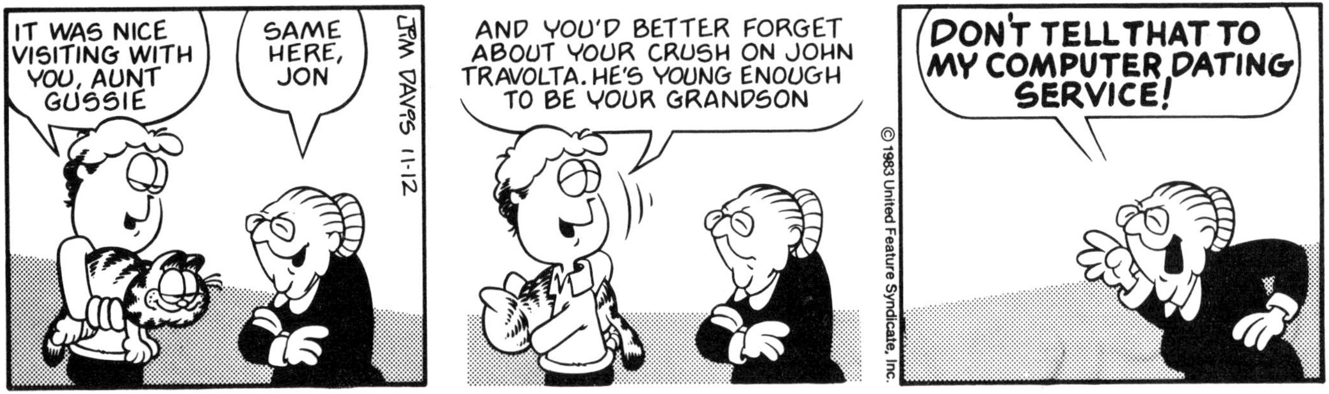
IT WAS NICE VISITING WITH YOU, AUNT GUSSIE
SAME HERE, JON
JIM DAVIS 11-12
AND YOU'D BETTER FORGET ABOUT YOUR CRUSH ON JOHN TRAVOLTA. HE'S YOUNG ENOUGH TO BE YOUR GRANDSON
© 1983 United Feature Syndicate, Inc.
DON'T TELL THAT TO MY COMPUTER DATING SERVICE!

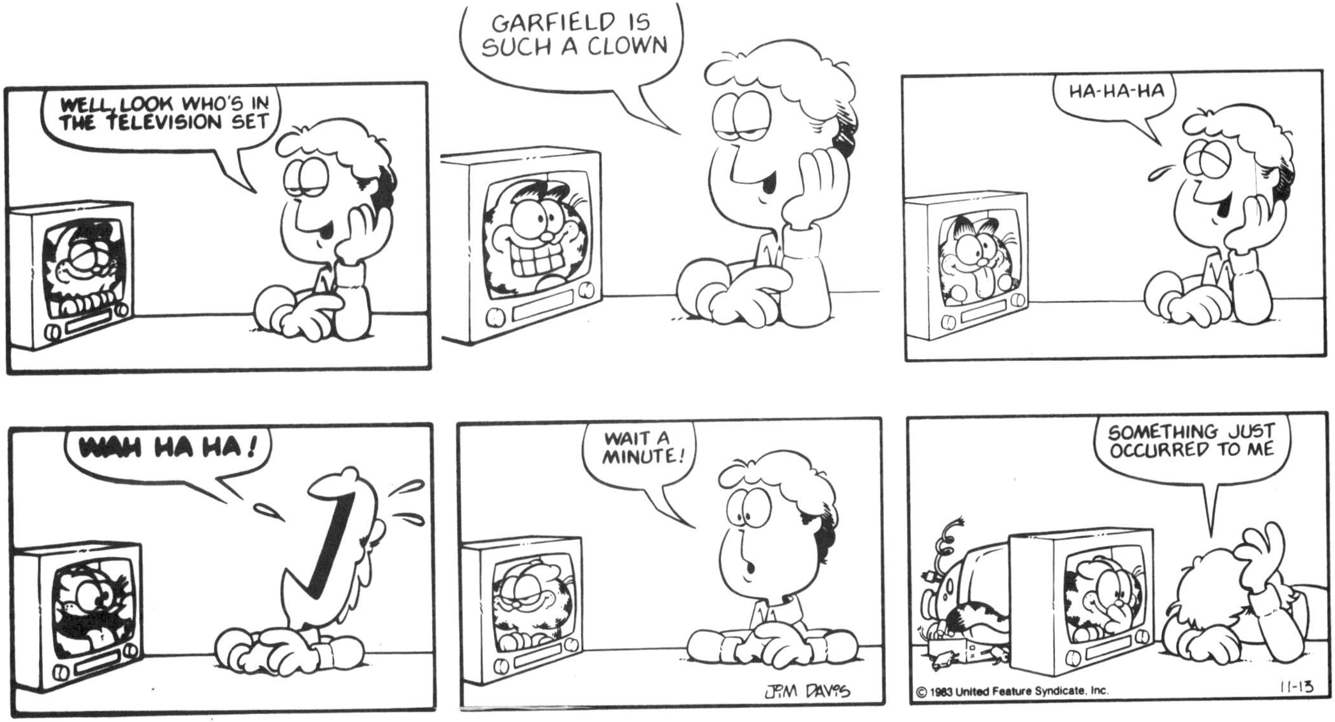
WELL, LOOK WHO'S IN THE TELEVISION SET
GARFIELD IS SUCH A CLOWN
HA-HA-HA
WAH HA HA!
WAIT A MINUTE!
JPM DAVPS
SOMETHING JUST OCCURRED TO ME
© 1983 United Feature Syndicate, Inc.
11-13

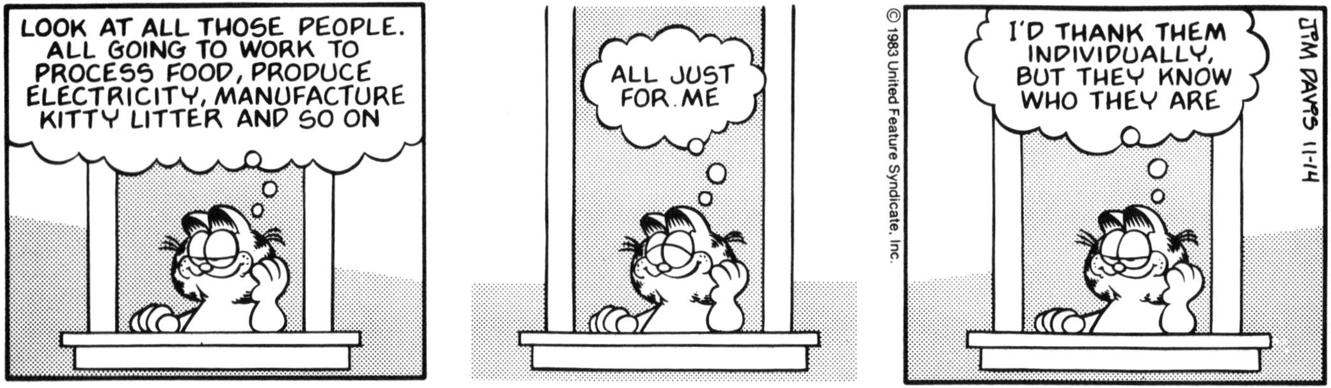
LOOK AT ALL THOSE PEOPLE. ALL GOING TO WORK TO PROCESS FOOD, PRODUCE ELECTRICITY, MANUFACTURE KITTY LITTER AND SO ON
ALL JUST FOR ME
© 1983 United Feature Syndicate, Inc.
I'D THANK THEM INDIVIDUALLY, BUT THEY KNOW WHO THEY ARE
JIM DAVIS 11-14

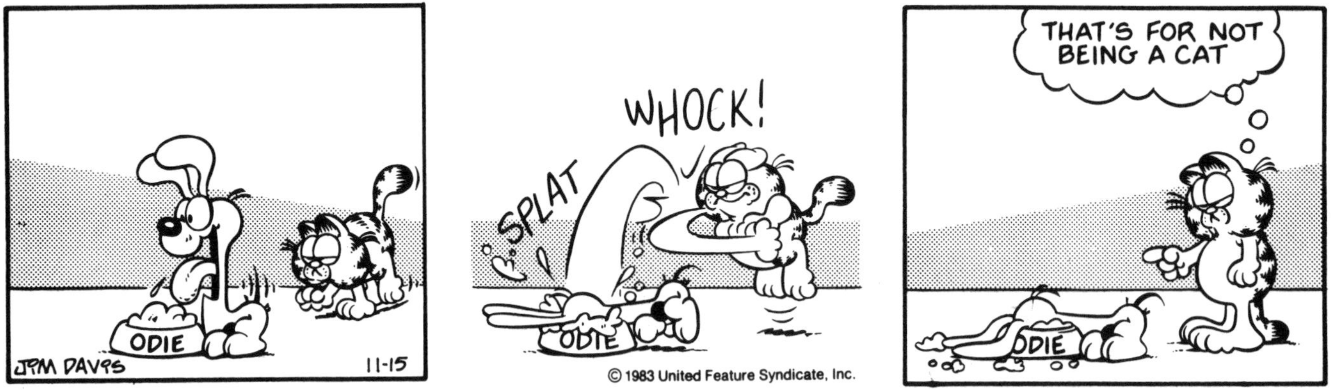
ODIE
JIM DAVIS
11-15
WHOCK!
SPLAT
ODIE
© 1983 United Feature Syndicate, Inc.
THAT'S FOR NOT BEING A CAT
ODIE

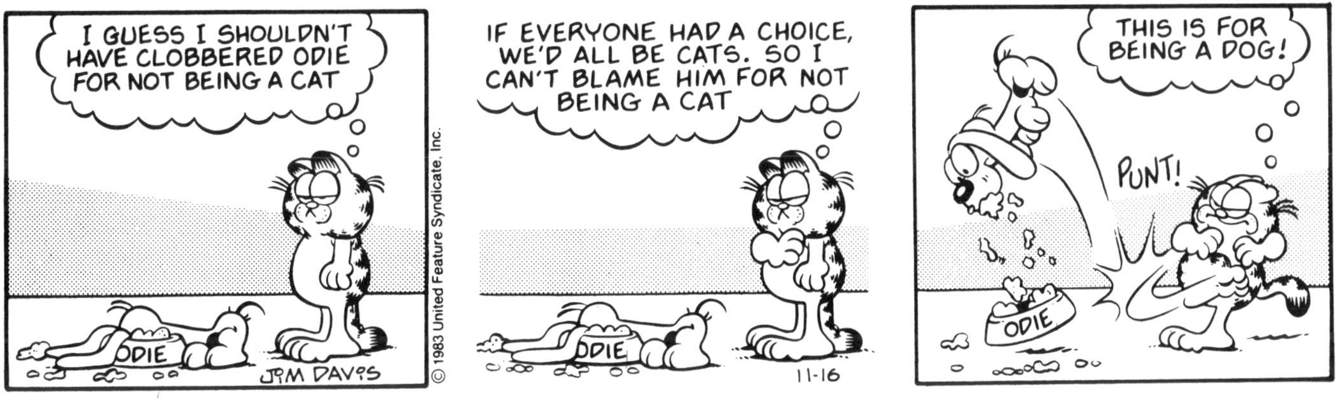
I GUESS I SHOULDN'T HAVE CLOBBERED ODIE FOR NOT BEING A CAT
ODIE
JIM DAVIS
IF EVERYONE HAD A CHOICE, WE'D ALL BE CATS. SO I CAN'T BLAME HIM FOR NOT BEING A CAT
ODIE
11-16
THIS IS FOR BEING A DOG!
PUNT!
ODIE


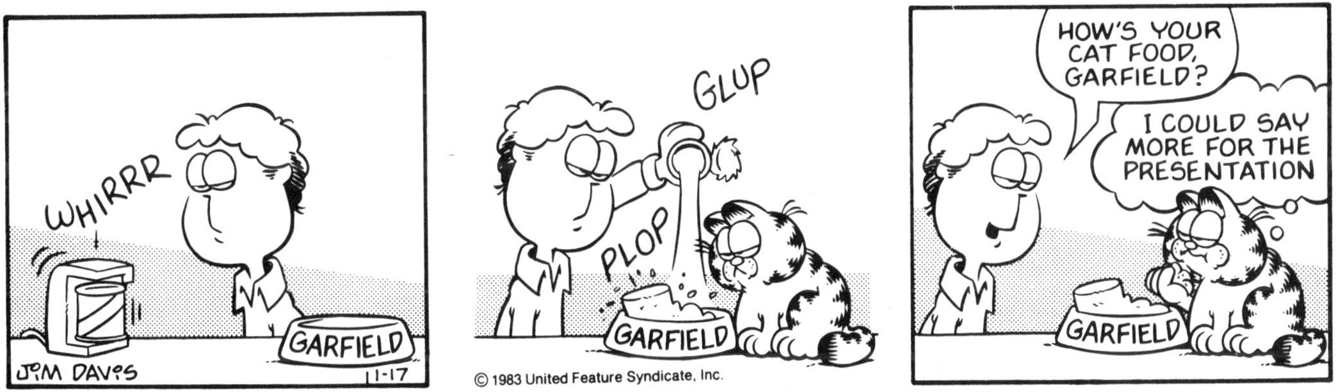
WHIRRR
GARFIELD
JIM DAVIS
11-17
GLUP
PLOP
GARFIELD
HOW'S YOUR CAT FOOD, GARFIELD?
I COULD SAY MORE FOR THE PRESENTATION
GARFIELD

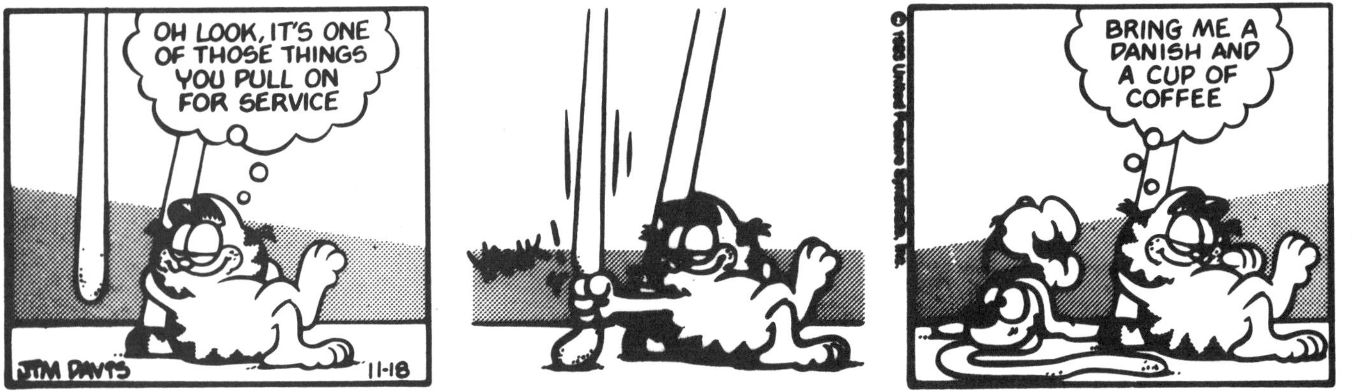
OH LOOK, IT'S ONE OF THOSE THINGS YOU PULL ON FOR SERVICE
JIM DAVIS
11-18
BRING ME A DANISH AND A CUP OF COFFEE

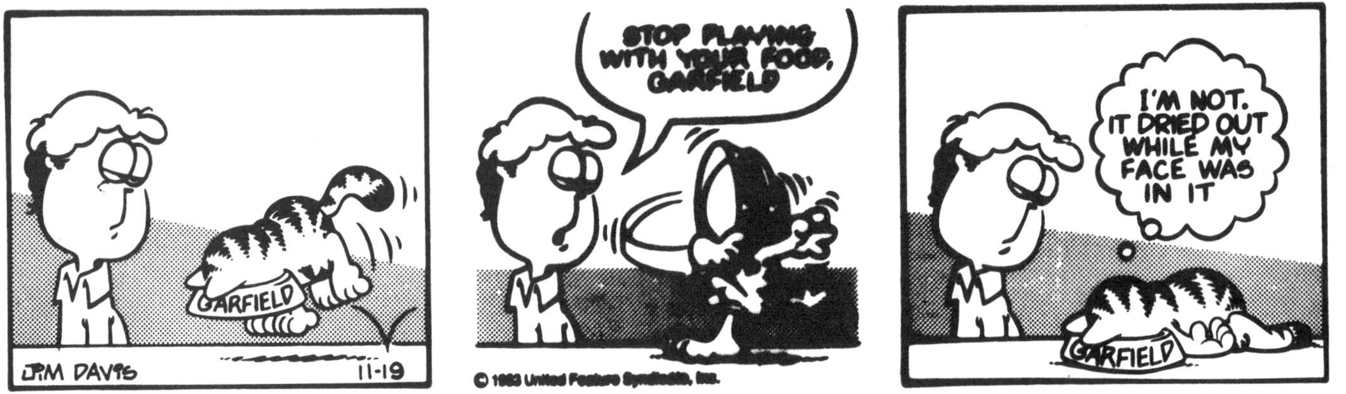
JIM DAVIS
11-19
GARFIELD
STOP PLAYING WITH YOUR FOOD, GARFIELD
I'M NOT. IT DRIED OUT WHILE MY FACE WAS IN IT
GARFIELD

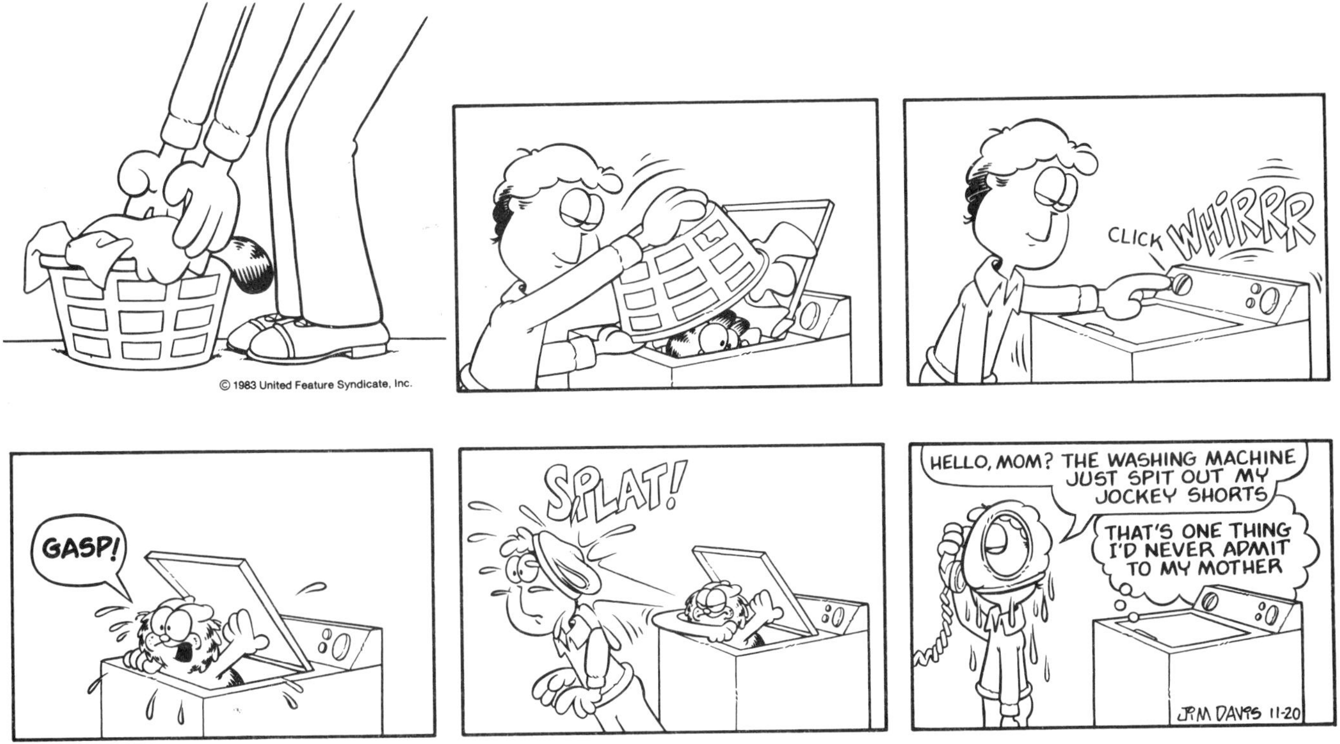
CLICK
WHIRRR
GASP!
SPLAT!
HELLO, MOM? THE WASHING MACHINE JUST SPIT OUT MY JOCKEY SHORTS
THAT'S ONE THING I'D NEVER ADMIT TO MY MOTHER
JIM DAVIS 11-20

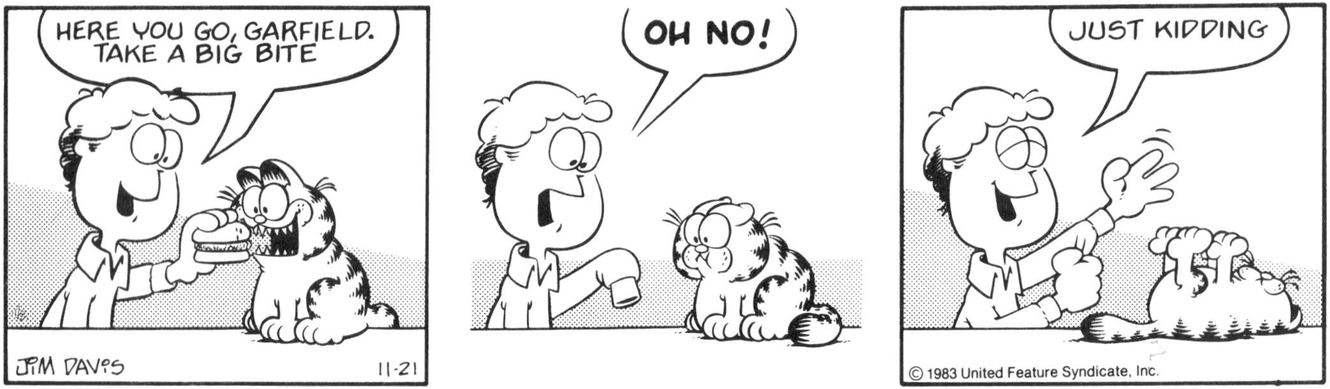
HERE YOU GO, GARFIELD. TAKE A BIG BITE
OH NO!
JUST KIDDING
JIM DAVIS
11-21
© 1983 United Feature Syndicate, Inc.

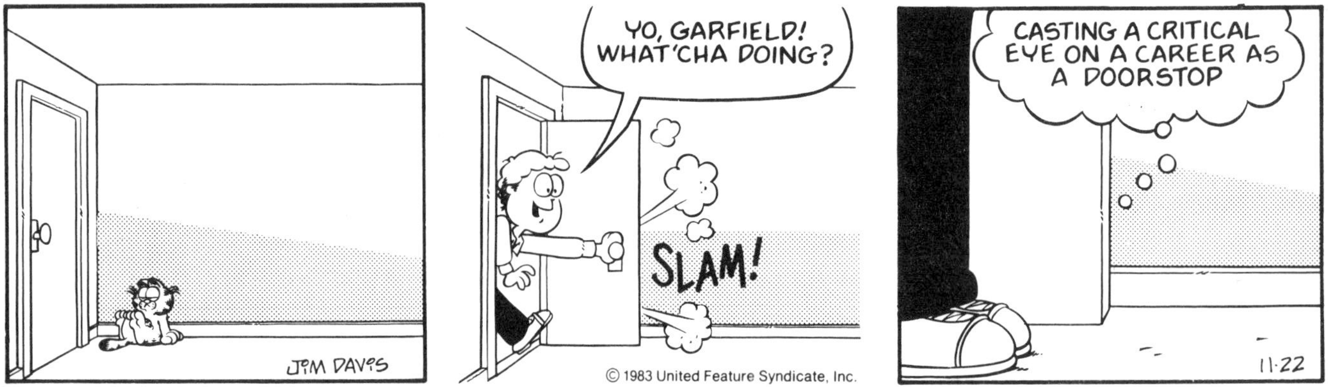
JIM DAVIS
YO, GARFIELD! WHAT'CHA DOING?
SLAM!
© 1983 United Feature Syndicate, Inc.
CASTING A CRITICAL EYE ON A CAREER AS A DOORSTOP
11-22

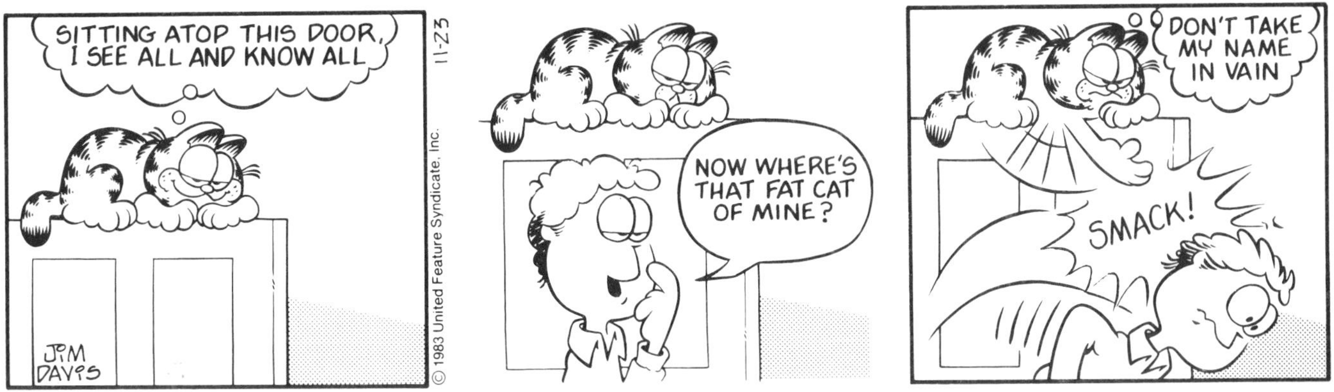
SITTING ATOP THIS DOOR, I SEE ALL AND KNOW ALL
JIM DAVIS
11-23
© 1983 United Feature Syndicate, Inc.
NOW WHERE'S THAT FAT CAT OF MINE?
DON'T TAKE MY NAME IN VAIN
SMACK!

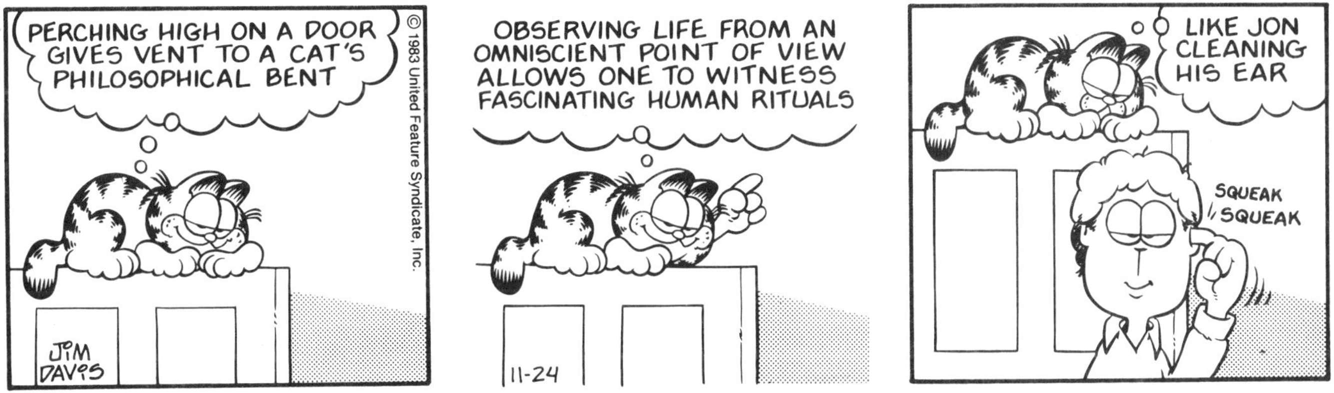
PERCHING HIGH ON A DOOR GIVES VENT TO A CAT'S PHILOSOPHICAL BENT
JIM DAVIS
© 1983 United Feature Syndicate, Inc.
OBSERVING LIFE FROM AN OMNISCIENT POINT OF VIEW ALLOWS ONE TO WITNESS FASCINATING HUMAN RITUALS
11-24
LIKE JON CLEANING HIS EAR
SQUEAK
SQUEAK

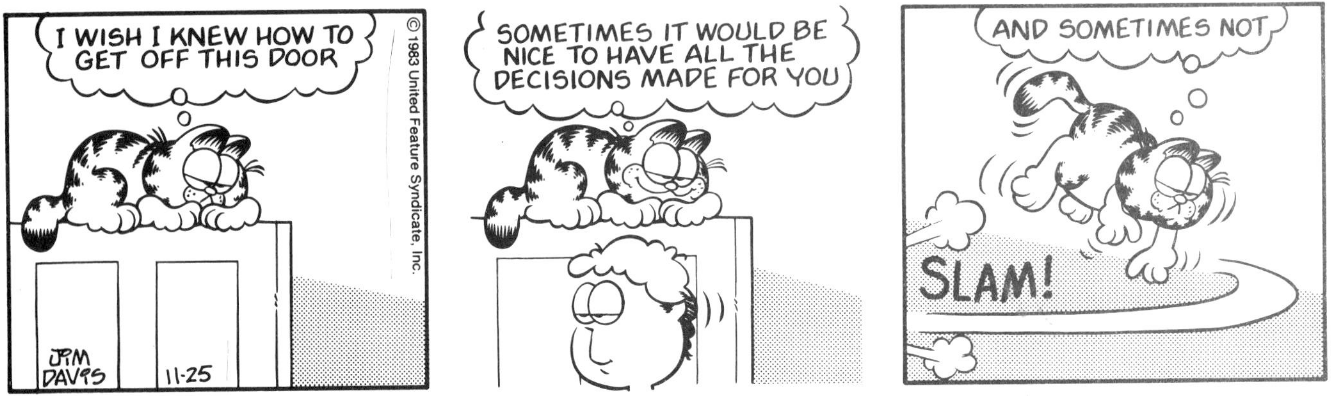

I WISH I KNEW HOW TO GET OFF THIS DOOR
© 1983 United Feature Syndicate, Inc.
JIM DAVIS
11-25
SOMETIMES IT WOULD BE NICE TO HAVE ALL THE DECISIONS MADE FOR YOU
AND SOMETIMES NOT
SLAM!


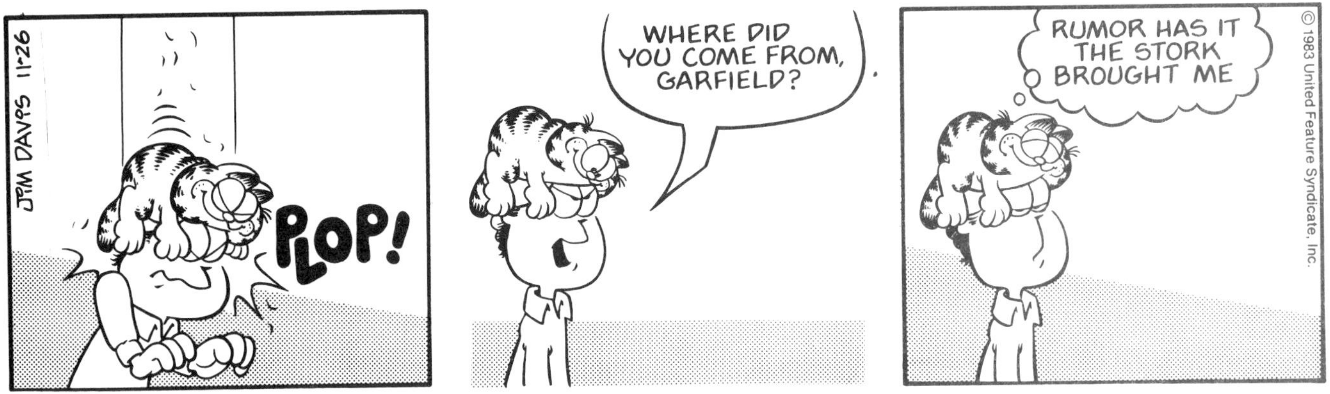

JIM DAVIS 11-26
PLOP!
WHERE DID YOU COME FROM, GARFIELD?
RUMOR HAS IT THE STORK BROUGHT ME
© 1983 United Feature Syndicate, Inc.

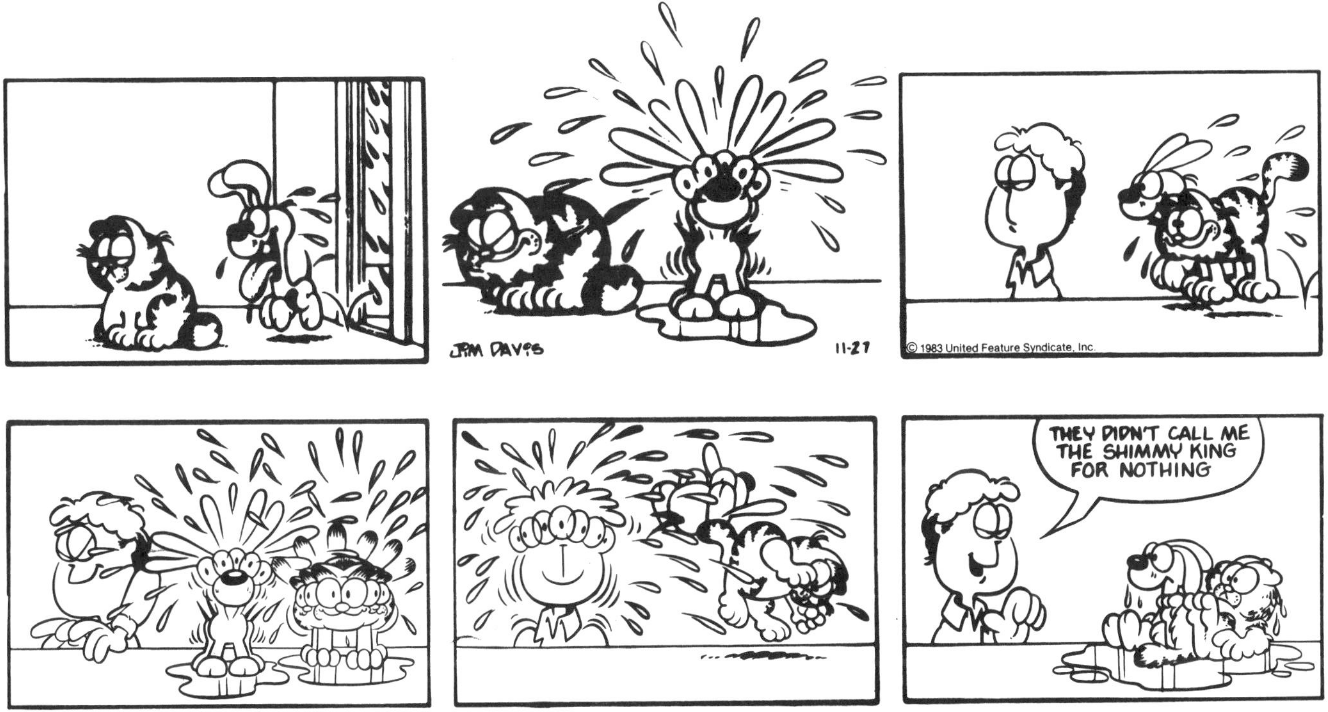
JIM DAVIS
11-27
© 1983 United Feature Syndicate, Inc.
THEY DIDN'T CALL ME THE SHIMMY KING FOR NOTHING

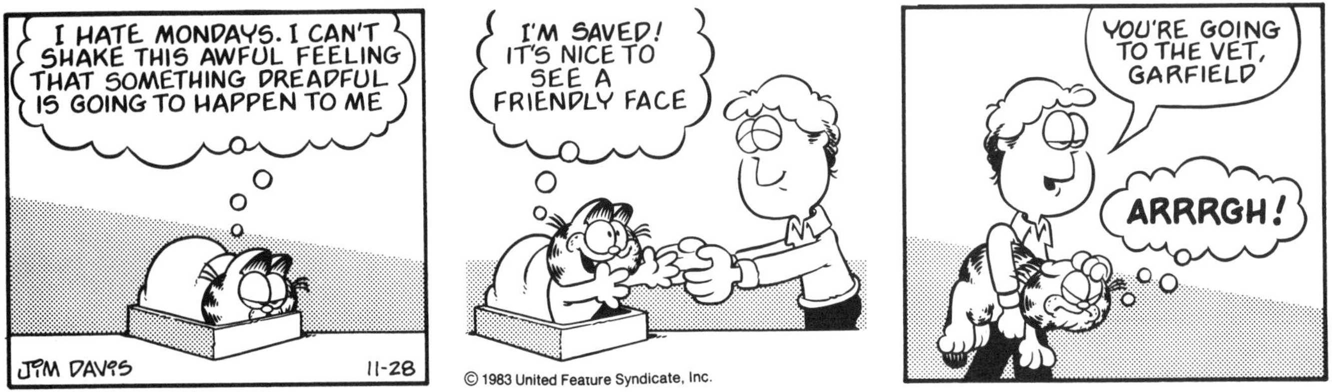
I HATE MONDAYS. I CAN'T SHAKE THIS AWFUL FEELING THAT SOMETHING DREADFUL IS GOING TO HAPPEN TO ME
JIM DAVIS
11-28
I'M SAVED! IT'S NICE TO SEE A FRIENDLY FACE
© 1983 United Feature Syndicate, Inc.
YOU'RE GOING TO THE VET, GARFIELD
ARRRGH!

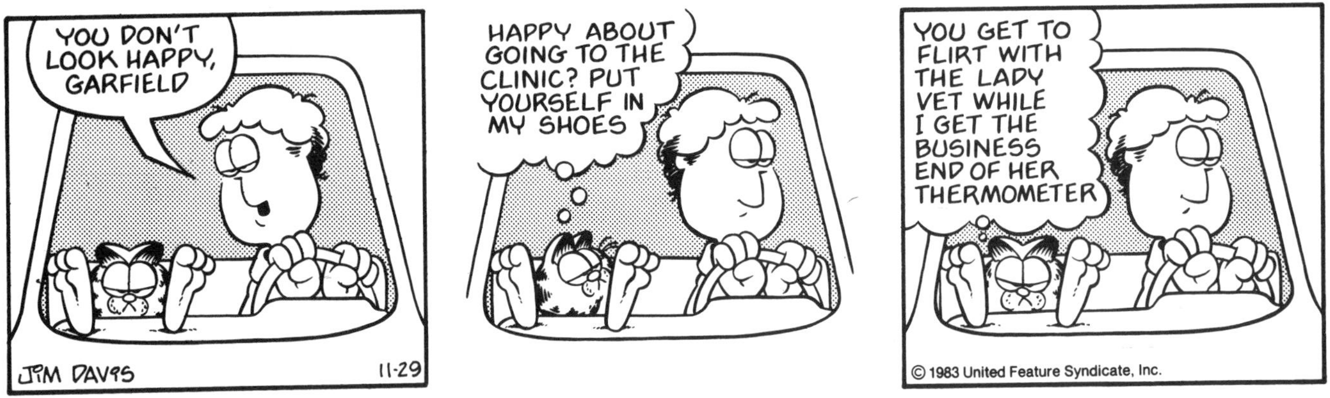
YOU DON'T LOOK HAPPY, GARFIELD
JIM DAVIS
11-29
HAPPY ABOUT GOING TO THE CLINIC? PUT YOURSELF IN MY SHOES
YOU GET TO FLIRT WITH THE LADY VET WHILE I GET THE BUSINESS END OF HER THERMOMETER
© 1983 United Feature Syndicate, Inc.

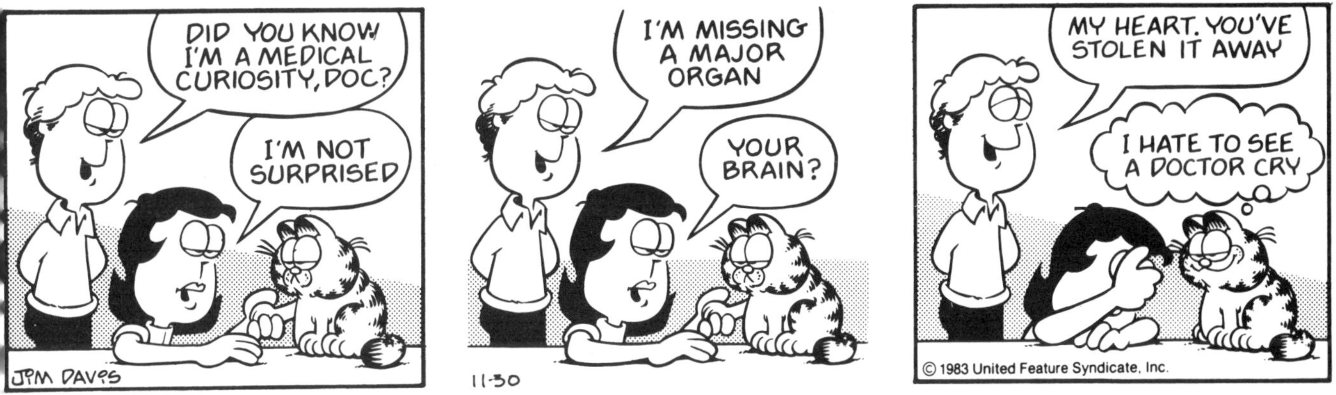
DID YOU KNOW I'M A MEDICAL CURIOSITY, DOC?
I'M NOT SURPRISED
JIM DAVIS
I'M MISSING A MAJOR ORGAN
YOUR BRAIN?
11-30
MY HEART. YOU'VE STOLEN IT AWAY
I HATE TO SEE A DOCTOR CRY
© 1983 United Feature Syndicate, Inc.

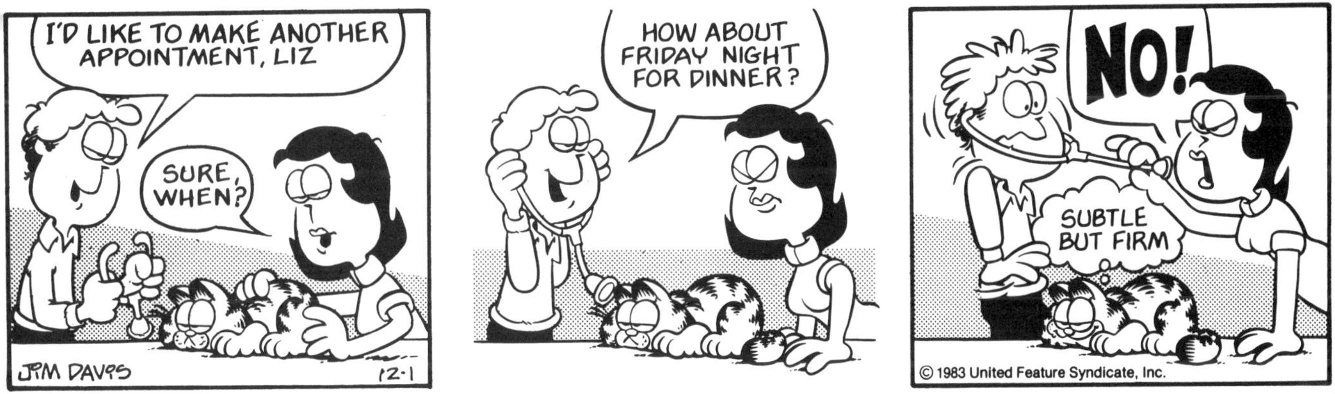
I'D LIKE TO MAKE ANOTHER APPOINTMENT, LIZ
SURE, WHEN?
JIM DAVIS
12-1
HOW ABOUT FRIDAY NIGHT FOR DINNER?
NO!
SUBTLE BUT FIRM
© 1983 United Feature Syndicate, Inc.

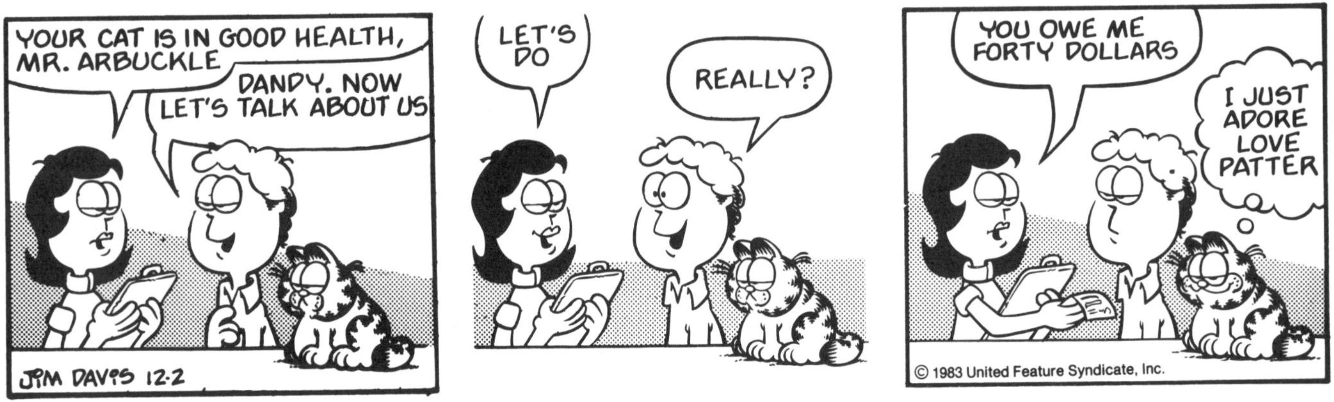
YOUR CAT IS IN GOOD HEALTH, MR. ARBUCKLE
DANDY. NOW LET'S TALK ABOUT US
JIM DAVIS 12-2
LET'S DO
REALLY?
YOU OWE ME FORTY DOLLARS
I JUST ADORE LOVE PATTER
© 1983 United Feature Syndicate, Inc.

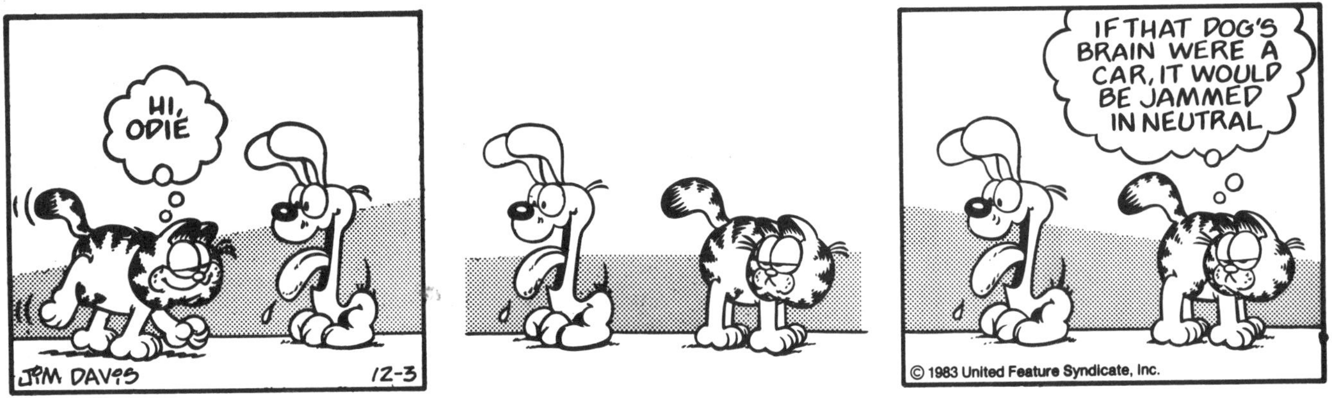
HI, ODIE
JIM DAVIS
12-3
IF THAT DOG'S BRAIN WERE A CAR, IT WOULD BE JAMMED IN NEUTRAL
© 1983 United Feature Syndicate, Inc.

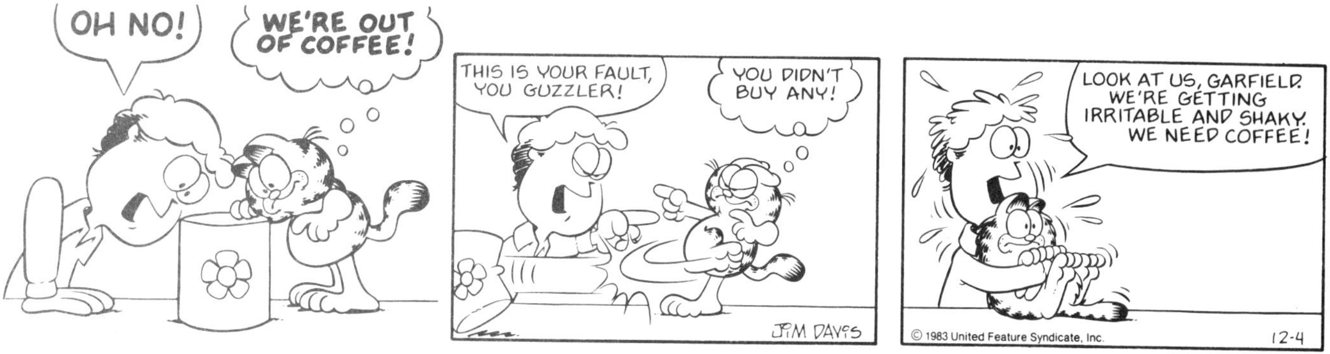
OH NO!
WE'RE OUT OF COFFEE!
THIS IS YOUR FAULT, YOU GUZZLER!
YOU DIDN'T BUY ANY!
JIM DAVIS
LOOK AT US, GARFIELD. WE'RE GETTING IRRITABLE AND SHAKY. WE NEED COFFEE!
© 1983 United Feature Syndicate, Inc.
12-4

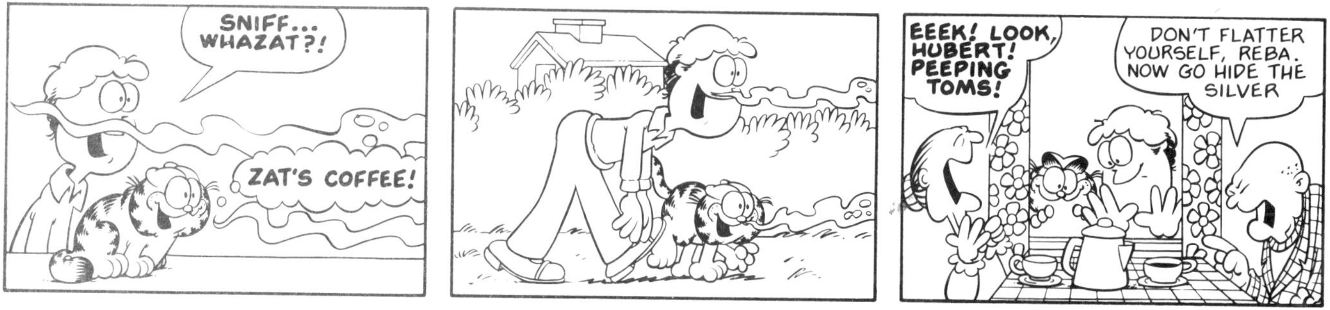
SNIFF... WHAZAT?!
ZAT'S COFFEE!
EEEK! LOOK, HUBERT! PEEPING TOMS!
DON'T FLATTER YOURSELF, REBA. NOW GO HIDE THE SILVER

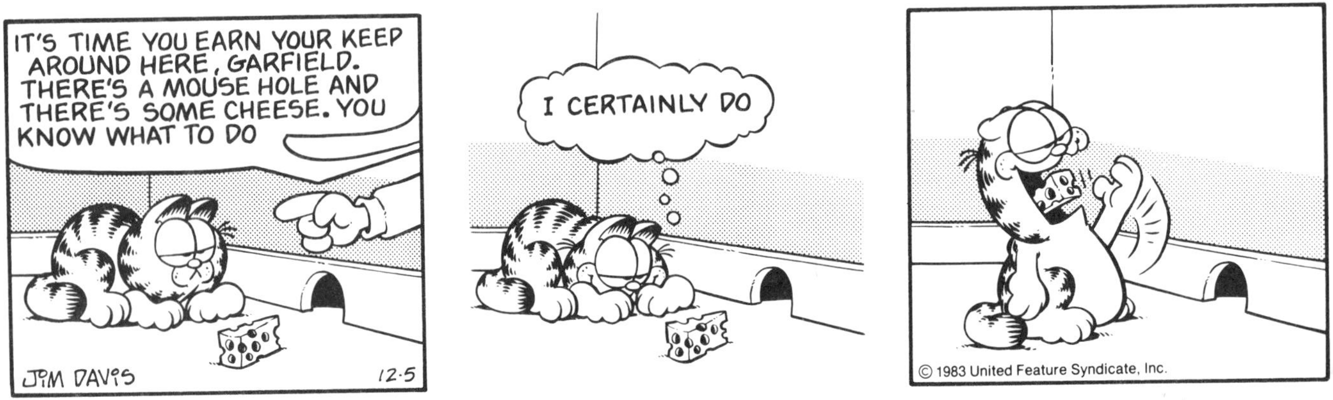
IT'S TIME YOU EARN YOUR KEEP AROUND HERE, GARFIELD. THERE'S A MOUSE HOLE AND THERE'S SOME CHEESE. YOU KNOW WHAT TO DO
JIM DAVIS
12-5
I CERTAINLY DO
© 1983 United Feature Syndicate, Inc.

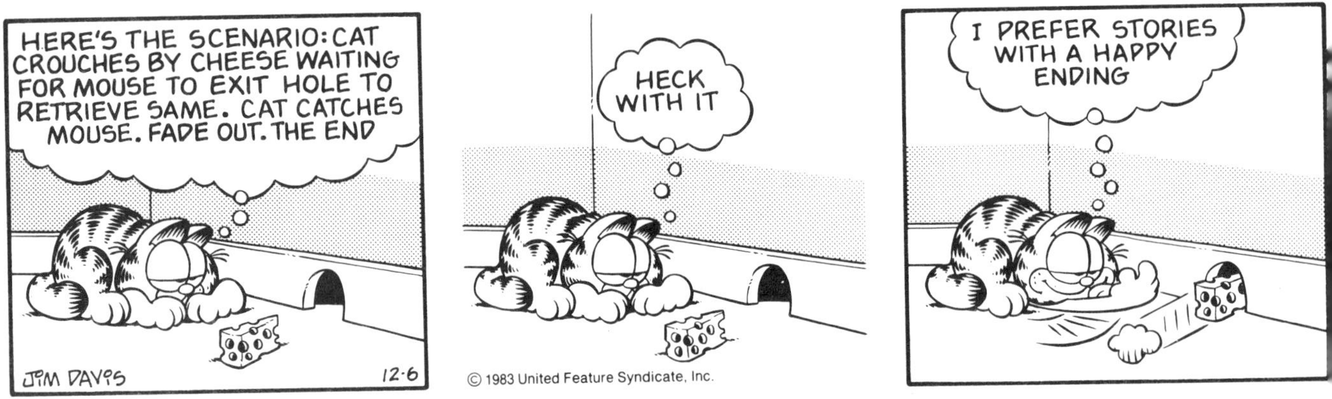
HERE'S THE SCENARIO: CAT CROUCHES BY CHEESE WAITING FOR MOUSE TO EXIT HOLE TO RETRIEVE SAME. CAT CATCHES MOUSE. FADE OUT. THE END
JIM DAVIS
12-6
HECK WITH IT
© 1983 United Feature Syndicate, Inc.
I PREFER STORIES WITH A HAPPY ENDING

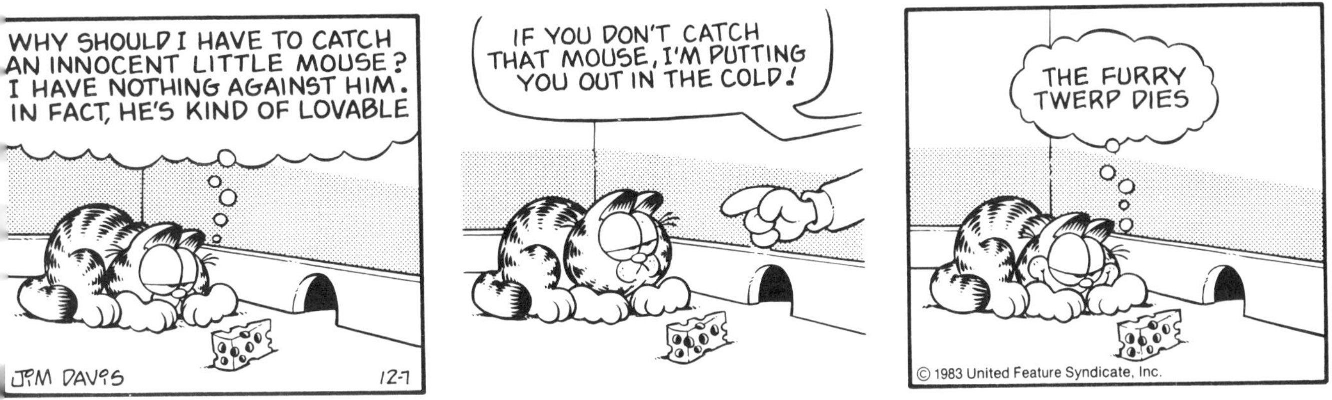
WHY SHOULD I HAVE TO CATCH AN INNOCENT LITTLE MOUSE? I HAVE NOTHING AGAINST HIM. IN FACT, HE'S KIND OF LOVABLE
JIM DAVIS
12-7
IF YOU DON'T CATCH THAT MOUSE, I'M PUTTING YOU OUT IN THE COLD!
THE FURRY TWERP DIES
© 1983 United Feature Syndicate, Inc.

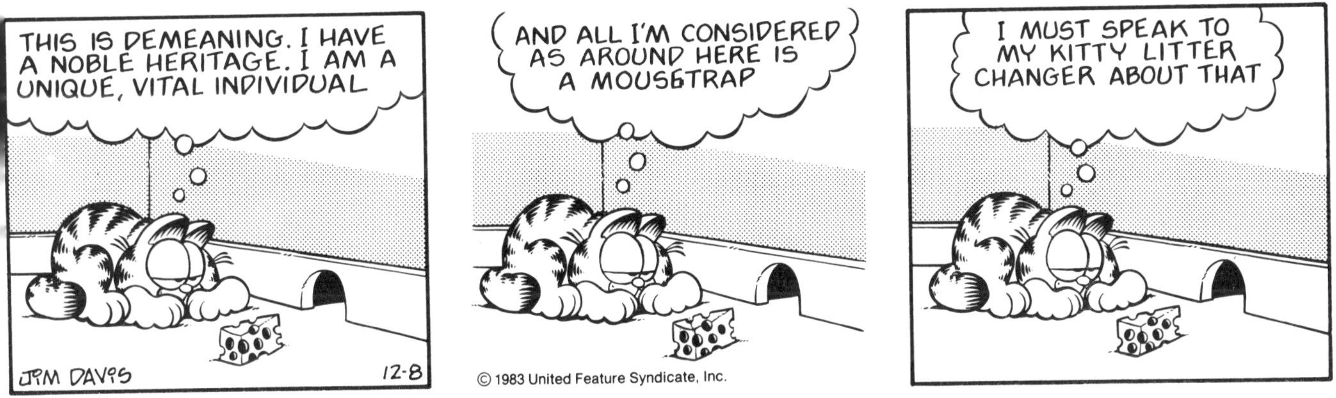
THIS IS DEMEANING. I HAVE A NOBLE HERITAGE. I AM A UNIQUE, VITAL INDIVIDUAL
JIM DAVIS
12-8
AND ALL I'M CONSIDERED AS AROUND HERE IS A MOUSETRAP
© 1983 United Feature Syndicate, Inc.
I MUST SPEAK TO MY KITTY LITTER CHANGER ABOUT THAT

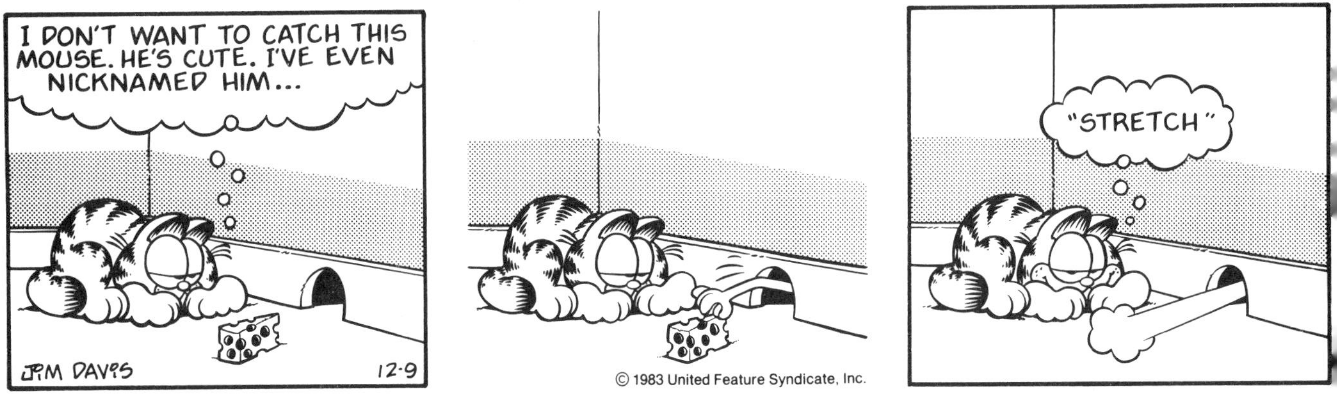
I DON'T WANT TO CATCH THIS MOUSE. HE'S CUTE. I'VE EVEN NICKNAMED HIM...
JIM DAVIS
12-9
© 1983 United Feature Syndicate, Inc.
"STRETCH"

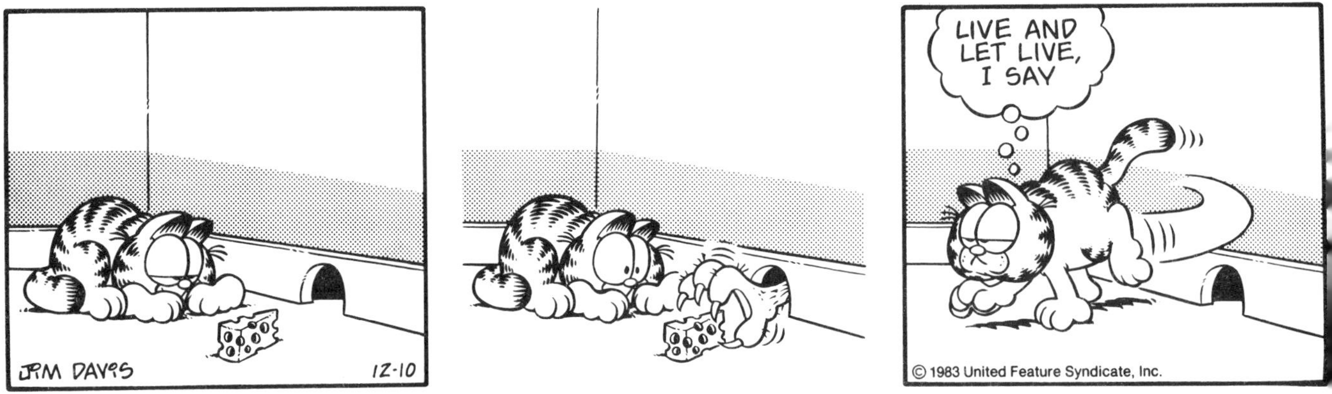
JIM DAVIS
12-10
LIVE AND LET LIVE, I SAY
© 1983 United Feature Syndicate, Inc.

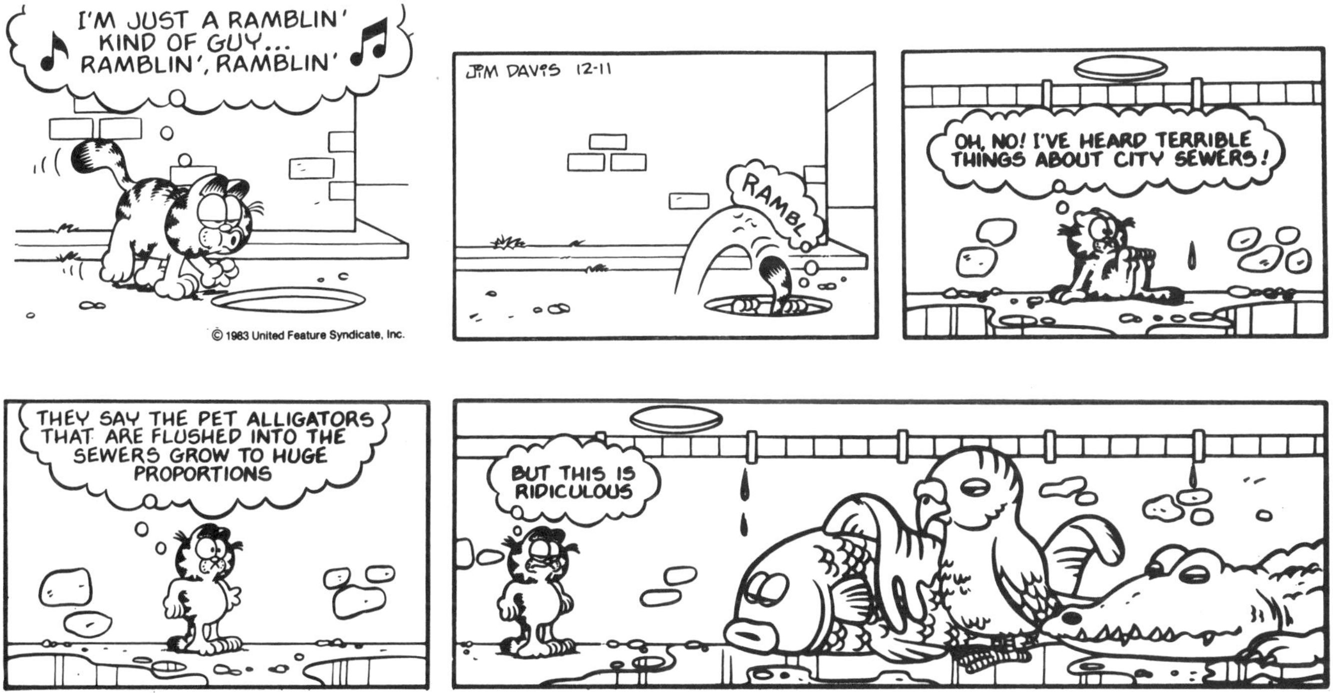
I'M JUST A RAMBLIN' KIND OF GUY... RAMBLIN', RAMBLIN'
JIM DAVIS 12-11
RAMBL
OH, NO! I'VE HEARD TERRIBLE THINGS ABOUT CITY SEWERS!
THEY SAY THE PET ALLIGATORS THAT ARE FLUSHED INTO THE SEWERS GROW TO HUGE PROPORTIONS
BUT THIS IS RIDICULOUS

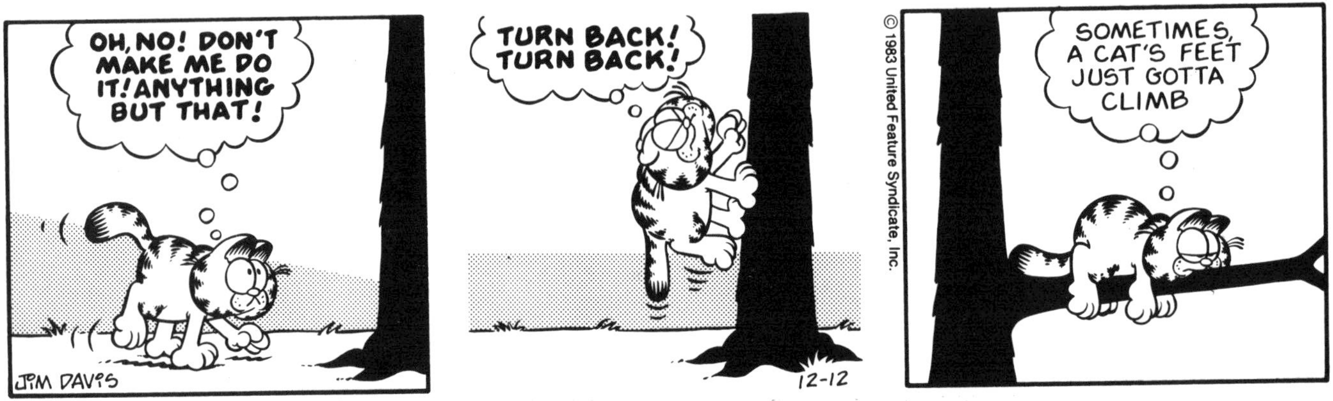
OH, NO! DON'T MAKE ME DO IT! ANYTHING BUT THAT!
JIM DAVIS
TURN BACK! TURN BACK!
12-12
© 1983 United Feature Syndicate, Inc.
SOMETIMES, A CAT'S FEET JUST GOTTA CLIMB

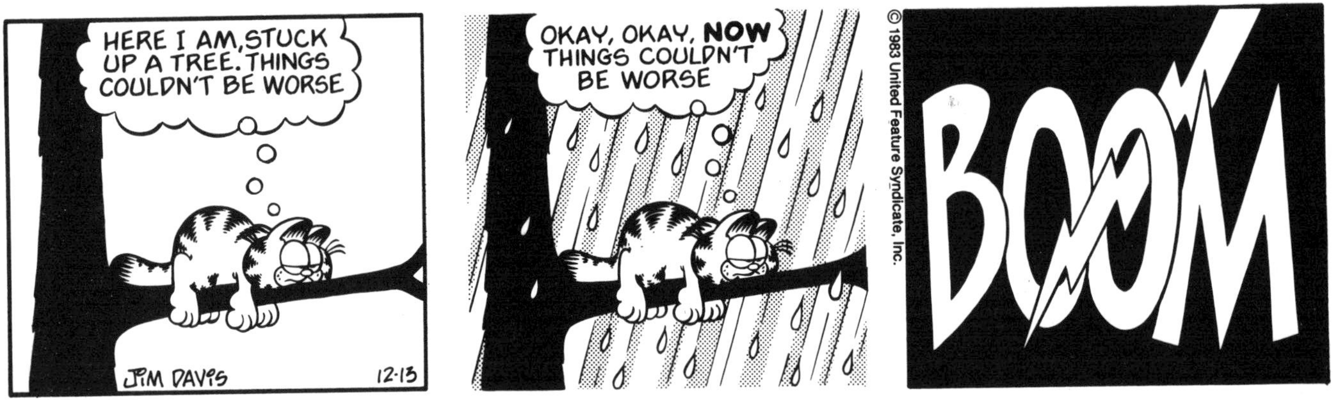
HERE I AM, STUCK UP A TREE. THINGS COULDN'T BE WORSE
JIM DAVIS
12-13
OKAY, OKAY, NOW THINGS COULDN'T BE WORSE
© 1983 United Feature Syndicate, Inc.
BOOM

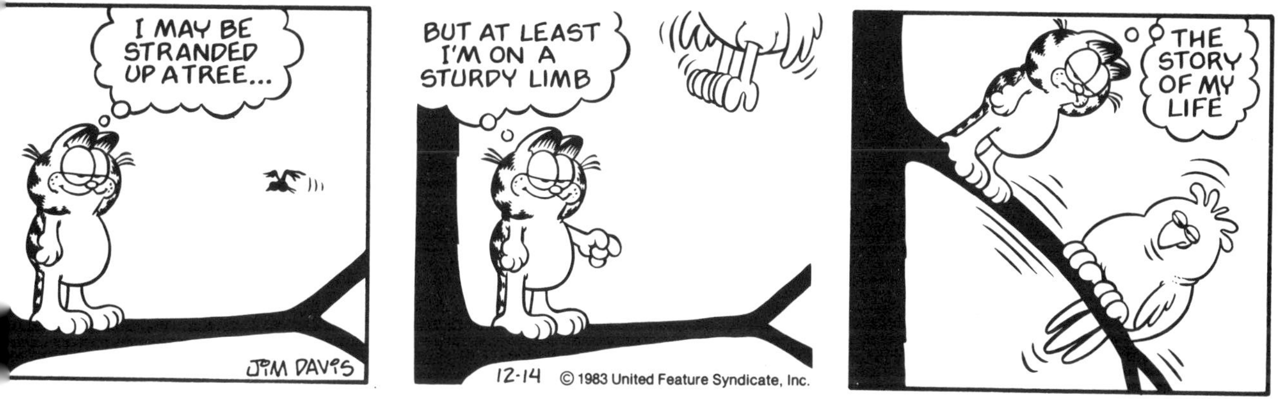
I MAY BE STRANDED UP A TREE...
JIM DAVIS
BUT AT LEAST I'M ON A STURDY LIMB
12-14
© 1983 United Feature Syndicate, Inc.
THE STORY OF MY LIFE

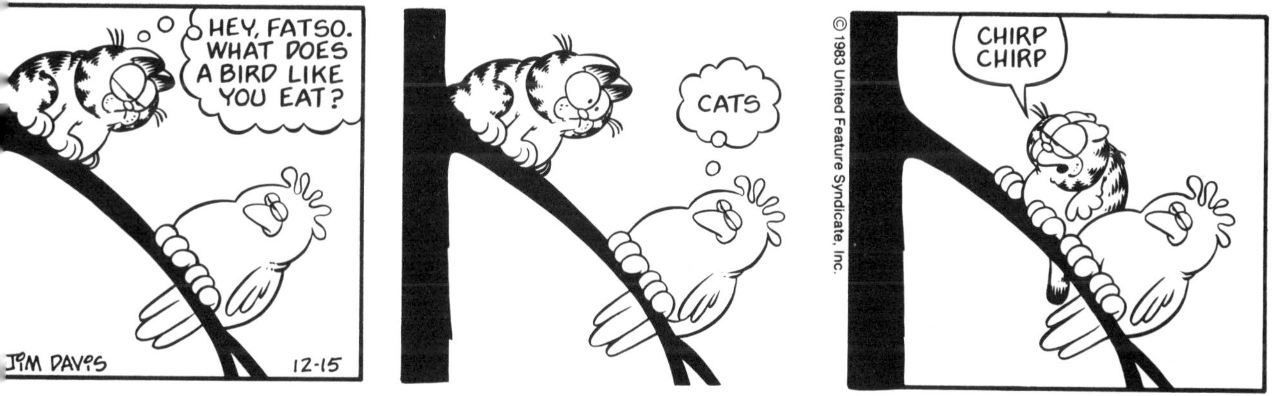
HEY, FATSO. WHAT DOES A BIRD LIKE YOU EAT?
JIM DAVIS
12-15
CATS
© 1983 United Feature Syndicate, Inc.
CHIRP CHIRP

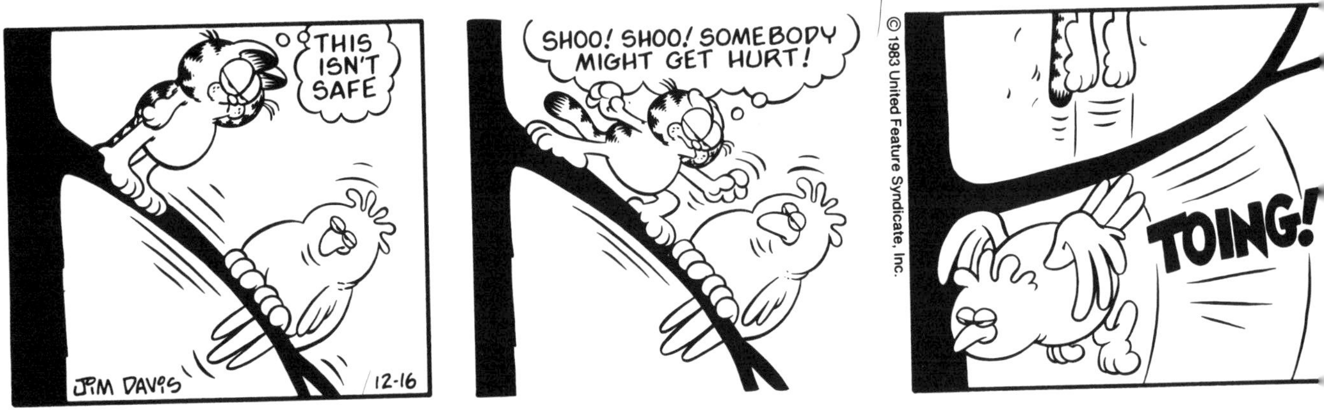
THIS ISN'T SAFE
JIM DAVIS
12-16
SHOO! SHOO! SOMEBODY MIGHT GET HURT!
© 1983 United Feature Syndicate, Inc.
TOING!

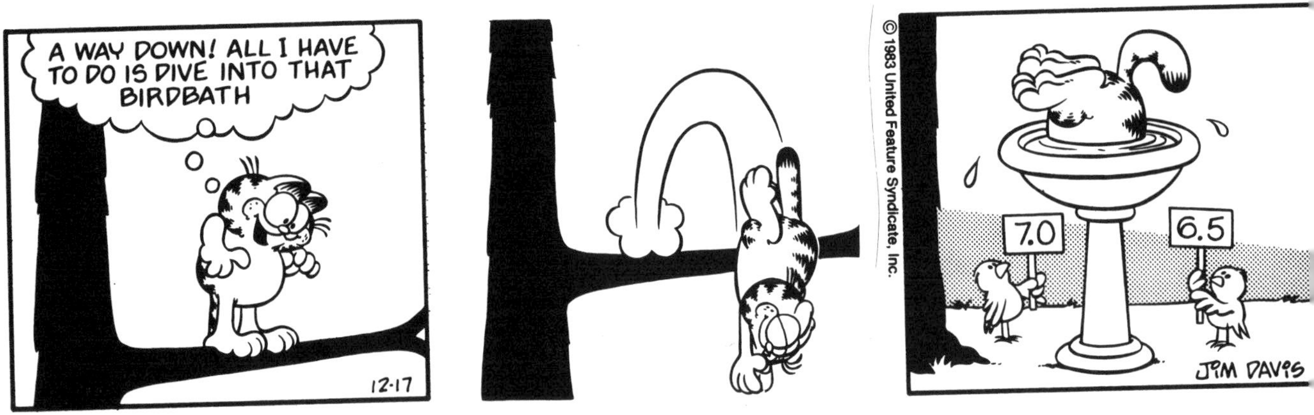
A WAY DOWN! ALL I HAVE TO DO IS DIVE INTO THAT BIRDBATH
12-17
© 1983 United Feature Syndicate, Inc.
7.0
6.5
JIM DAVIS

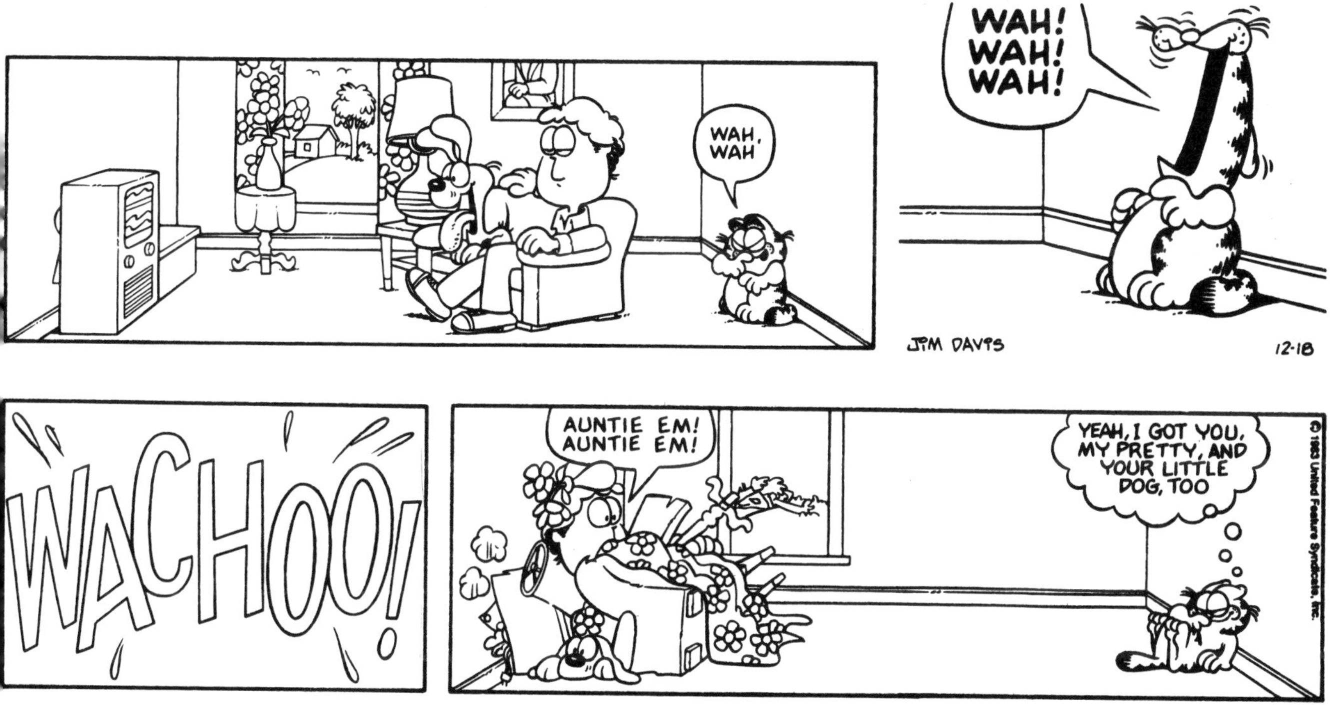
WAH, WAH
WAH! WAH! WAH!
JIM DAVIS
12-18
WACHOO!
AUNTIE EM! AUNTIE EM!
YEAH, I GOT YOU, MY PRETTY, AND YOUR LITTLE DOG, TOO
© 1983 United Feature Syndicate, Inc.

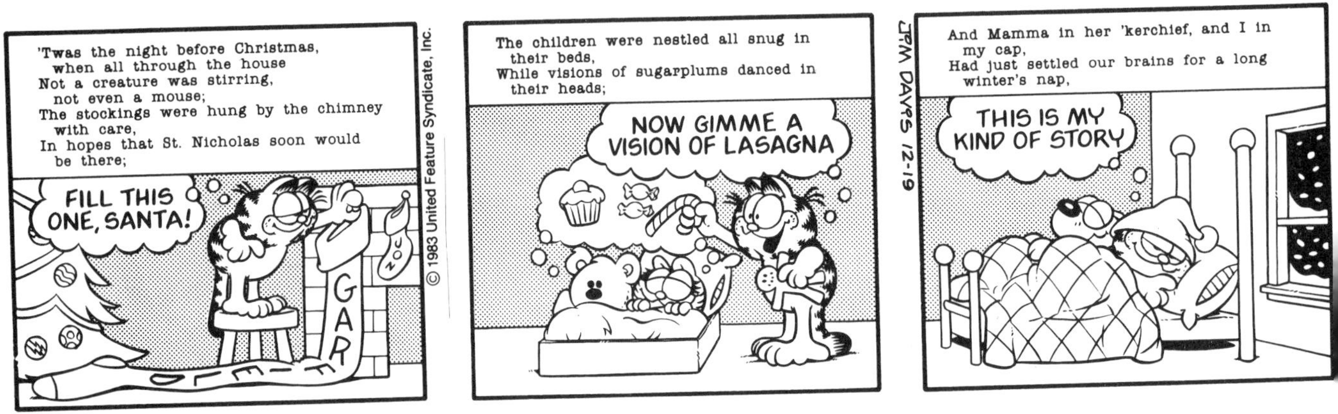
'Twas the night before Christmas, when all through the house
Not a creature was stirring, not even a mouse;
The stockings were hung by the chimney with care,
In hopes that St. Nicholas soon would be there;
FILL THIS ONE, SANTA!
GARFIELD
© 1983 United Feature Syndicate, Inc.
The children were nestled all snug in their beds,
While visions of sugarplums danced in their heads;
NOW GIMME A VISION OF LASAGNA
JIM DAVIS 12-19
And Mamma in her 'kerchief, and I in my cap,
Had just settled our brains for a long winter's nap,
THIS IS MY KIND OF STORY

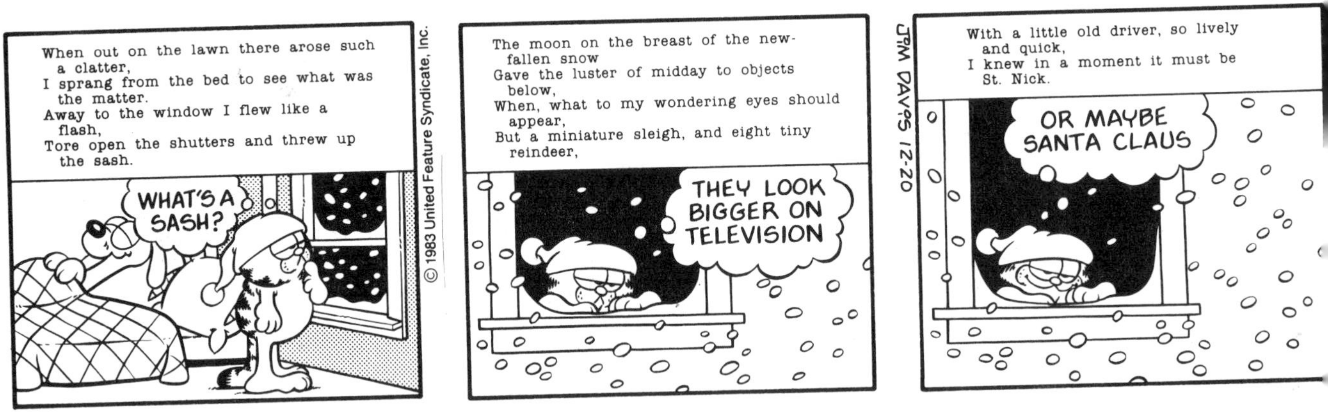
When out on the lawn there arose such a clatter,
I sprang from the bed to see what was the matter.
Away to the window I flew like a flash,
Tore open the shutters and threw up the sash.
WHAT'S A SASH?
© 1983 United Feature Syndicate, Inc.
The moon on the breast of the new-fallen snow
Gave the luster of midday to objects below,
When, what to my wondering eyes should appear,
But a miniature sleigh, and eight tiny reindeer,
THEY LOOK BIGGER ON TELEVISION
JIM DAVIS 12-20
With a little old driver, so lively and quick,
I knew in a moment it must be St. Nick.
OR MAYBE SANTA CLAUS

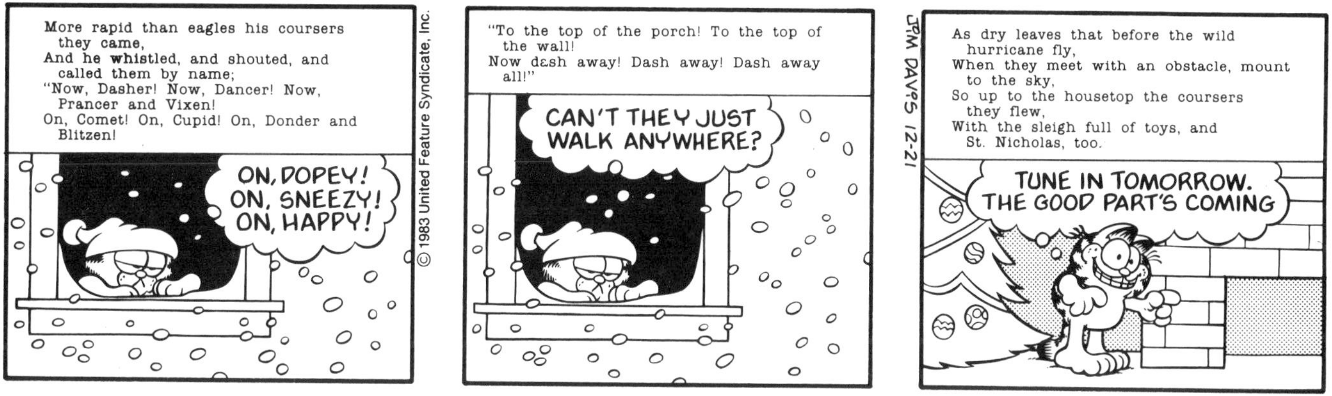
More rapid than eagles his coursers they came,
And he whistled, and shouted, and called them by name;
"Now, Dasher! Now, Dancer! Now, Prancer and Vixen!
On, Comet! On, Cupid! On, Donder and Blitzen!
ON, DOPEY! ON, SNEEZY! ON, HAPPY!
© 1983 United Feature Syndicate, Inc.
"To the top of the porch! To the top of the wall!
Now dash away! Dash away! Dash away all!"
CAN'T THEY JUST WALK ANYWHERE?
JIM DAVIS 12-21
As dry leaves that before the wild hurricane fly,
When they meet with an obstacle, mount to the sky,
So up to the housetop the coursers they flew,
With the sleigh full of toys, and St. Nicholas, too.
TUNE IN TOMORROW. THE GOOD PART'S COMING

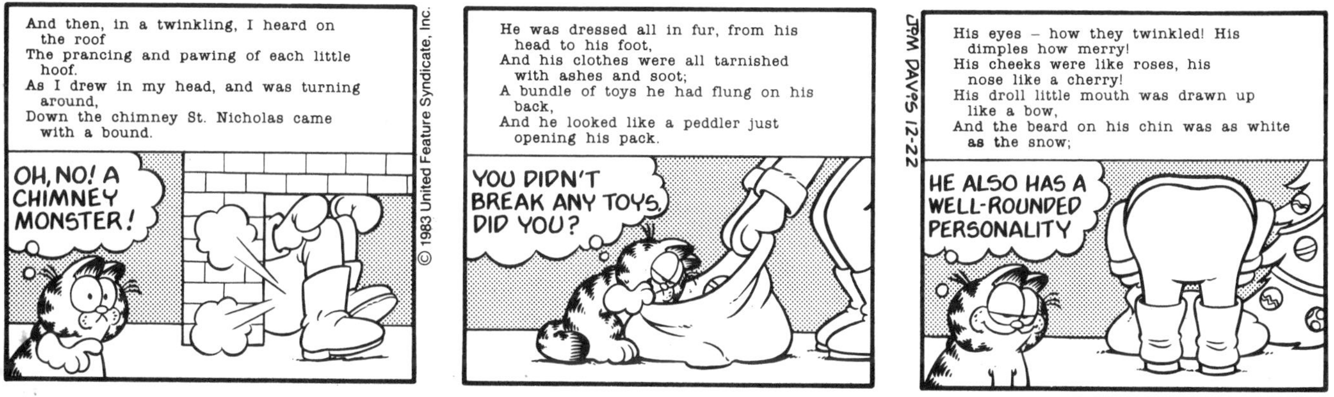
And then, in a twinkling, I heard on the roof
The prancing and pawing of each little hoof.
As I drew in my head, and was turning around,
Down the chimney St. Nicholas came with a bound.
OH, NO! A CHIMNEY MONSTER!
© 1983 United Feature Syndicate, Inc.
He was dressed all in fur, from his head to his foot,
And his clothes were all tarnished with ashes and soot;
A bundle of toys he had flung on his back,
And he looked like a peddler just opening his pack.
YOU DIDN'T BREAK ANY TOYS, DID YOU?
JIM DAVIS 12-22
His eyes – how they twinkled! His dimples how merry!
His cheeks were like roses, his nose like a cherry!
His droll little mouth was drawn up like a bow,
And the beard on his chin was as white as the snow;
HE ALSO HAS A WELL-ROUNDED PERSONALITY

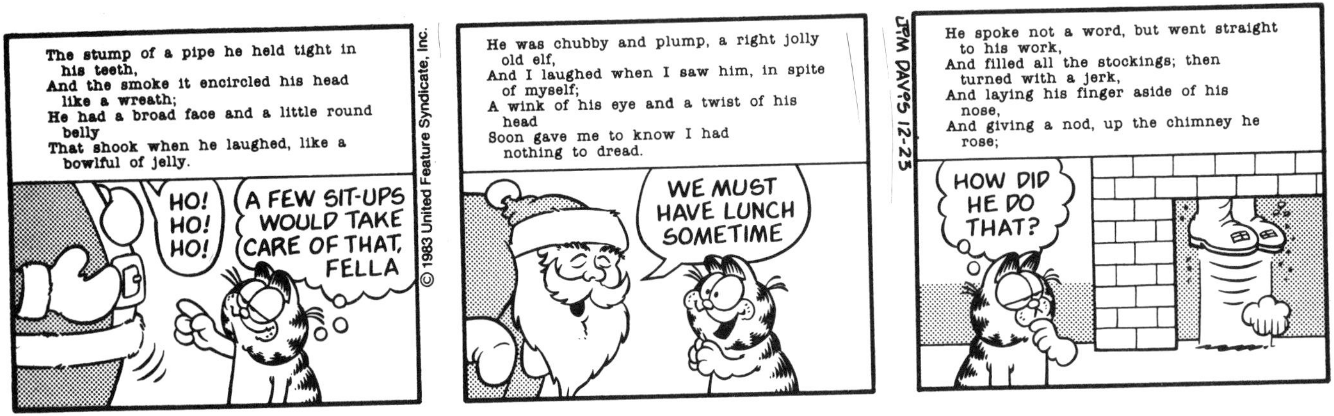
The stump of a pipe he held tight in his teeth,
And the smoke it encircled his head like a wreath;
He had a broad face and a little round belly
That shook when he laughed, like a bowlful of jelly.
HO! HO! HO!
A FEW SIT-UPS WOULD TAKE CARE OF THAT, FELLA
© 1983 United Feature Syndicate, Inc.
He was chubby and plump, a right jolly old elf,
And I laughed when I saw him, in spite of myself;
A wink of his eye and a twist of his head
Soon gave me to know I had nothing to dread.
WE MUST HAVE LUNCH SOMETIME
JPM DAVIS 12-23
He spoke not a word, but went straight to his work,
And filled all the stockings; then turned with a jerk,
And laying his finger aside of his nose,
And giving a nod, up the chimney he rose;
HOW DID HE DO THAT?

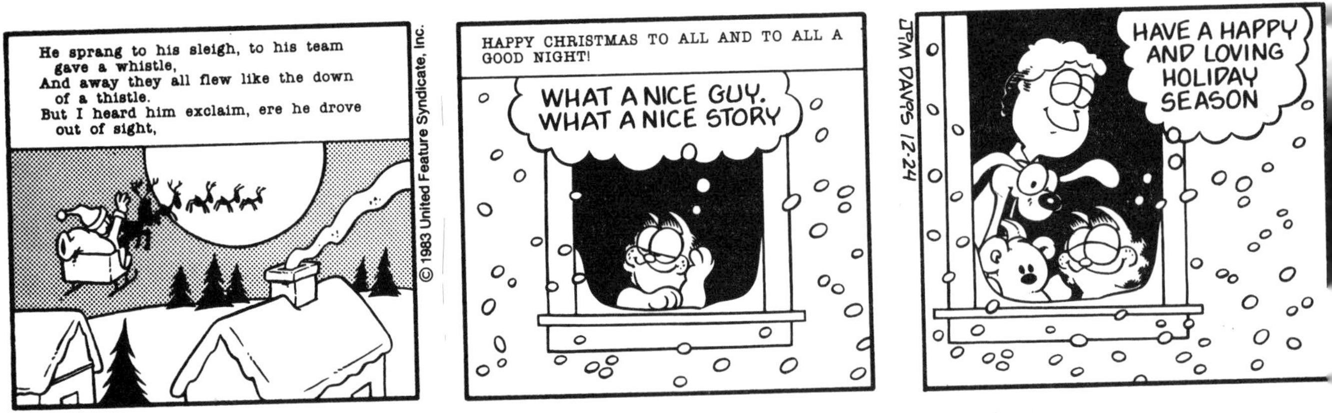
He sprang to his sleigh, to his team gave a whistle,
And away they all flew like the down of a thistle.
But I heard him exclaim, ere he drove out of sight,
© 1983 United Feature Syndicate, Inc.
HAPPY CHRISTMAS TO ALL AND TO ALL A GOOD NIGHT!
WHAT A NICE GUY. WHAT A NICE STORY
JPM DAVIS 12-24
HAVE A HAPPY AND LOVING HOLIDAY SEASON

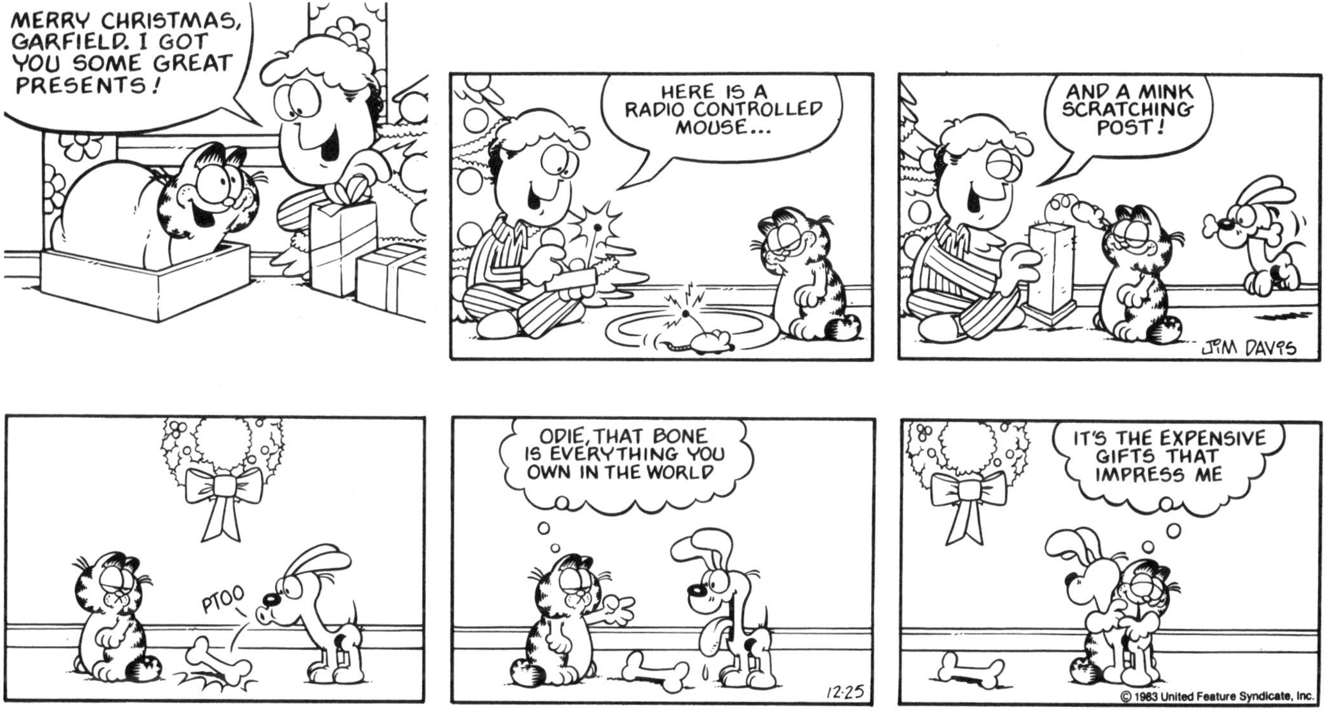

MERRY CHRISTMAS, GARFIELD. I GOT YOU SOME GREAT PRESENTS!
HERE IS A RADIO CONTROLLED MOUSE...
AND A MINK SCRATCHING POST!
JIM DAVIS
PTOO
ODIE, THAT BONE IS EVERYTHING YOU OWN IN THE WORLD
12-25
IT'S THE EXPENSIVE GIFTS THAT IMPRESS ME
© 1983 United Feature Syndicate, Inc.

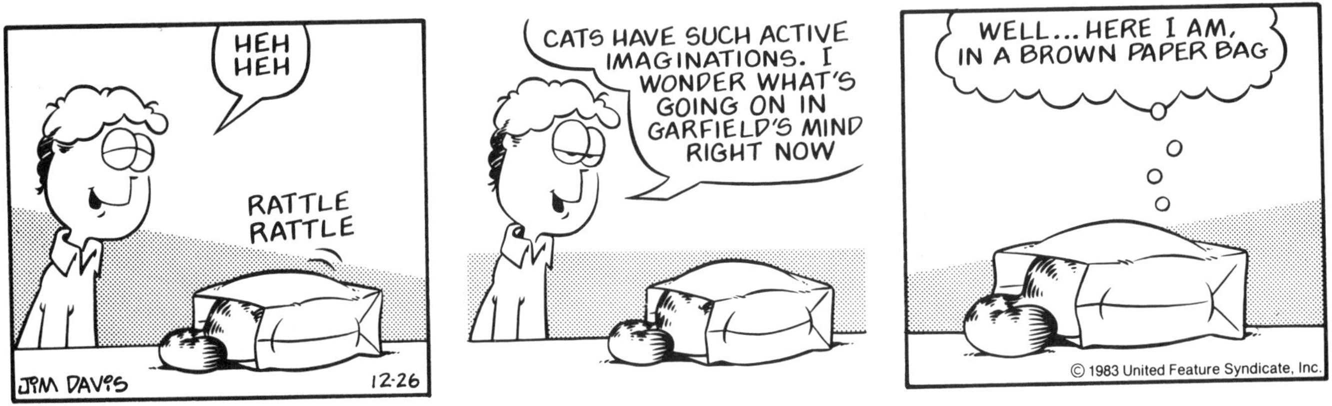
HEH HEH
RATTLE RATTLE
JIM DAVIS
12-26
CATS HAVE SUCH ACTIVE IMAGINATIONS. I WONDER WHAT'S GOING ON IN GARFIELD'S MIND RIGHT NOW
WELL... HERE I AM, IN A BROWN PAPER BAG
© 1983 United Feature Syndicate, Inc.

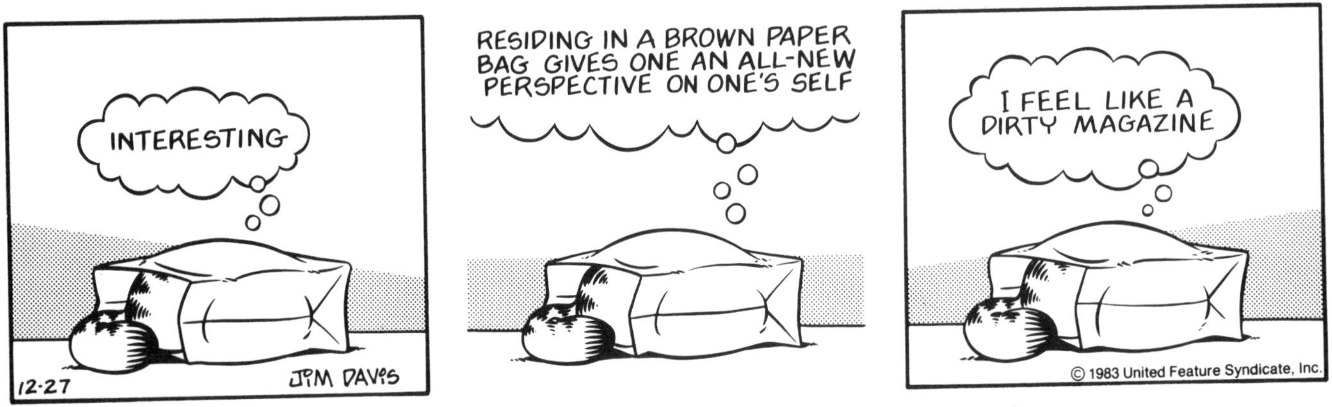
INTERESTING
12-27
JIM DAVIS
RESIDING IN A BROWN PAPER BAG GIVES ONE AN ALL-NEW PERSPECTIVE ON ONE'S SELF
I FEEL LIKE A DIRTY MAGAZINE
© 1983 United Feature Syndicate, Inc.

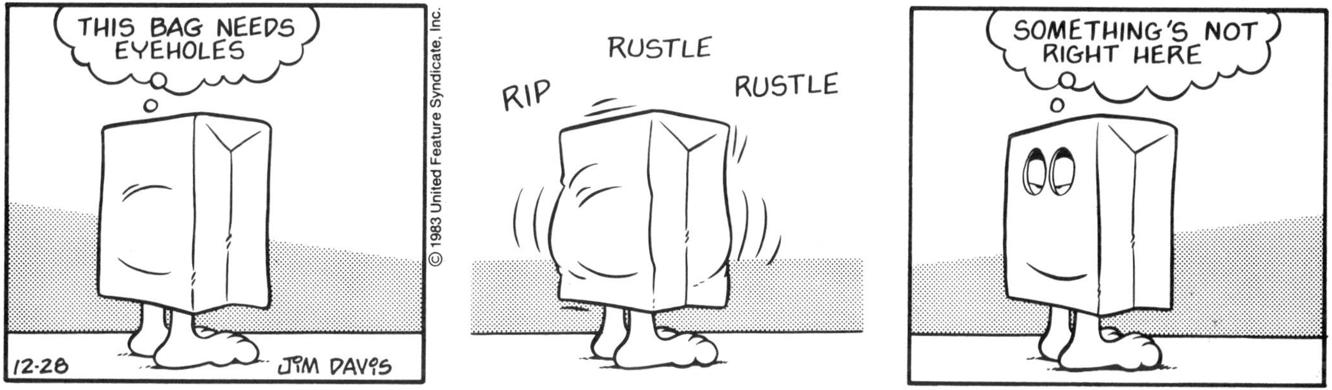
THIS BAG NEEDS EYEHOLES
12-28
JIM DAVIS
RIP
RUSTLE
RUSTLE
SOMETHING'S NOT RIGHT HERE


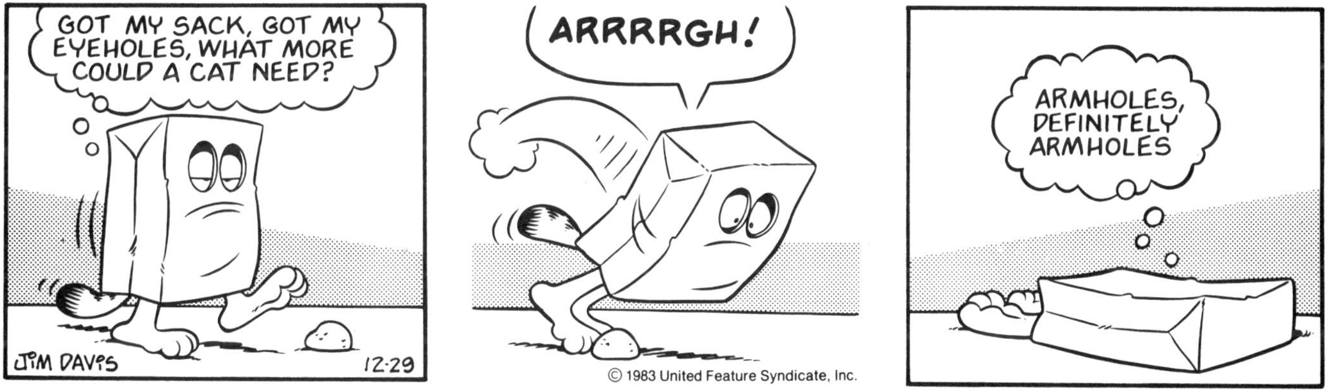
GOT MY SACK, GOT MY EYEHOLES, WHAT MORE COULD A CAT NEED?
JIM DAVIS
12-29
ARRRRGH!
ARMHOLES, DEFINITELY ARMHOLES

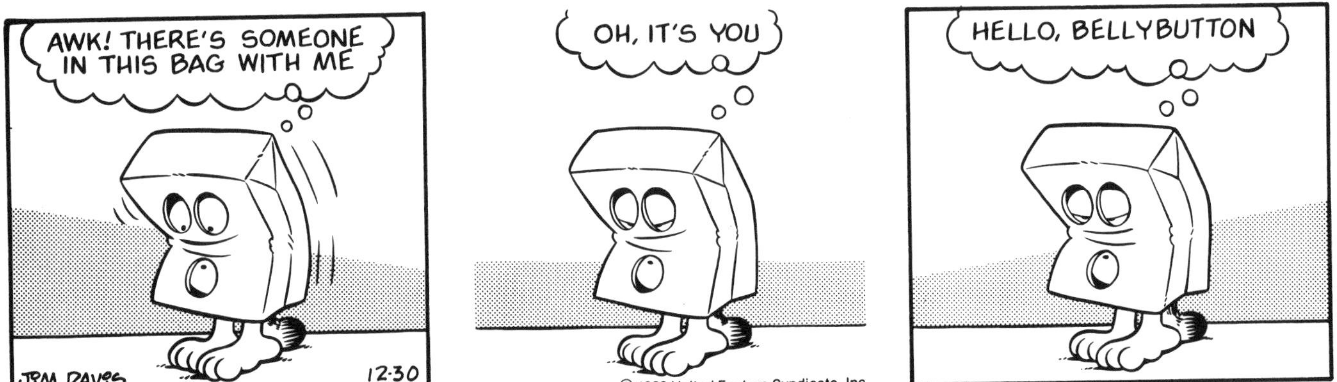
AWK! THERE'S SOMEONE IN THIS BAG WITH ME
JIM DAVIS
12-30
OH, IT'S YOU
HELLO, BELLYBUTTON



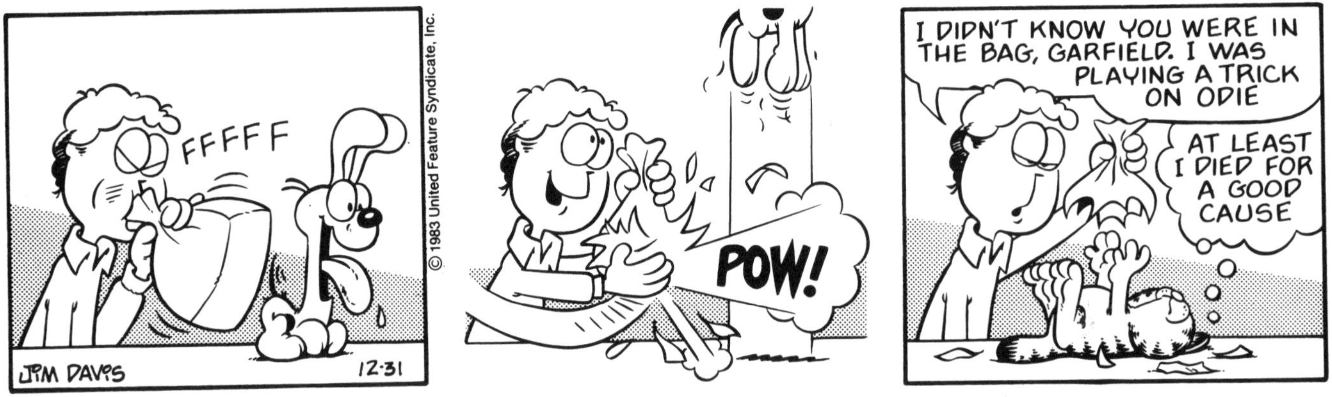
FFFFF
JIM DAVIS
12-31
POW!
I DIDN'T KNOW YOU WERE IN THE BAG, GARFIELD. I WAS PLAYING A TRICK ON ODIE
AT LEAST I DIED FOR A GOOD CAUSE

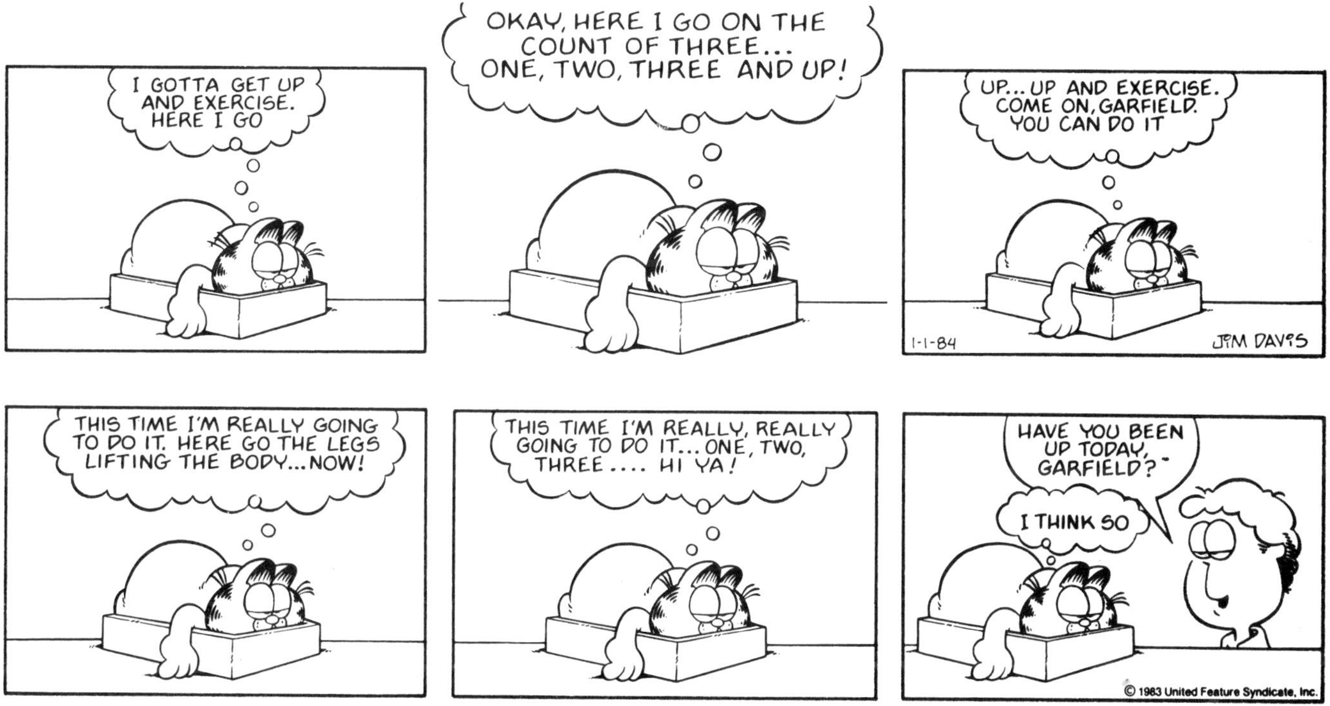

I GOTTA GET UP AND EXERCISE. HERE I GO
OKAY, HERE I GO ON THE COUNT OF THREE... ONE, TWO, THREE AND UP!
UP... UP AND EXERCISE. COME ON, GARFIELD. YOU CAN DO IT
1-1-84
JIM DAVIS
THIS TIME I'M REALLY GOING TO DO IT. HERE GO THE LEGS LIFTING THE BODY... NOW!
THIS TIME I'M REALLY, REALLY GOING TO DO IT... ONE, TWO, THREE.... HI YA!
HAVE YOU BEEN UP TODAY, GARFIELD?
I THINK SO
© 1983 United Feature Syndicate, Inc.

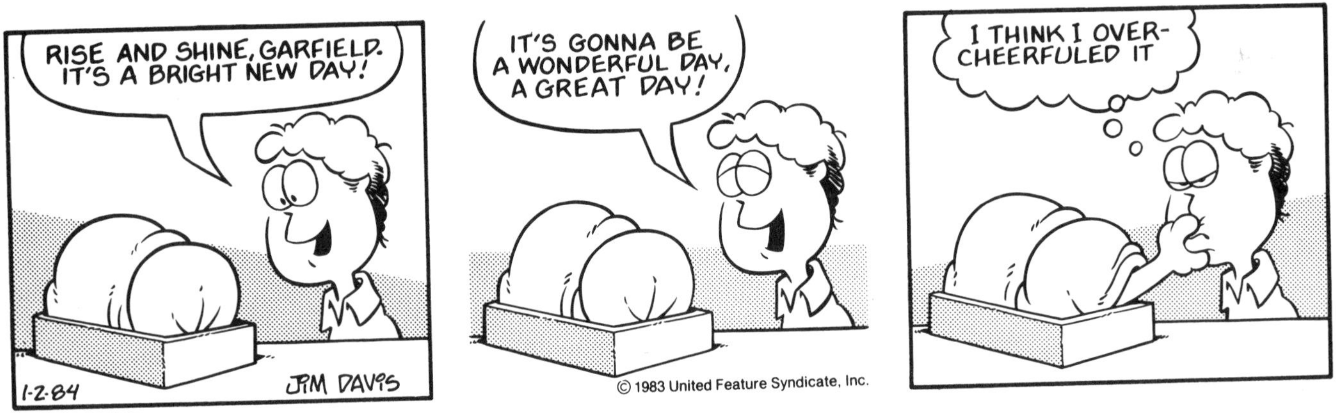
RISE AND SHINE, GARFIELD. IT'S A BRIGHT NEW DAY!
1-2-84
JIM DAVIS
IT'S GONNA BE A WONDERFUL DAY, A GREAT DAY!
I THINK I OVER-CHEERFULED IT


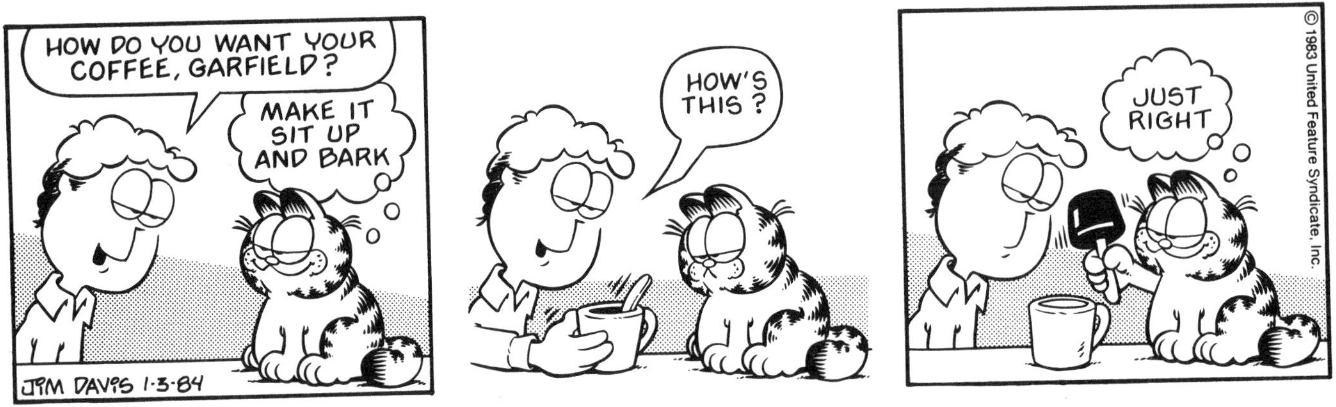
HOW DO YOU WANT YOUR COFFEE, GARFIELD?
MAKE IT SIT UP AND BARK
JIM DAVIS 1-3-84
HOW'S THIS?
JUST RIGHT

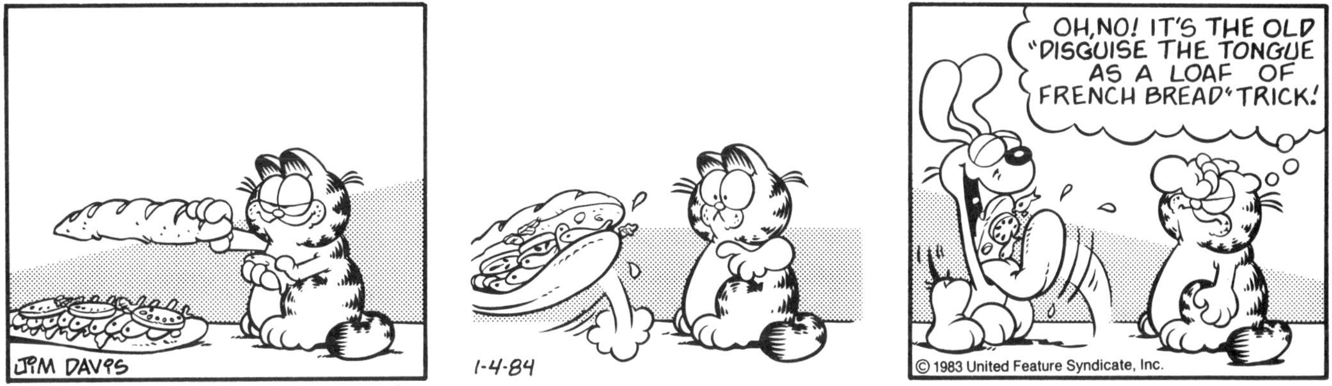
JIM DAVIS
1-4-84
OH, NO! IT'S THE OLD "DISGUISE THE TONGUE AS A LOAF OF FRENCH BREAD" TRICK!
© 1983 United Feature Syndicate, Inc.

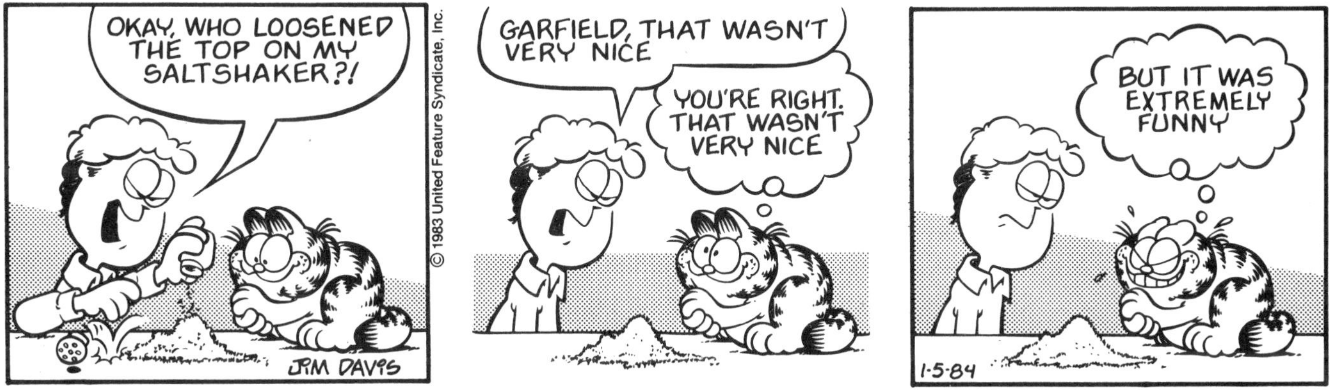
OKAY, WHO LOOSENED THE TOP ON MY SALTSHAKER?!
JIM DAVIS
© 1983 United Feature Syndicate, Inc.
GARFIELD, THAT WASN'T VERY NICE
YOU'RE RIGHT. THAT WASN'T VERY NICE
BUT IT WAS EXTREMELY FUNNY
1-5-84

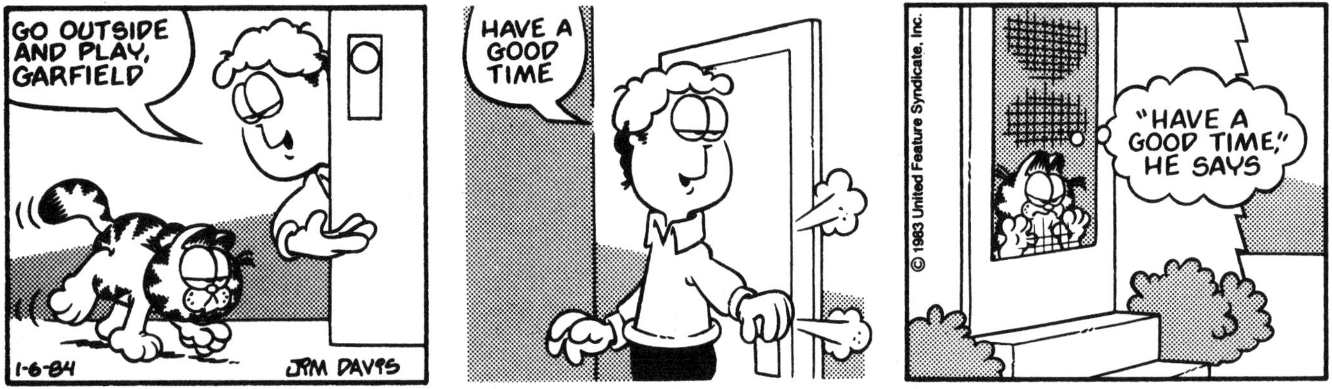
GO OUTSIDE AND PLAY, GARFIELD
1-6-84
JIM DAVIS
HAVE A GOOD TIME
© 1983 United Feature Syndicate, Inc.
"HAVE A GOOD TIME," HE SAYS

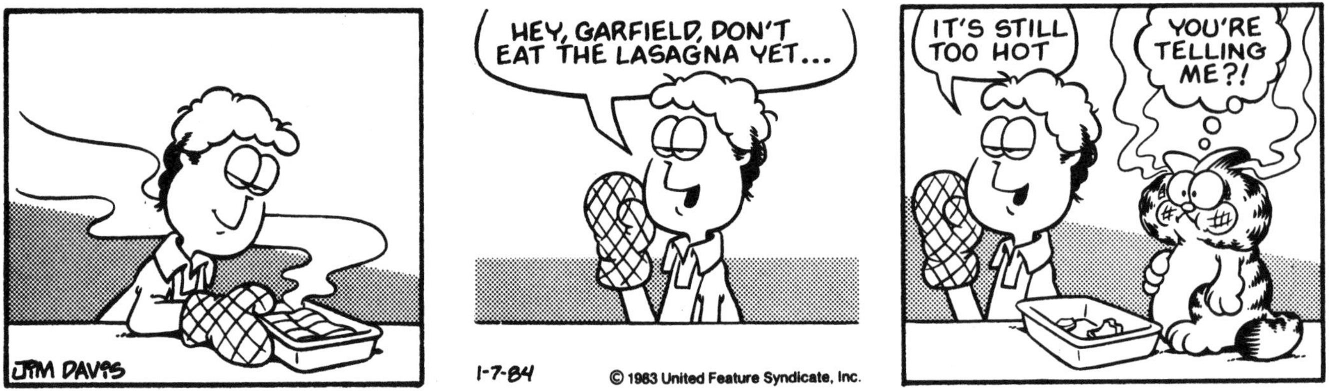
JIM DAVIS
HEY, GARFIELD, DON'T EAT THE LASAGNA YET...
1-7-84
© 1983 United Feature Syndicate, Inc.
IT'S STILL TOO HOT
YOU'RE TELLING ME?!

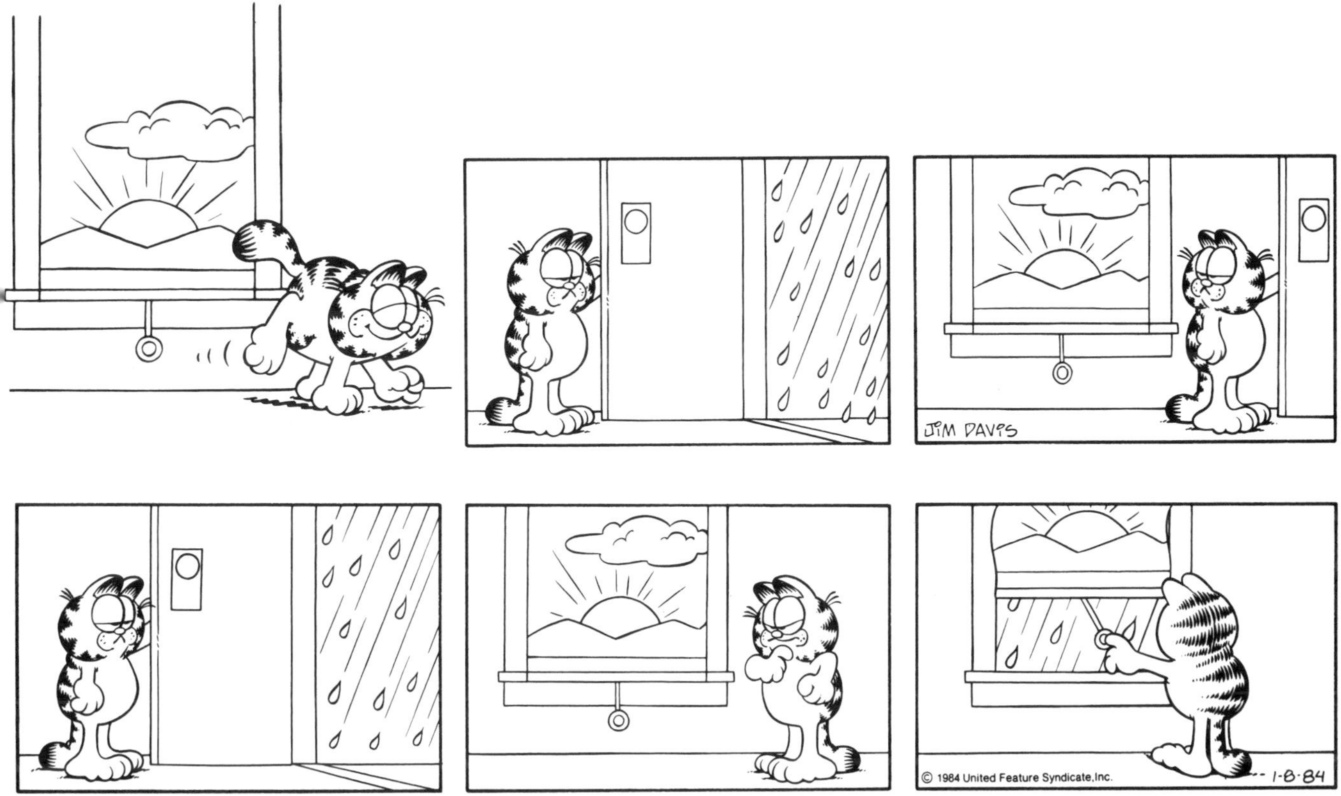
JIM DAVIS
© 1984 United Feature Syndicate, Inc.
1-8-84

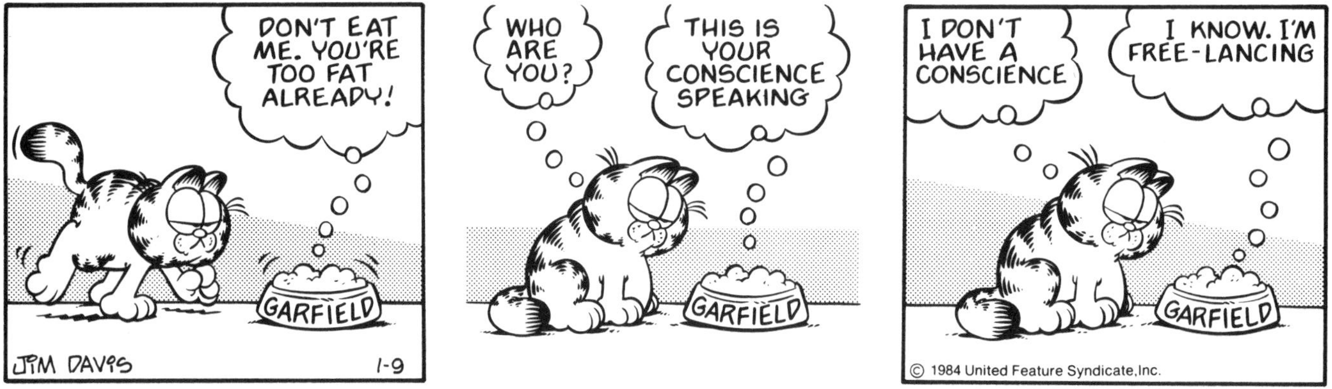
DON'T EAT ME. YOU'RE TOO FAT ALREADY!
JIM DAVIS
1-9
WHO ARE YOU?
THIS IS YOUR CONSCIENCE SPEAKING
I DON'T HAVE A CONSCIENCE
I KNOW. I'M FREE-LANCING
GARFIELD
© 1984 United Feature Syndicate, Inc.

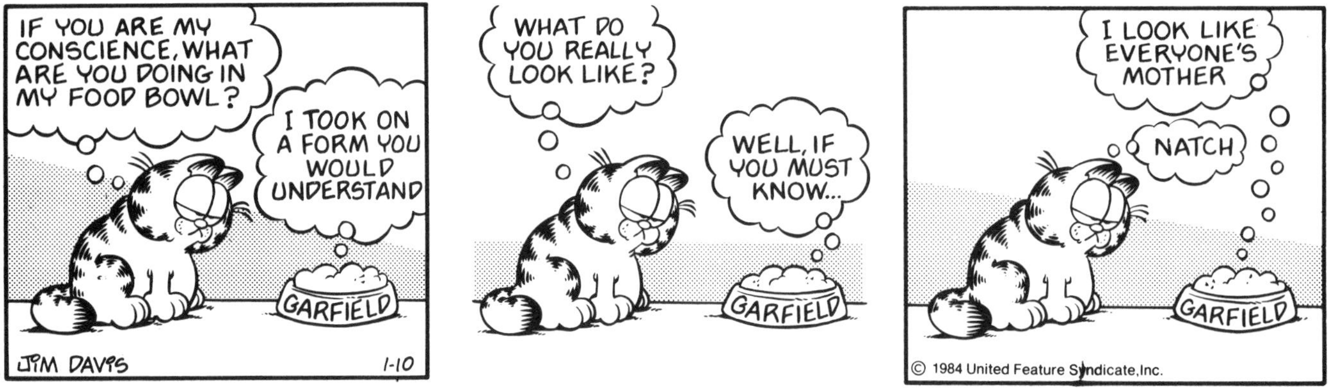
IF YOU ARE MY CONSCIENCE, WHAT ARE YOU DOING IN MY FOOD BOWL?
I TOOK ON A FORM YOU WOULD UNDERSTAND
JIM DAVIS
1-10
WHAT DO YOU REALLY LOOK LIKE?
WELL, IF YOU MUST KNOW...
I LOOK LIKE EVERYONE'S MOTHER
NATCH
GARFIELD
© 1984 United Feature Syndicate, Inc.

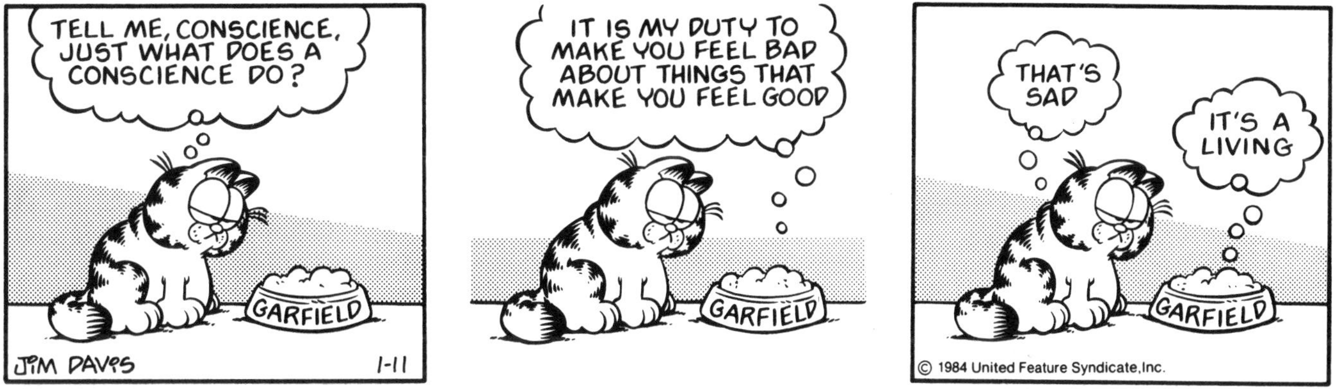
TELL ME, CONSCIENCE, JUST WHAT DOES A CONSCIENCE DO?
IT IS MY DUTY TO MAKE YOU FEEL BAD ABOUT THINGS THAT MAKE YOU FEEL GOOD
THAT'S SAD
IT'S A LIVING
GARFIELD
JIM DAVIS
1-11
© 1984 United Feature Syndicate, Inc.

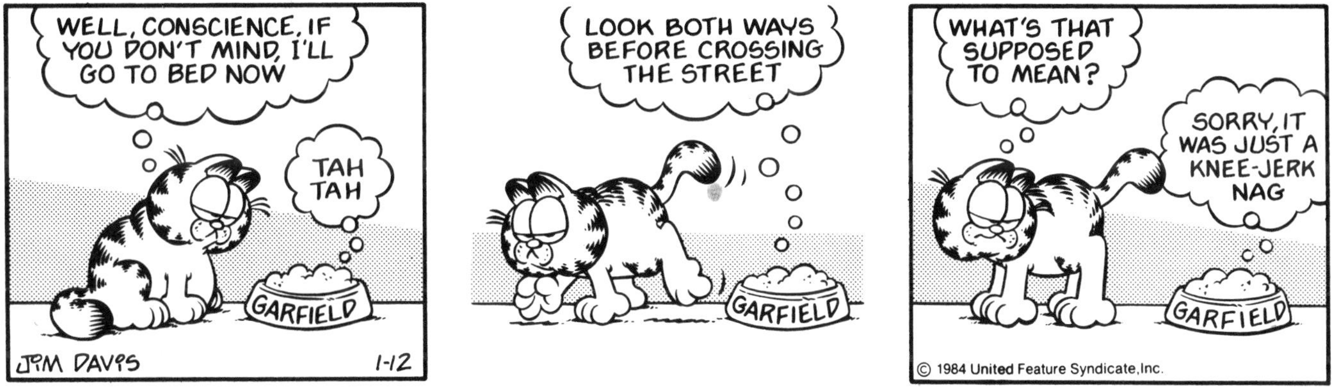
WELL, CONSCIENCE, IF YOU DON'T MIND, I'LL GO TO BED NOW
TAH TAH
LOOK BOTH WAYS BEFORE CROSSING THE STREET
WHAT'S THAT SUPPOSED TO MEAN?
SORRY, IT WAS JUST A KNEE-JERK NAG
GARFIELD
JIM DAVIS
1-12
© 1984 United Feature Syndicate, Inc.

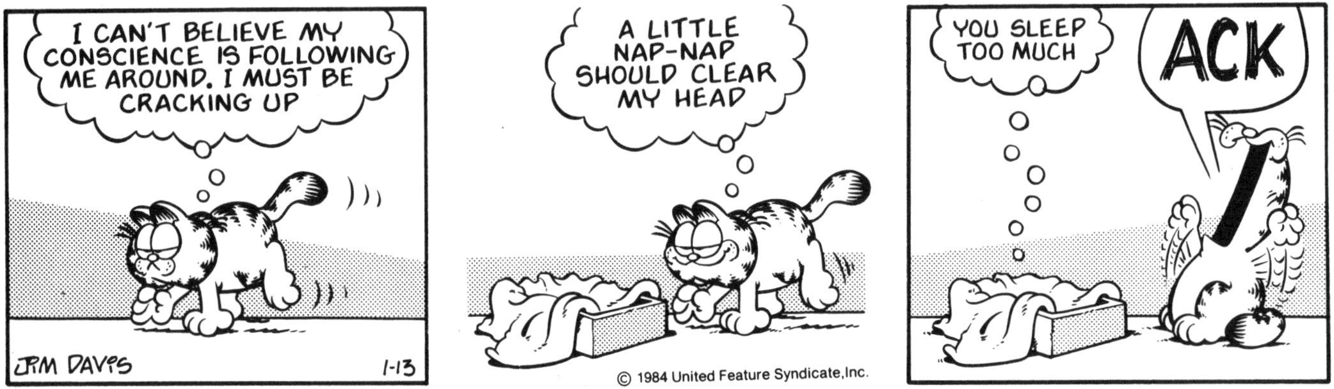
I CAN'T BELIEVE MY CONSCIENCE IS FOLLOWING ME AROUND. I MUST BE CRACKING UP
JIM DAVIS
1-13
A LITTLE NAP-NAP SHOULD CLEAR MY HEAD
© 1984 United Feature Syndicate, Inc.
YOU SLEEP TOO MUCH
ACK

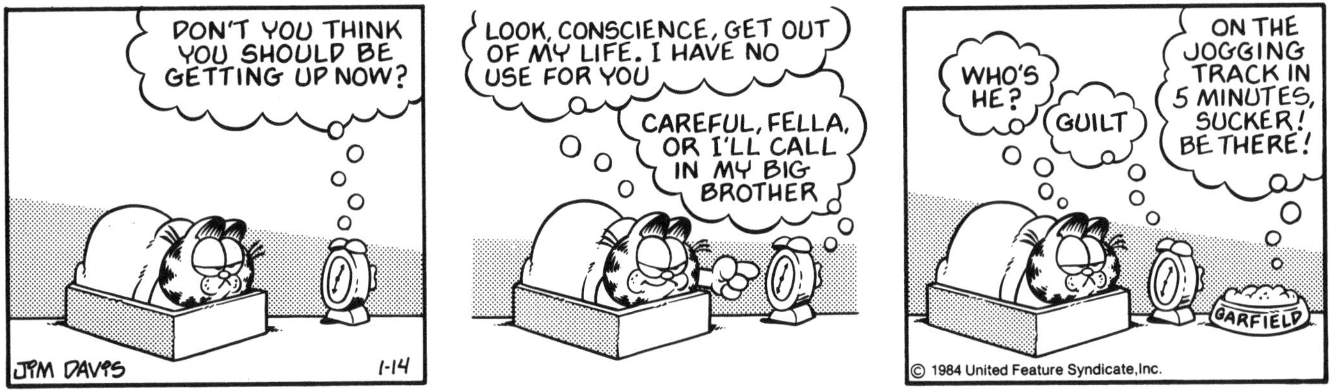
DON'T YOU THINK YOU SHOULD BE GETTING UP NOW?
JIM DAVIS
1-14
LOOK, CONSCIENCE, GET OUT OF MY LIFE. I HAVE NO USE FOR YOU
CAREFUL, FELLA, OR I'LL CALL IN MY BIG BROTHER
WHO'S HE?
GUILT
ON THE JOGGING TRACK IN 5 MINUTES, SUCKER! BE THERE!
GARFIELD
© 1984 United Feature Syndicate, Inc.

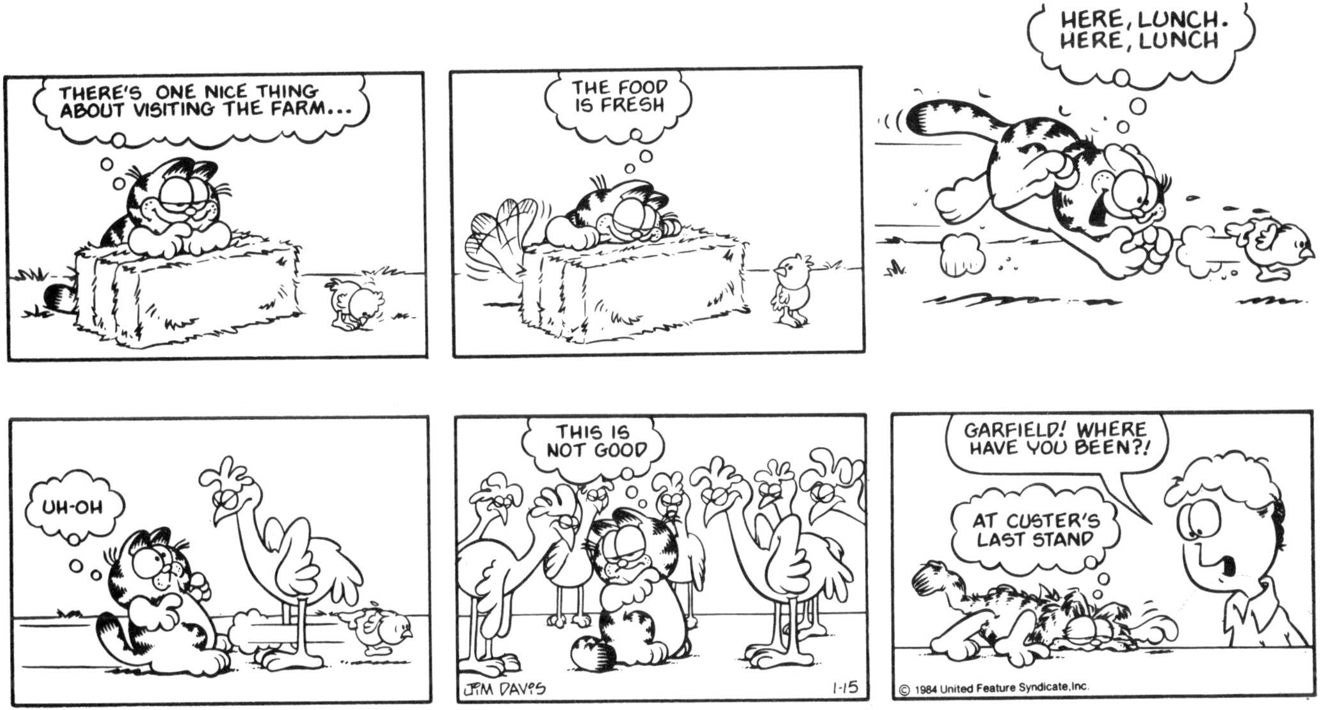
THERE'S ONE NICE THING ABOUT VISITING THE FARM...
THE FOOD IS FRESH
HERE, LUNCH. HERE, LUNCH
UH-OH
THIS IS NOT GOOD
JIM DAVIS
1-15
GARFIELD! WHERE HAVE YOU BEEN?!
AT CUSTER'S LAST STAND
© 1984 United Feature Syndicate, Inc.

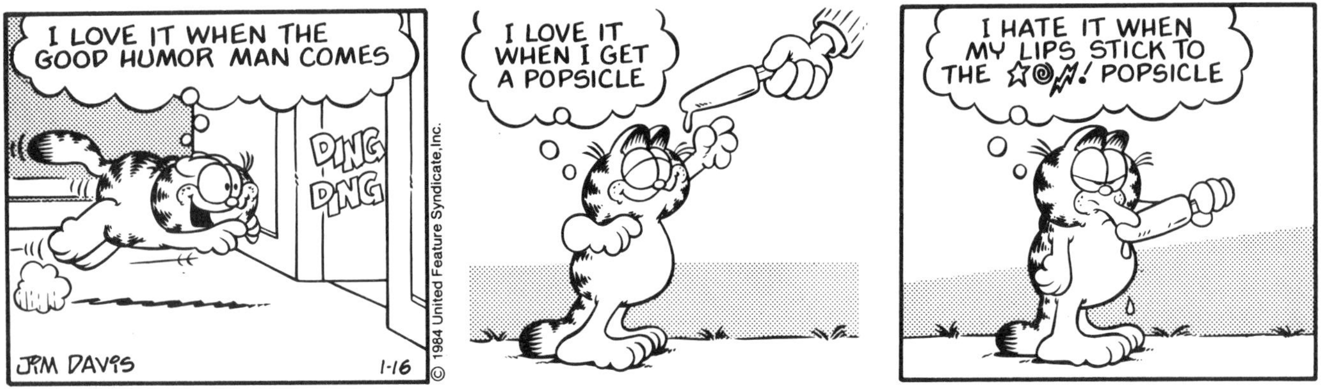
I LOVE IT WHEN THE GOOD HUMOR MAN COMES
DING DING
JIM DAVIS
1-16
© 1984 United Feature Syndicate, Inc.
I LOVE IT WHEN I GET A POPSICLE
I HATE IT WHEN MY LIPS STICK TO THE ☆◎ϟ! POPSICLE

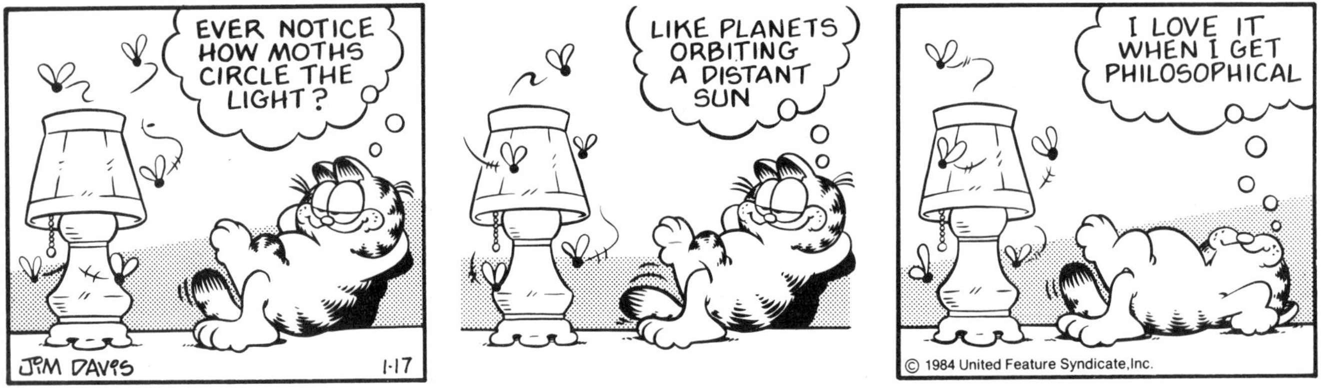
EVER NOTICE HOW MOTHS CIRCLE THE LIGHT?
JIM DAVIS
1-17
LIKE PLANETS ORBITING A DISTANT SUN
I LOVE IT WHEN I GET PHILOSOPHICAL
© 1984 United Feature Syndicate, Inc.

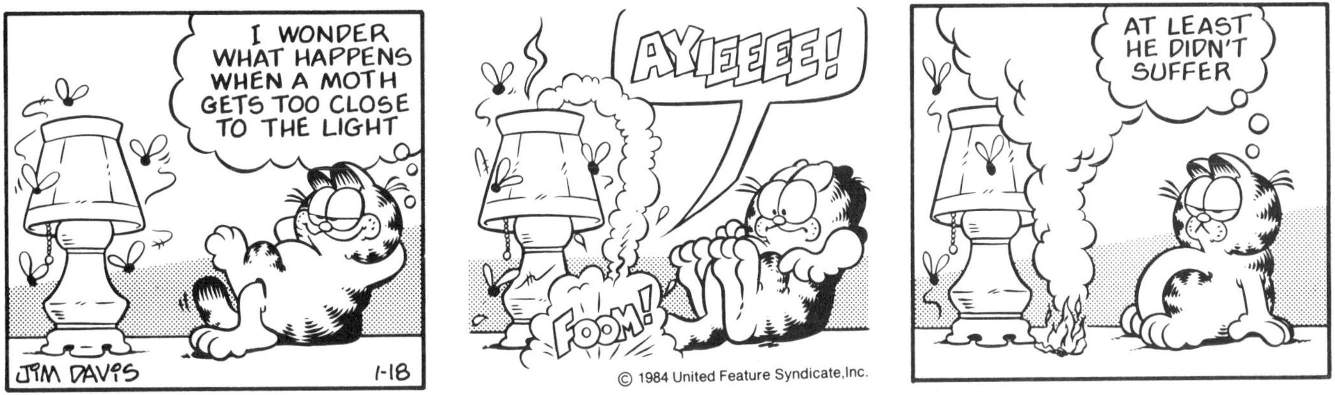
I WONDER WHAT HAPPENS WHEN A MOTH GETS TOO CLOSE TO THE LIGHT
JIM DAVIS
1-18
AYIEEEEE!
FOOM!
© 1984 United Feature Syndicate,Inc.
AT LEAST HE DIDN'T SUFFER

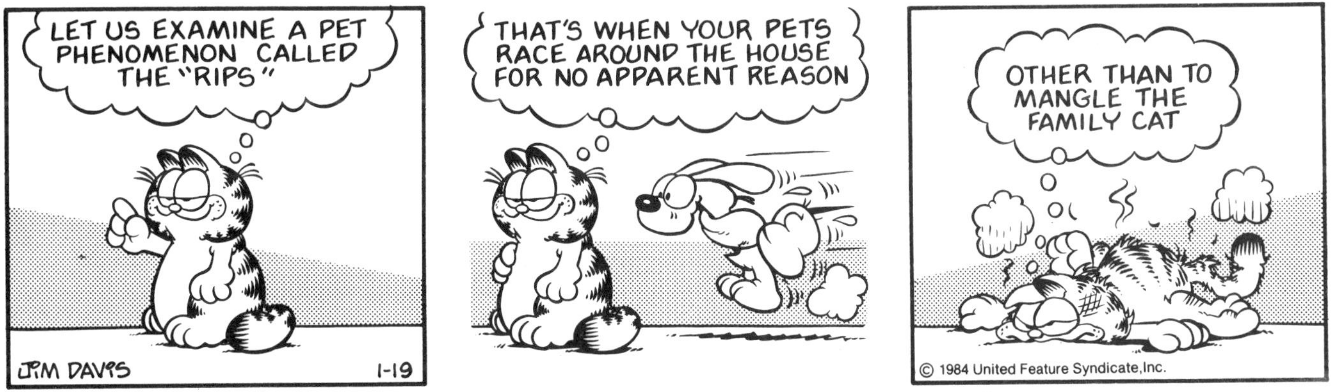
LET US EXAMINE A PET PHENOMENON CALLED THE "RIPS"
JIM DAVIS
1-19
THAT'S WHEN YOUR PETS RACE AROUND THE HOUSE FOR NO APPARENT REASON
OTHER THAN TO MANGLE THE FAMILY CAT
© 1984 United Feature Syndicate,Inc.

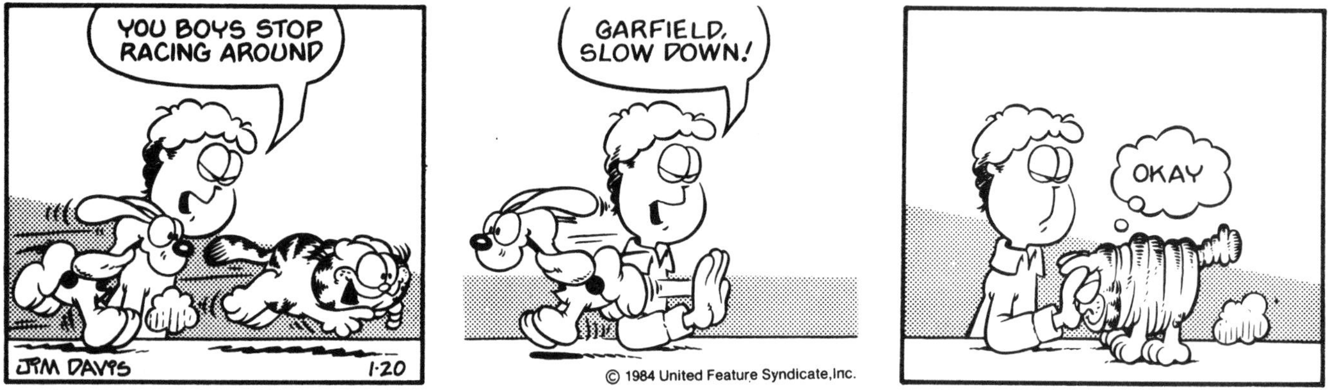
YOU BOYS STOP RACING AROUND
JIM DAVIS
1-20
GARFIELD, SLOW DOWN!
© 1984 United Feature Syndicate, Inc.
OKAY

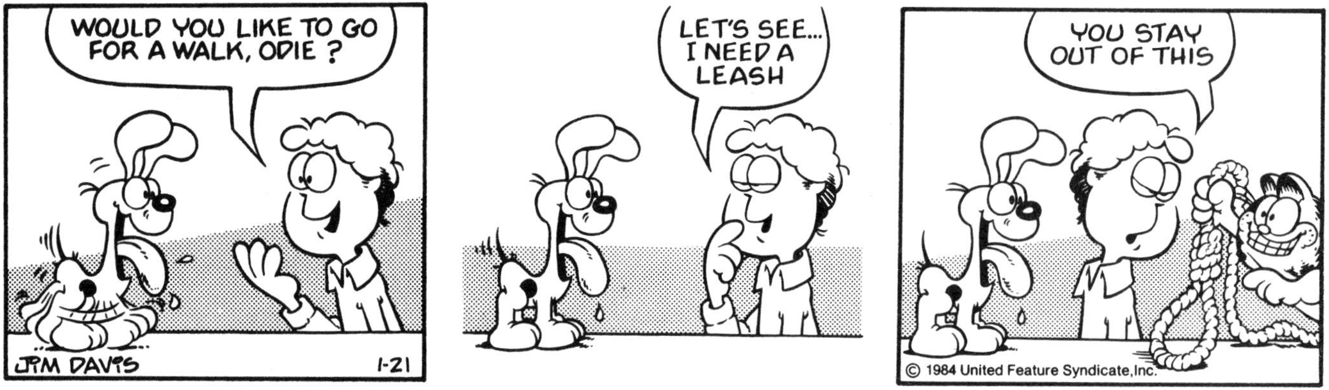
WOULD YOU LIKE TO GO FOR A WALK, ODIE ?
JIM DAVIS
1-21
LET'S SEE... I NEED A LEASH
YOU STAY OUT OF THIS
© 1984 United Feature Syndicate, Inc.

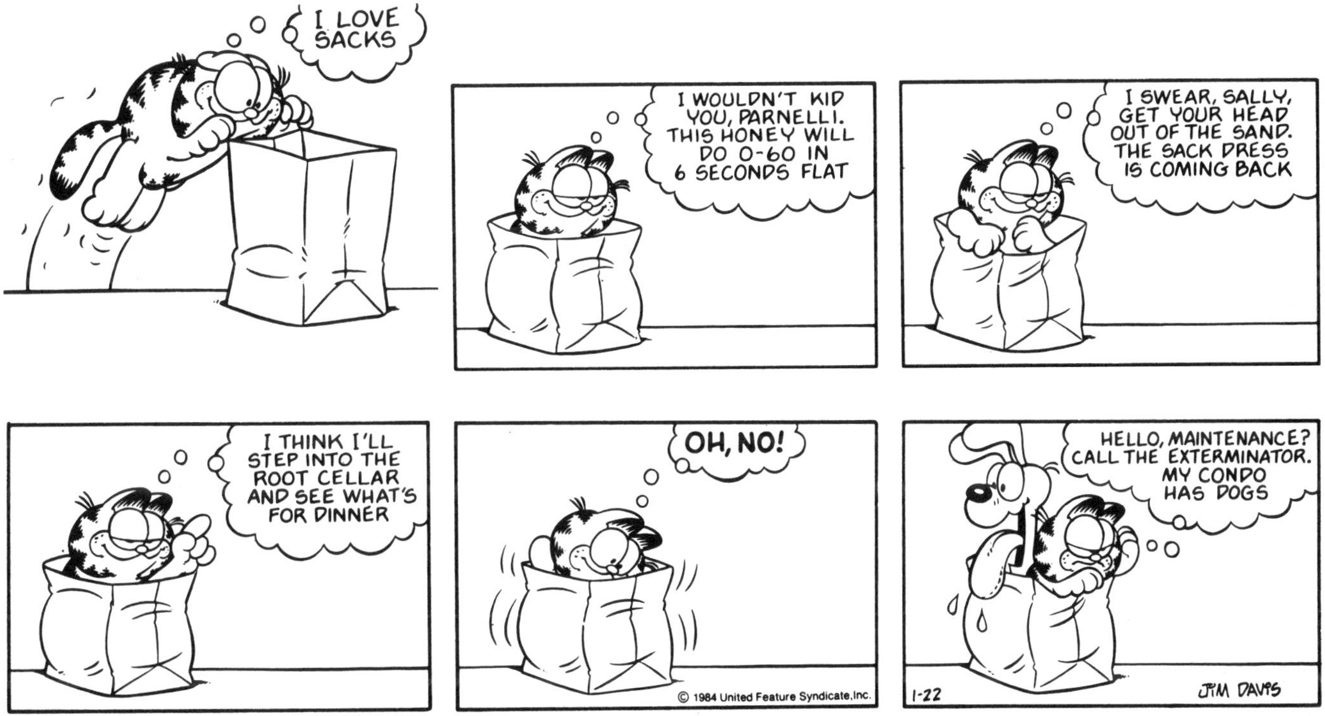
I LOVE SACKS
I WOULDN'T KID YOU, PARNELLI. THIS HONEY WILL DO 0-60 IN 6 SECONDS FLAT
I SWEAR, SALLY, GET YOUR HEAD OUT OF THE SAND. THE SACK DRESS IS COMING BACK
I THINK I'LL STEP INTO THE ROOT CELLAR AND SEE WHAT'S FOR DINNER
OH, NO!
HELLO, MAINTENANCE? CALL THE EXTERMINATOR. MY CONDO HAS DOGS
© 1984 United Feature Syndicate, Inc.
1-22
JIM DAVIS

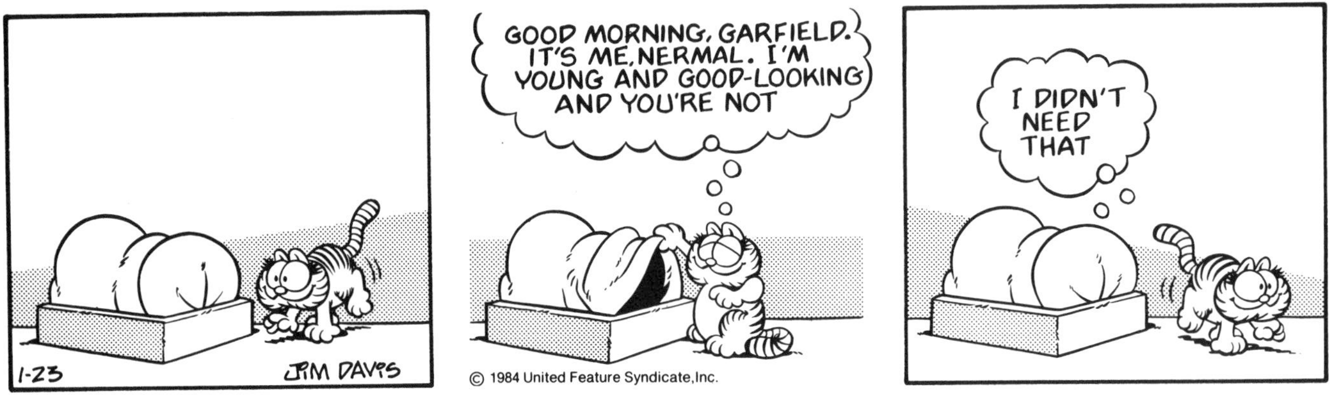
1-23
JIM DAVIS
GOOD MORNING, GARFIELD. IT'S ME, NERMAL. I'M YOUNG AND GOOD-LOOKING AND YOU'RE NOT
© 1984 United Feature Syndicate, Inc.
I DIDN'T NEED THAT

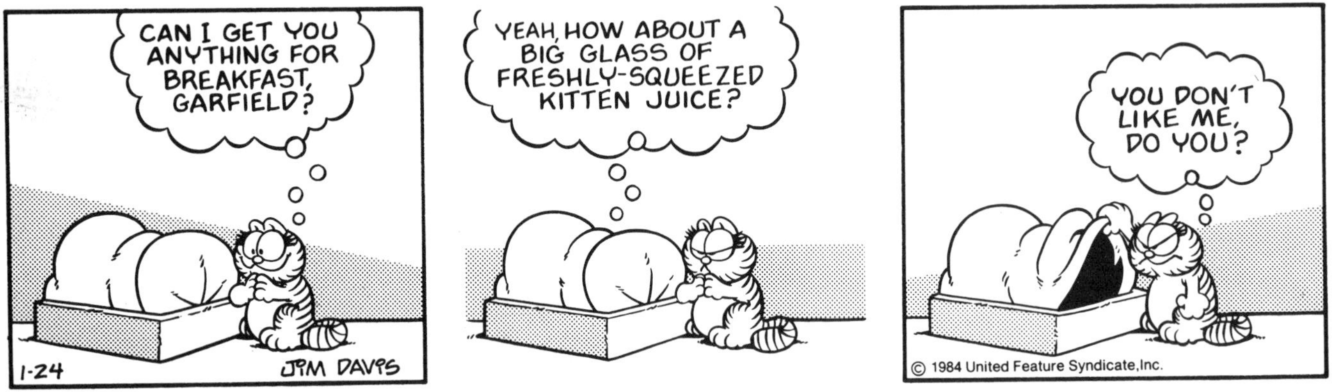
CAN I GET YOU ANYTHING FOR BREAKFAST, GARFIELD?
1-24
JIM DAVIS
YEAH, HOW ABOUT A BIG GLASS OF FRESHLY-SQUEEZED KITTEN JUICE?
YOU DON'T LIKE ME, DO YOU?
© 1984 United Feature Syndicate, Inc.

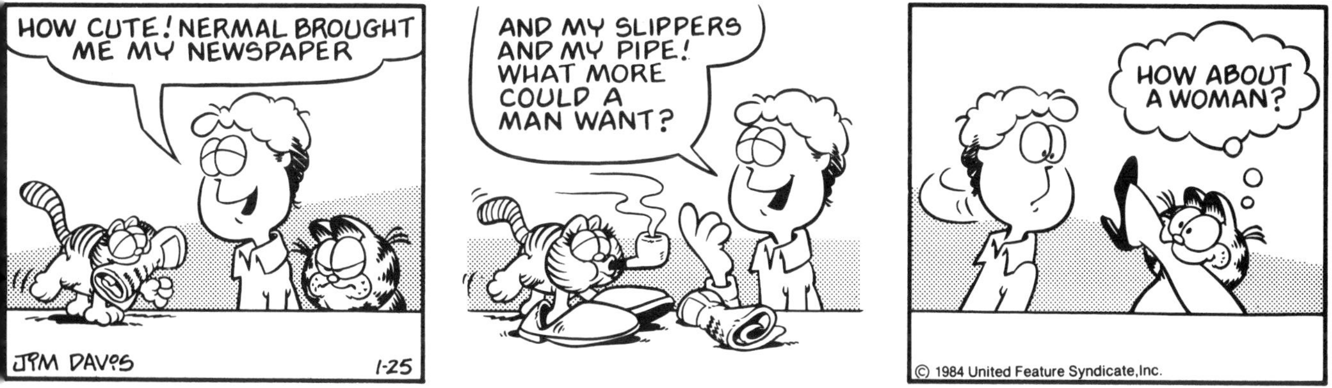
HOW CUTE! NERMAL BROUGHT ME MY NEWSPAPER
JIM DAVIS
1-25
AND MY SLIPPERS AND MY PIPE! WHAT MORE COULD A MAN WANT?
HOW ABOUT A WOMAN?
© 1984 United Feature Syndicate, Inc.

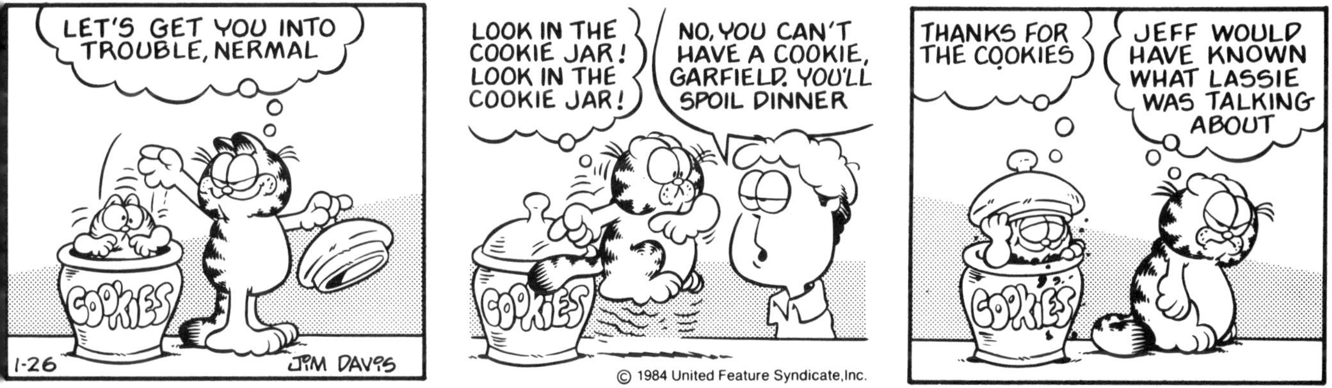
LET'S GET YOU INTO TROUBLE, NERMAL
COOKIES
1-26
JIM DAVIS
LOOK IN THE COOKIE JAR! LOOK IN THE COOKIE JAR!
NO, YOU CAN'T HAVE A COOKIE, GARFIELD. YOU'LL SPOIL DINNER
© 1984 United Feature Syndicate, Inc.
THANKS FOR THE COOKIES
JEFF WOULD HAVE KNOWN WHAT LASSIE WAS TALKING ABOUT

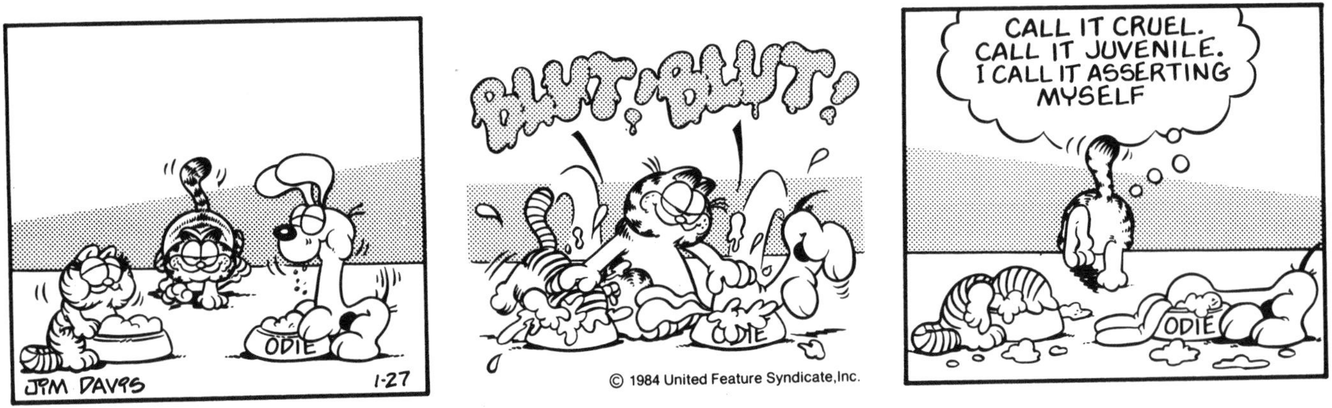
JIM DAVIS
1·27
ODIE
BLUT, BLUT!
© 1984 United Feature Syndicate,Inc.
CALL IT CRUEL. CALL IT JUVENILE. I CALL IT ASSERTING MYSELF
ODIE

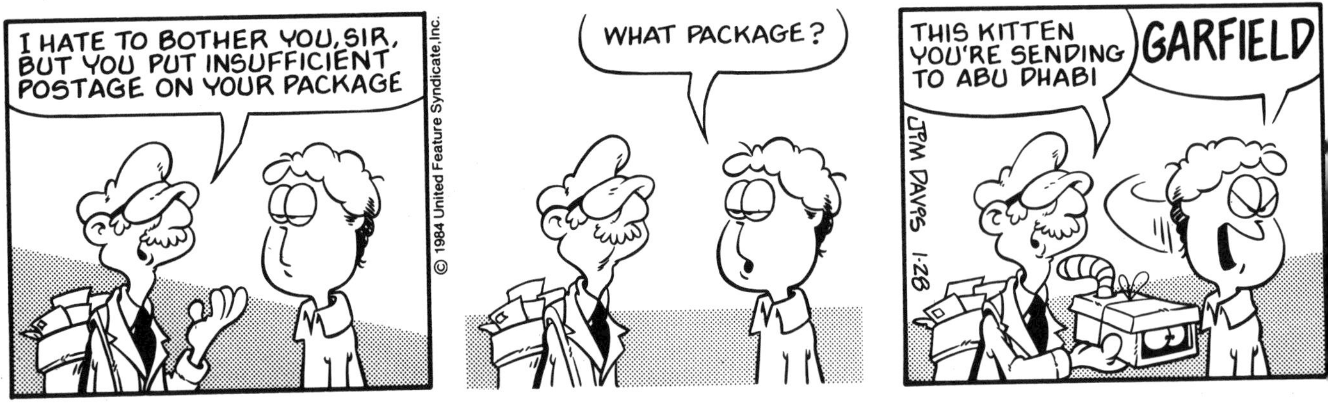
I HATE TO BOTHER YOU, SIR, BUT YOU PUT INSUFFICIENT POSTAGE ON YOUR PACKAGE
© 1984 United Feature Syndicate,Inc.
WHAT PACKAGE?
THIS KITTEN YOU'RE SENDING TO ABU DHABI
GARFIELD
JIM DAVIS 1·28

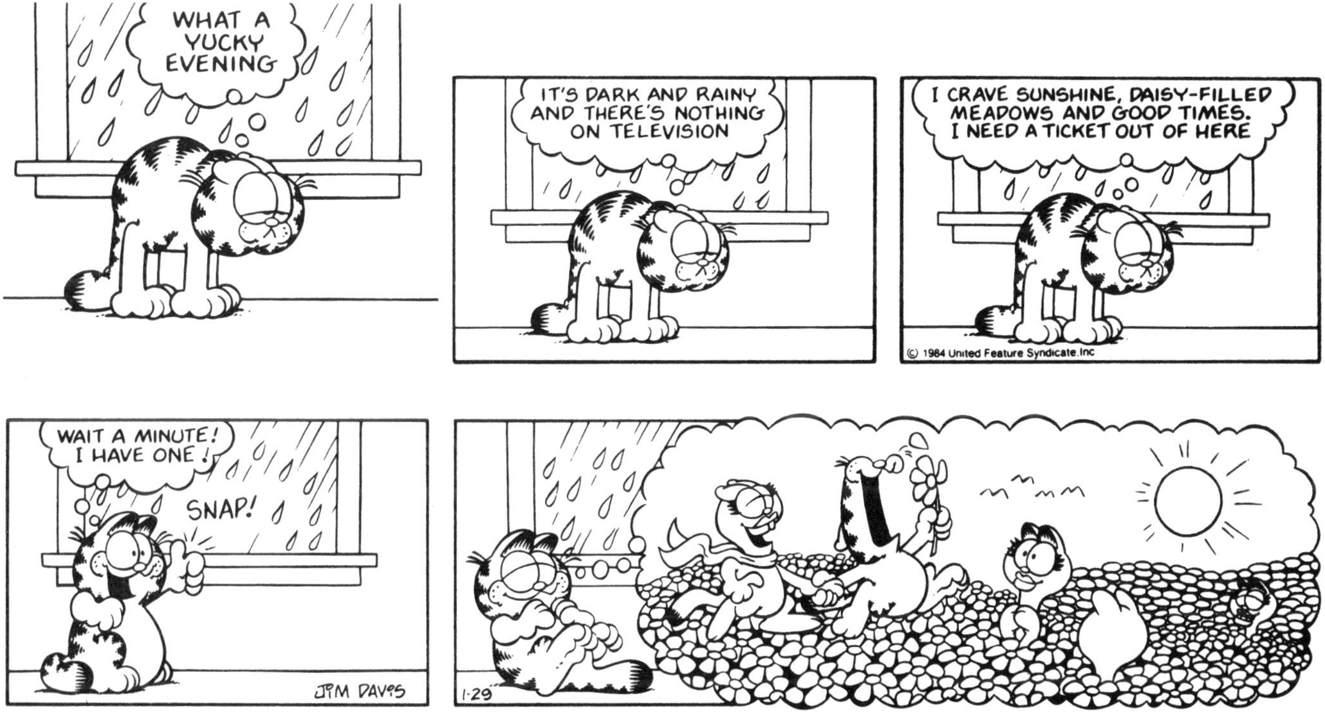

WHAT A YUCKY EVENING
IT'S DARK AND RAINY AND THERE'S NOTHING ON TELEVISION
I CRAVE SUNSHINE, DAISY-FILLED MEADOWS AND GOOD TIMES. I NEED A TICKET OUT OF HERE
© 1984 United Feature Syndicate, Inc
WAIT A MINUTE! I HAVE ONE!
SNAP!
JIM DAVIS
1-29

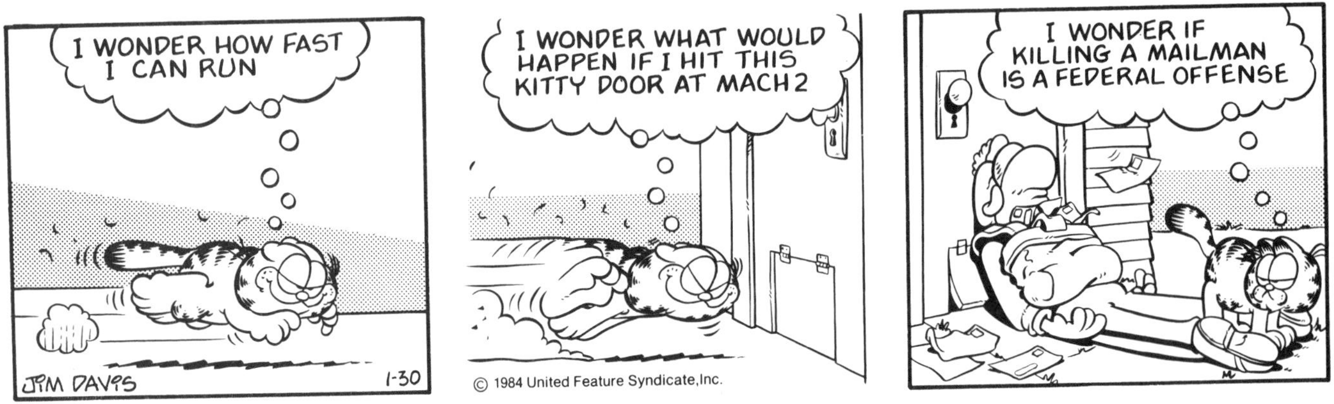
I WONDER HOW FAST I CAN RUN
JIM DAVIS
1-30
I WONDER WHAT WOULD HAPPEN IF I HIT THIS KITTY DOOR AT MACH 2
© 1984 United Feature Syndicate, Inc.
I WONDER IF KILLING A MAILMAN IS A FEDERAL OFFENSE

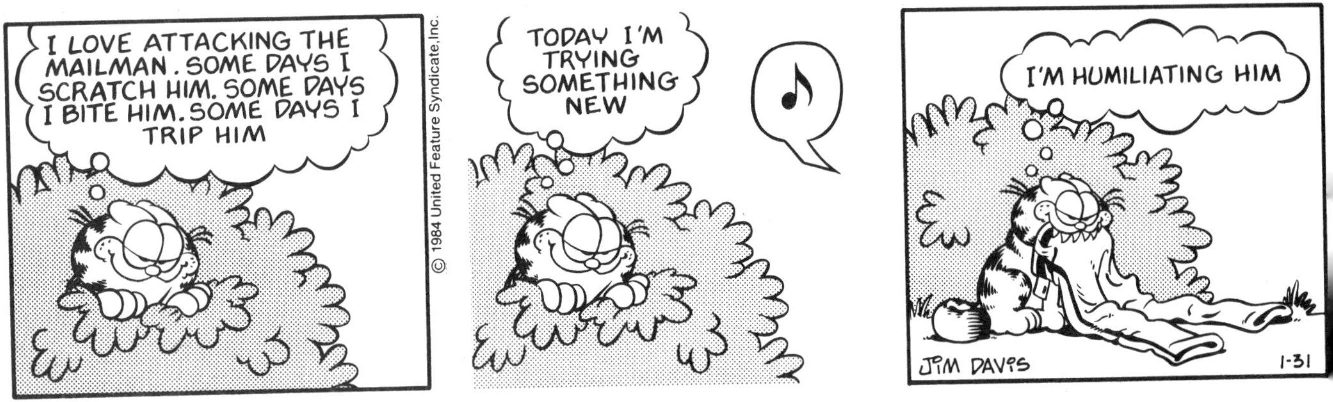
I LOVE ATTACKING THE MAILMAN. SOME DAYS I SCRATCH HIM. SOME DAYS I BITE HIM. SOME DAYS I TRIP HIM
© 1984 United Feature Syndicate, Inc.
TODAY I'M TRYING SOMETHING NEW
♪
I'M HUMILIATING HIM
JIM DAVIS
1-31

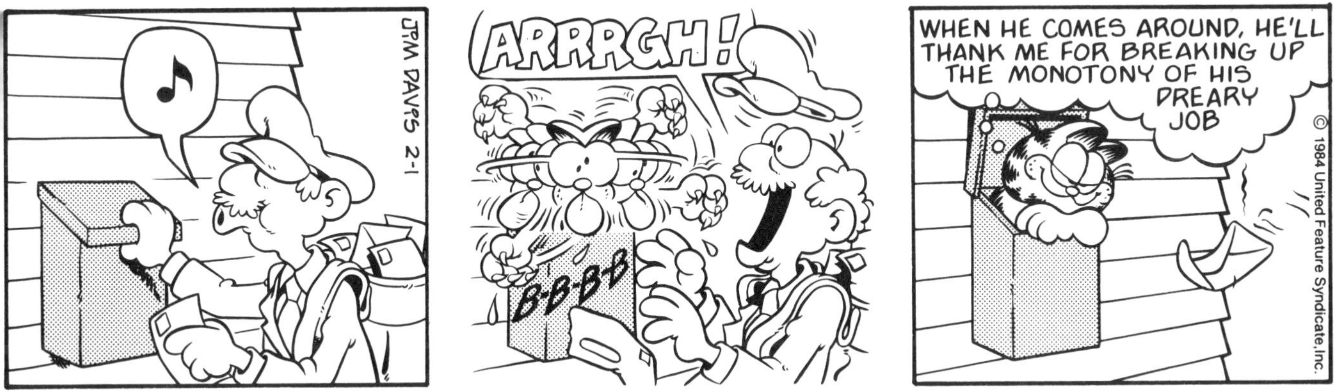
JIM DAVIS 2-1
ARRRGH!
B-B-B-B
WHEN HE COMES AROUND, HE'LL THANK ME FOR BREAKING UP THE MONOTONY OF HIS DREARY JOB
© 1984 United Feature Syndicate,Inc.

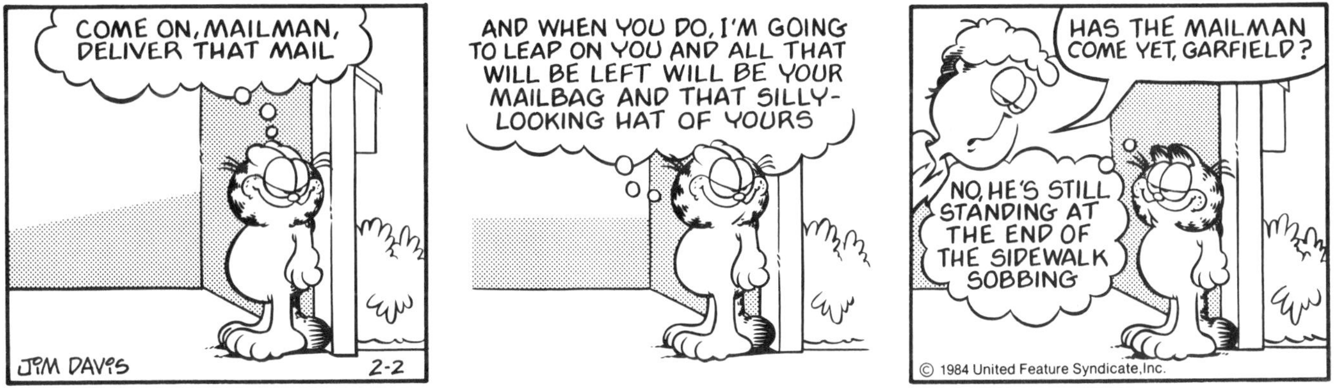
COME ON, MAILMAN, DELIVER THAT MAIL
JIM DAVIS
2-2
AND WHEN YOU DO, I'M GOING TO LEAP ON YOU AND ALL THAT WILL BE LEFT WILL BE YOUR MAILBAG AND THAT SILLY-LOOKING HAT OF YOURS
HAS THE MAILMAN COME YET, GARFIELD?
NO, HE'S STILL STANDING AT THE END OF THE SIDEWALK SOBBING
© 1984 United Feature Syndicate,Inc.

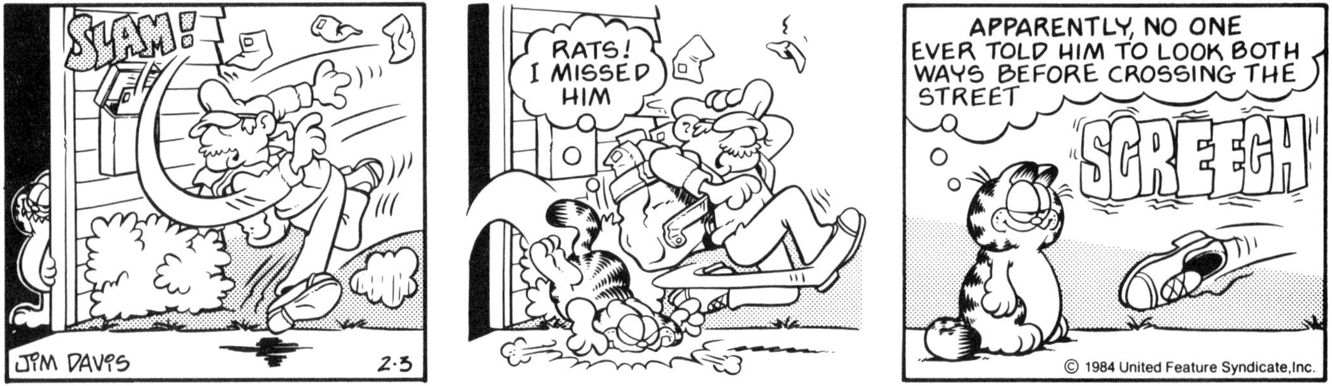
SLAM!
JIM DAVIS
2-3
RATS! I MISSED HIM
APPARENTLY, NO ONE EVER TOLD HIM TO LOOK BOTH WAYS BEFORE CROSSING THE STREET
SCREECH
© 1984 United Feature Syndicate, Inc.

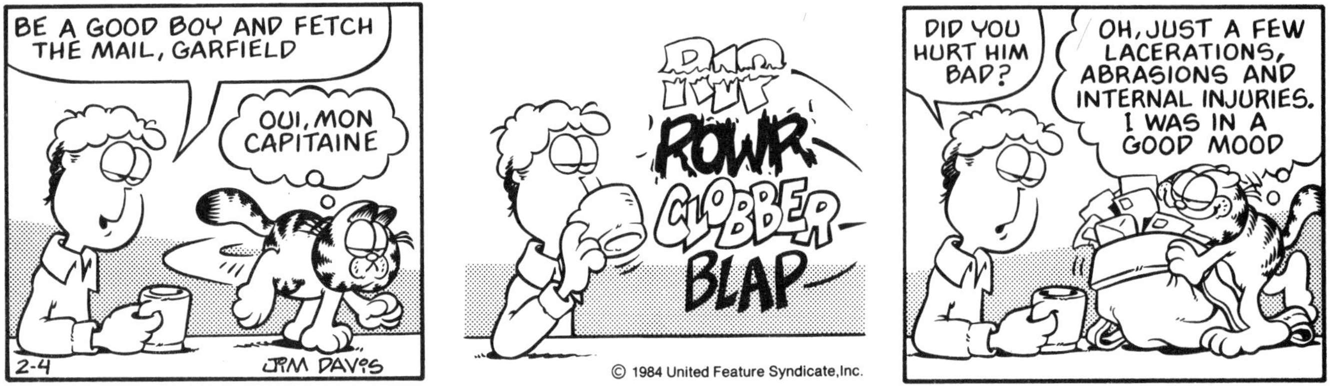
BE A GOOD BOY AND FETCH THE MAIL, GARFIELD
OUI, MON CAPITAINE
2-4
JIM DAVIS
RIP
ROWR
CLOBBER
BLAP
© 1984 United Feature Syndicate, Inc.
DID YOU HURT HIM BAD?
OH, JUST A FEW LACERATIONS, ABRASIONS AND INTERNAL INJURIES. I WAS IN A GOOD MOOD

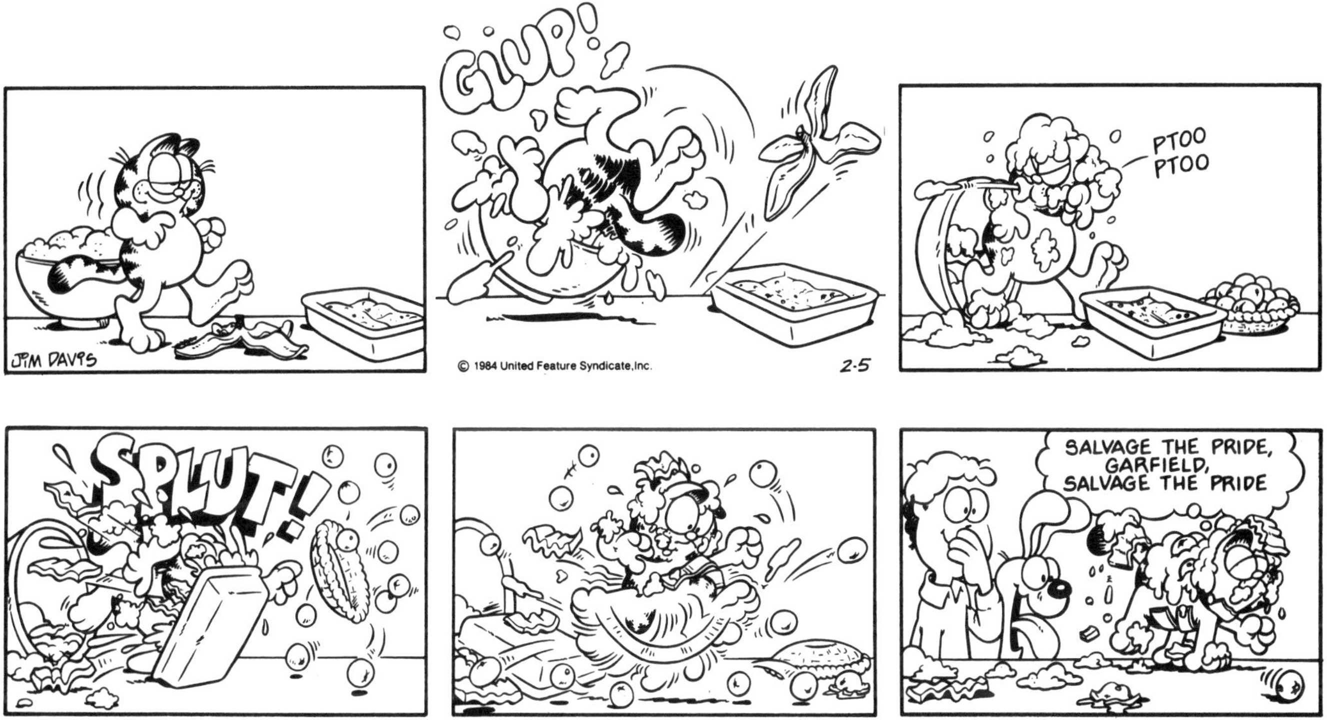
JIM DAVIS
GLUP!
© 1984 United Feature Syndicate, Inc.
2-5
PTOO
PTOO
SPLUT!
SALVAGE THE PRIDE,
GARFIELD,
SALVAGE THE PRIDE

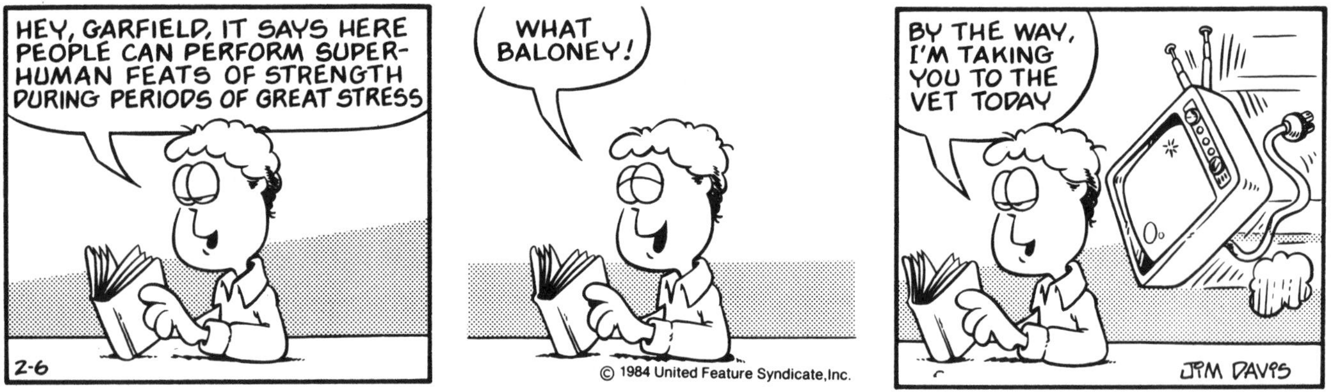
HEY, GARFIELD, IT SAYS HERE PEOPLE CAN PERFORM SUPER-HUMAN FEATS OF STRENGTH DURING PERIODS OF GREAT STRESS
2-6
WHAT BALONEY!
© 1984 United Feature Syndicate, Inc.
BY THE WAY, I'M TAKING YOU TO THE VET TODAY
JIM DAVIS

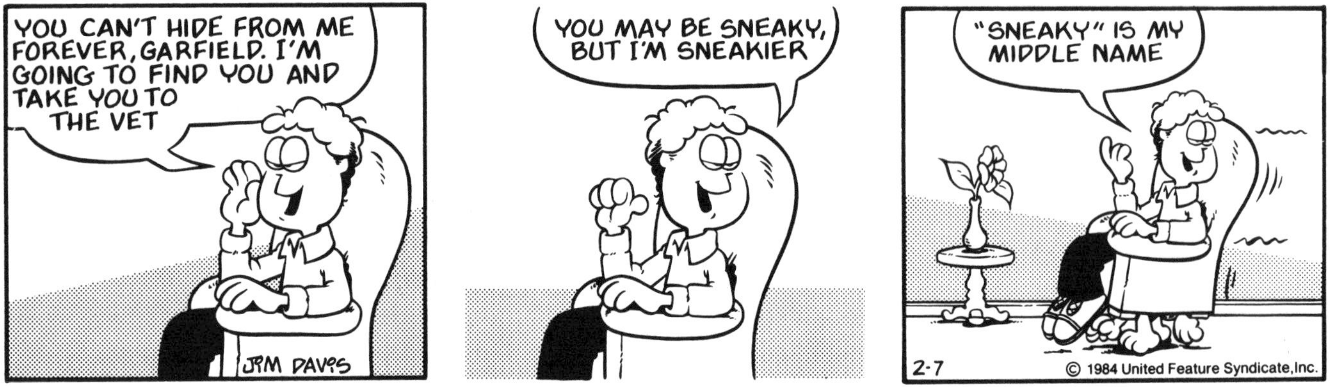
YOU CAN'T HIDE FROM ME FOREVER, GARFIELD. I'M GOING TO FIND YOU AND TAKE YOU TO THE VET
JIM DAVIS
YOU MAY BE SNEAKY, BUT I'M SNEAKIER
"SNEAKY" IS MY MIDDLE NAME
2-7
© 1984 United Feature Syndicate, Inc.

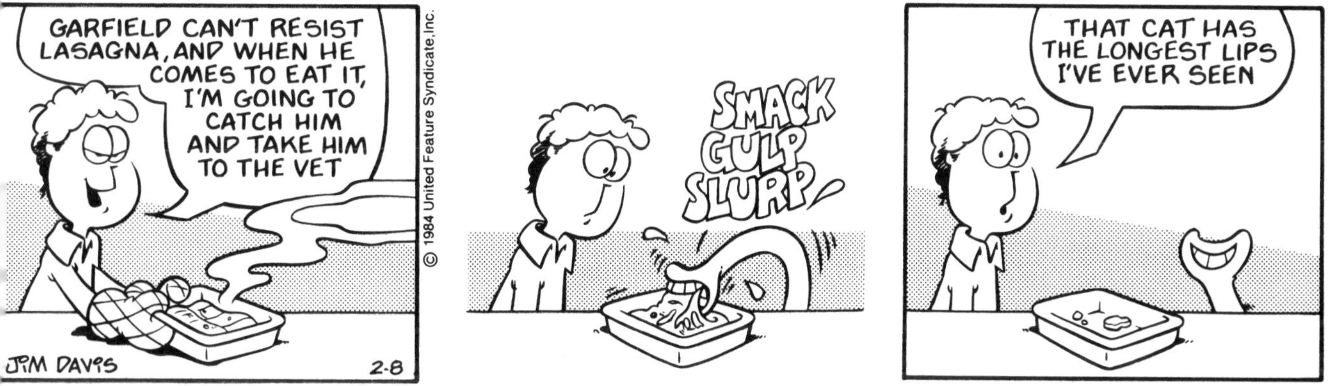
GARFIELD CAN'T RESIST LASAGNA, AND WHEN HE COMES TO EAT IT, I'M GOING TO CATCH HIM AND TAKE HIM TO THE VET
JIM DAVIS
2-8
© 1984 United Feature Syndicate, Inc.
SMACK GULP SLURP
THAT CAT HAS THE LONGEST LIPS I'VE EVER SEEN

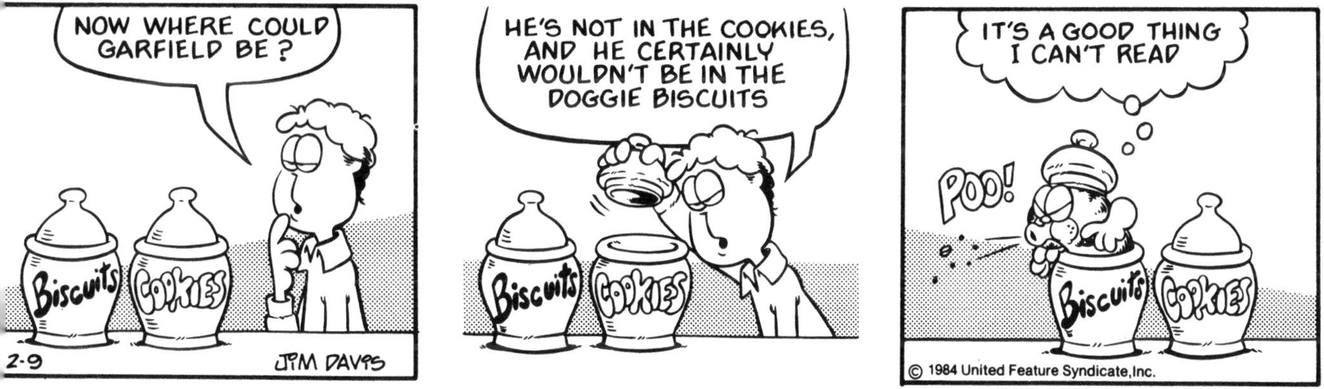
NOW WHERE COULD GARFIELD BE?
Biscuits
COOKIES
2-9
JIM DAVIS
HE'S NOT IN THE COOKIES, AND HE CERTAINLY WOULDN'T BE IN THE DOGGIE BISCUITS
Biscuits
COOKIES
IT'S A GOOD THING I CAN'T READ
POOF!
Biscuits
COOKIES
© 1984 United Feature Syndicate, Inc.

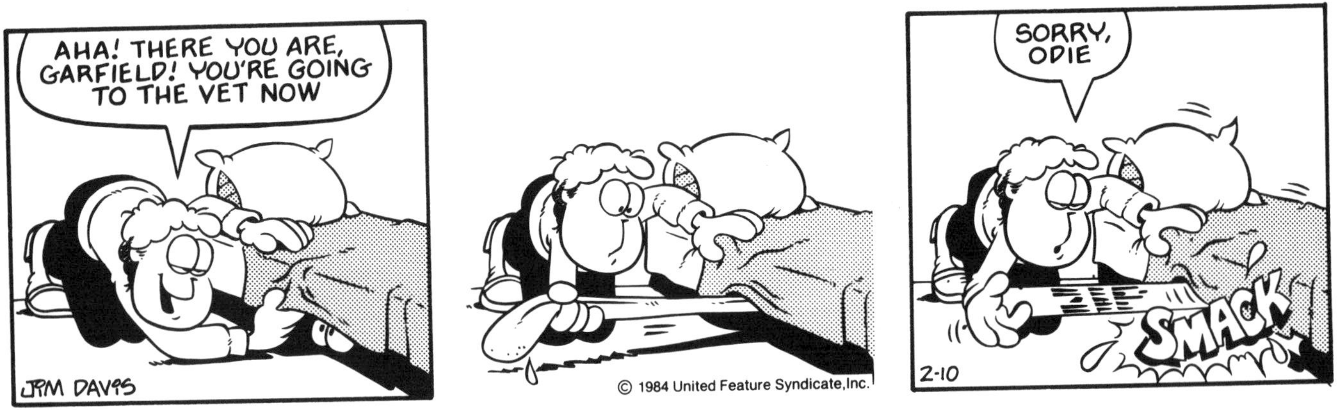
AHA! THERE YOU ARE, GARFIELD! YOU'RE GOING TO THE VET NOW
JIM DAVIS
© 1984 United Feature Syndicate, Inc.
SORRY, ODIE
SMACK
2-10

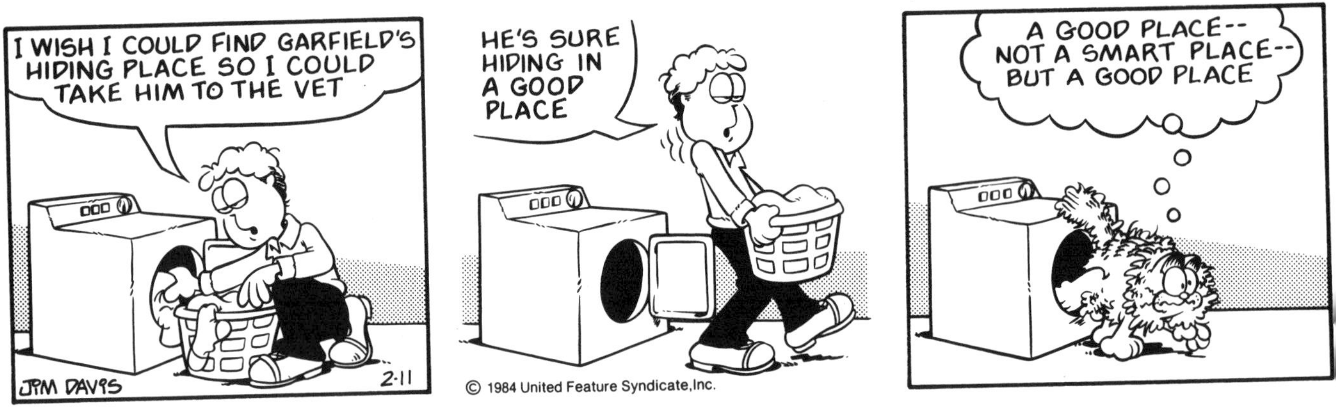
I WISH I COULD FIND GARFIELD'S HIDING PLACE SO I COULD TAKE HIM TO THE VET
JIM DAVIS
2-11
HE'S SURE HIDING IN A GOOD PLACE
© 1984 United Feature Syndicate, Inc.
A GOOD PLACE-- NOT A SMART PLACE-- BUT A GOOD PLACE

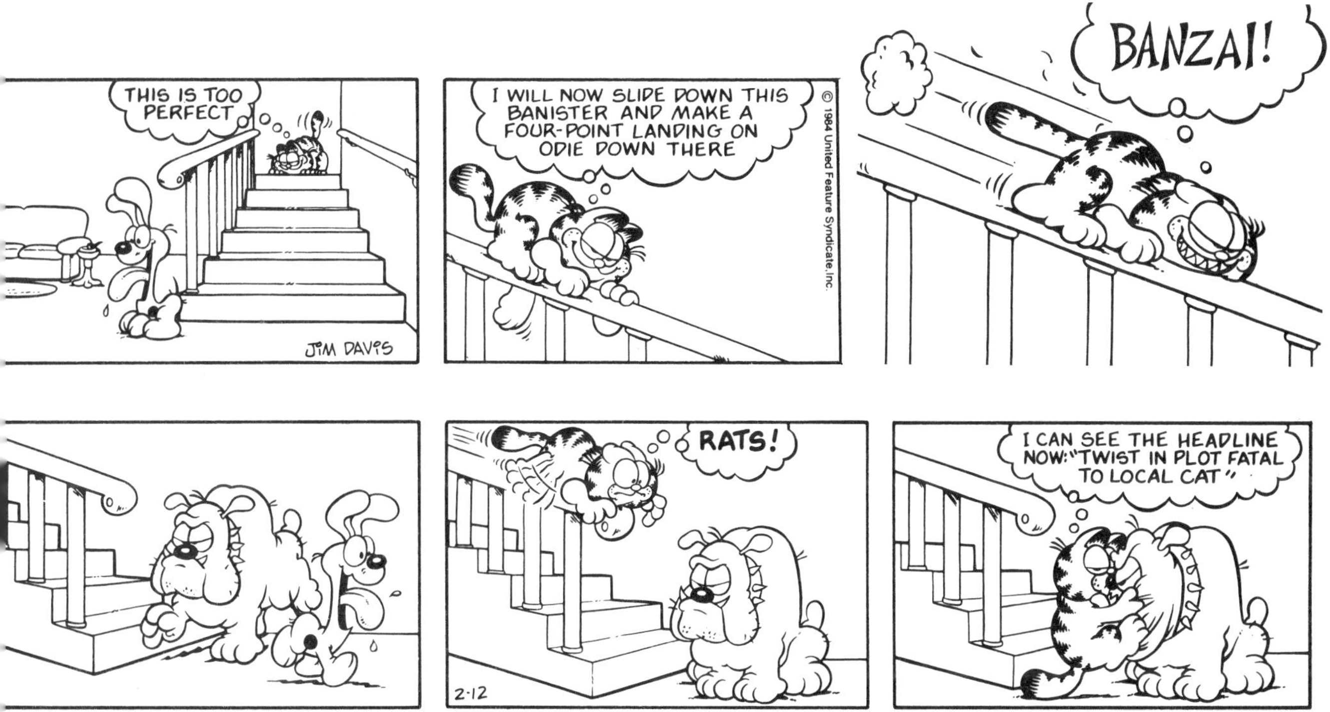
THIS IS TOO PERFECT
JIM DAVIS
I WILL NOW SLIDE DOWN THIS BANISTER AND MAKE A FOUR-POINT LANDING ON ODIE DOWN THERE
© 1984 United Feature Syndicate, Inc.
BANZAI!
RATS!
2-12
I CAN SEE THE HEADLINE NOW: "TWIST IN PLOT FATAL TO LOCAL CAT"

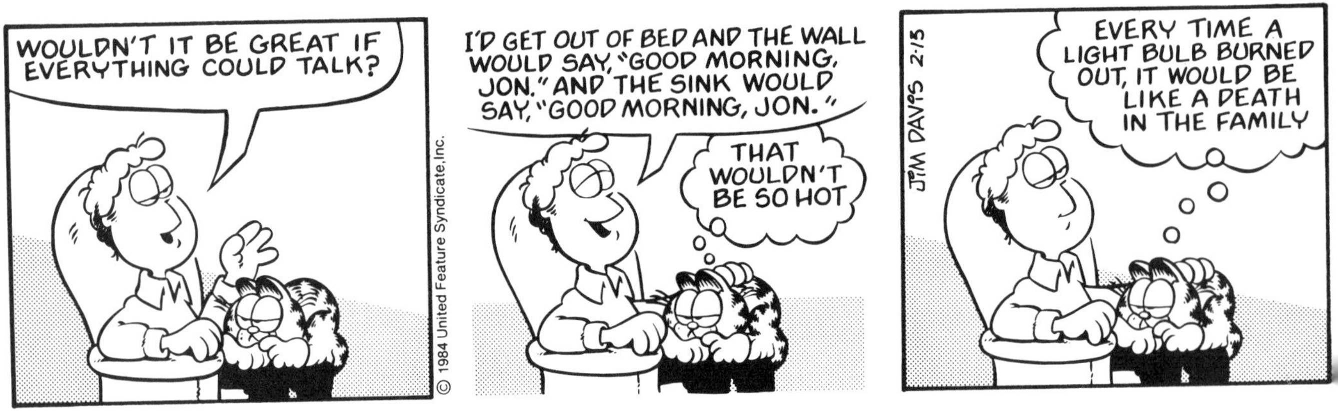
WOULDN'T IT BE GREAT IF EVERYTHING COULD TALK?
I'D GET OUT OF BED AND THE WALL WOULD SAY, "GOOD MORNING, JON." AND THE SINK WOULD SAY, "GOOD MORNING, JON."
THAT WOULDN'T BE SO HOT
JIM DAVIS 2·13
EVERY TIME A LIGHT BULB BURNED OUT, IT WOULD BE LIKE A DEATH IN THE FAMILY



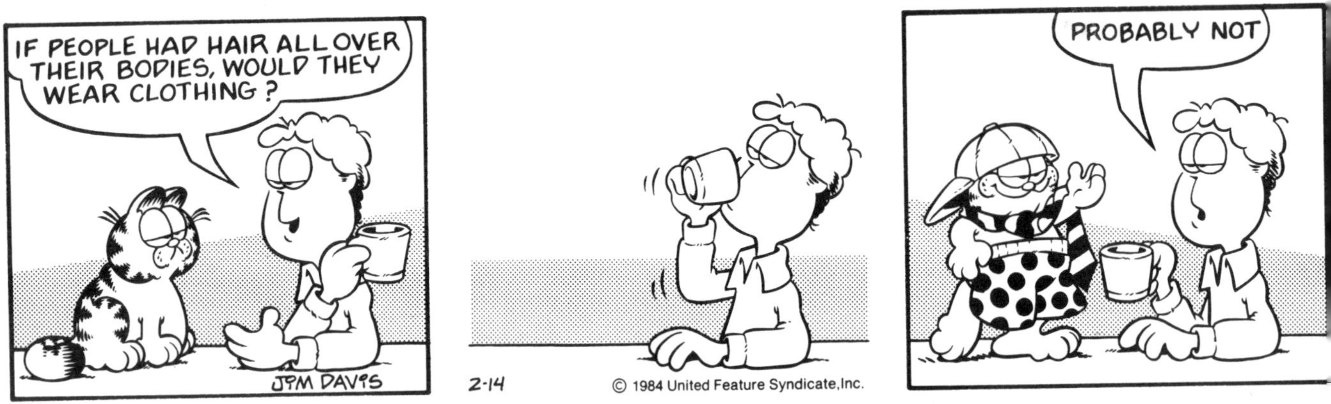
IF PEOPLE HAD HAIR ALL OVER THEIR BODIES, WOULD THEY WEAR CLOTHING?
JIM DAVIS
PROBABLY NOT

2-14

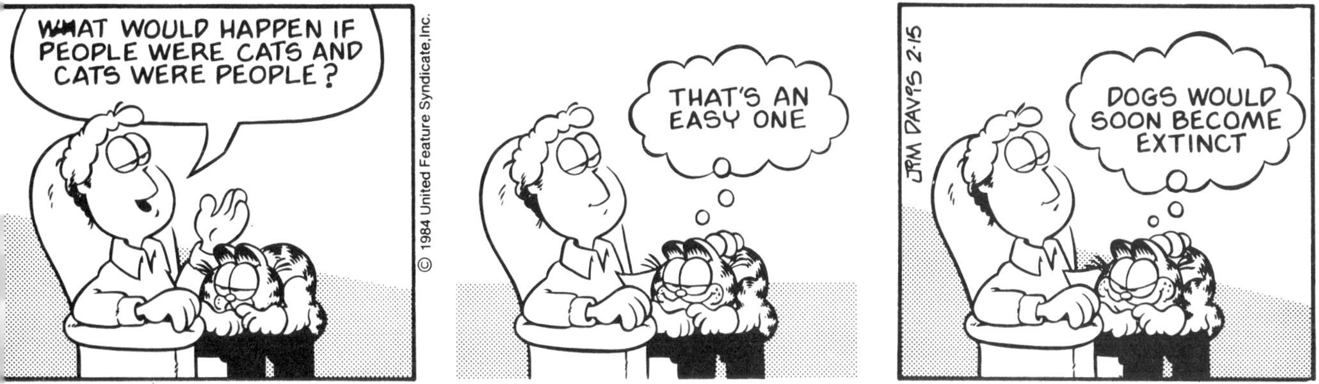
WHAT WOULD HAPPEN IF PEOPLE WERE CATS AND CATS WERE PEOPLE?
© 1984 United Feature Syndicate, Inc.
THAT'S AN EASY ONE
JIM DAVIS 2-15
DOGS WOULD SOON BECOME EXTINCT

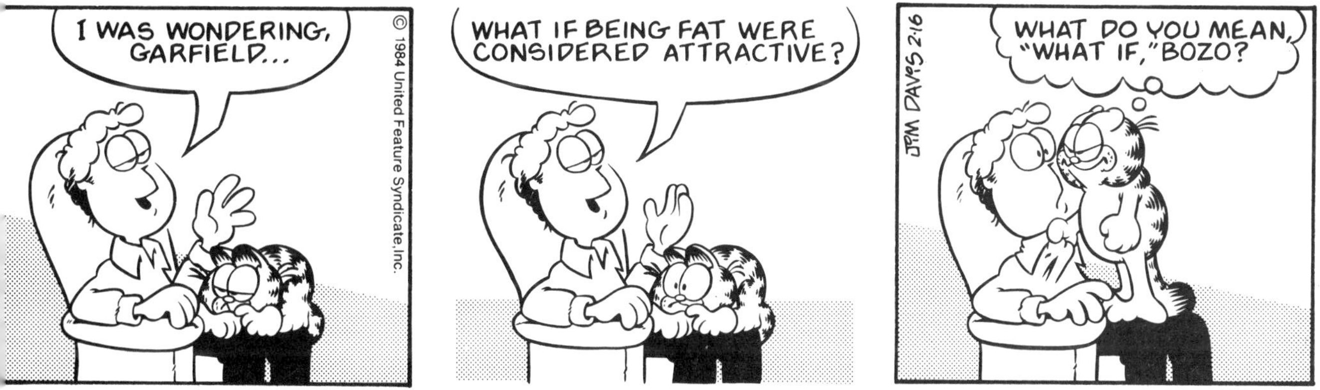
I WAS WONDERING, GARFIELD...
© 1984 United Feature Syndicate, Inc.
WHAT IF BEING FAT WERE CONSIDERED ATTRACTIVE?
JIM DAVIS 2-16
WHAT DO YOU MEAN, "WHAT IF," BOZO?

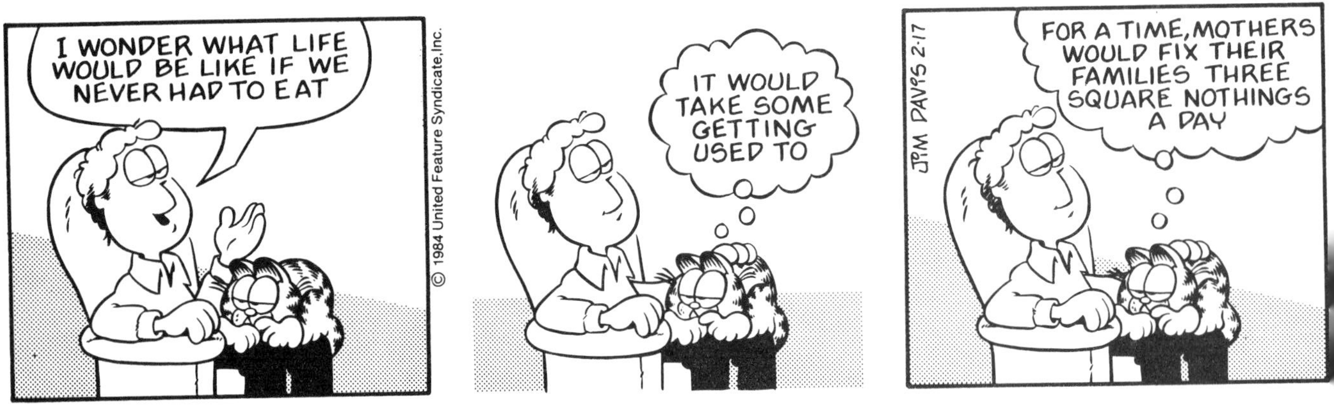
I WONDER WHAT LIFE WOULD BE LIKE IF WE NEVER HAD TO EAT
© 1984 United Feature Syndicate, Inc.
IT WOULD TAKE SOME GETTING USED TO
JIM DAVIS 2·17
FOR A TIME, MOTHERS WOULD FIX THEIR FAMILIES THREE SQUARE NOTHINGS A DAY

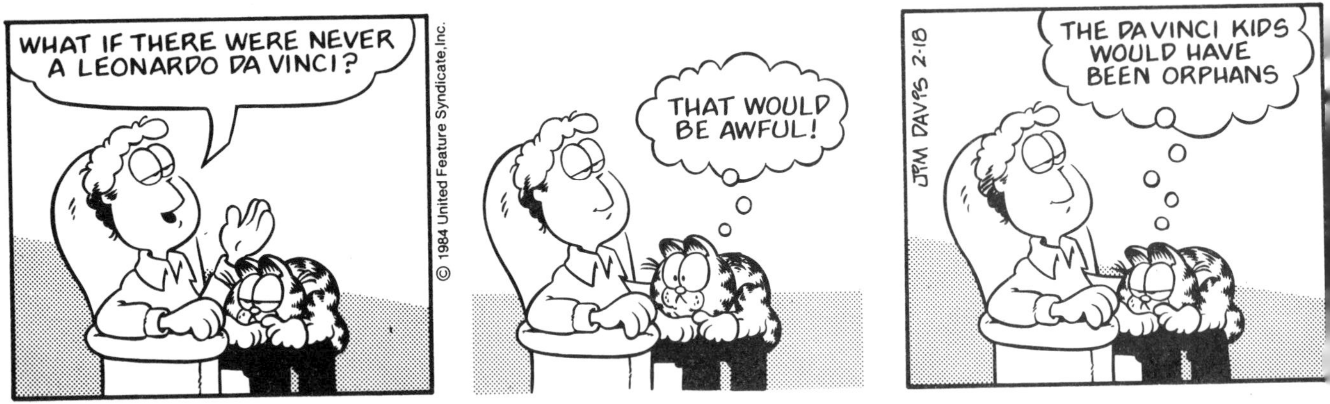
WHAT IF THERE WERE NEVER A LEONARDO DA VINCI?
© 1984 United Feature Syndicate, Inc.
THAT WOULD BE AWFUL!
JIM DAVIS 2·18
THE DA VINCI KIDS WOULD HAVE BEEN ORPHANS

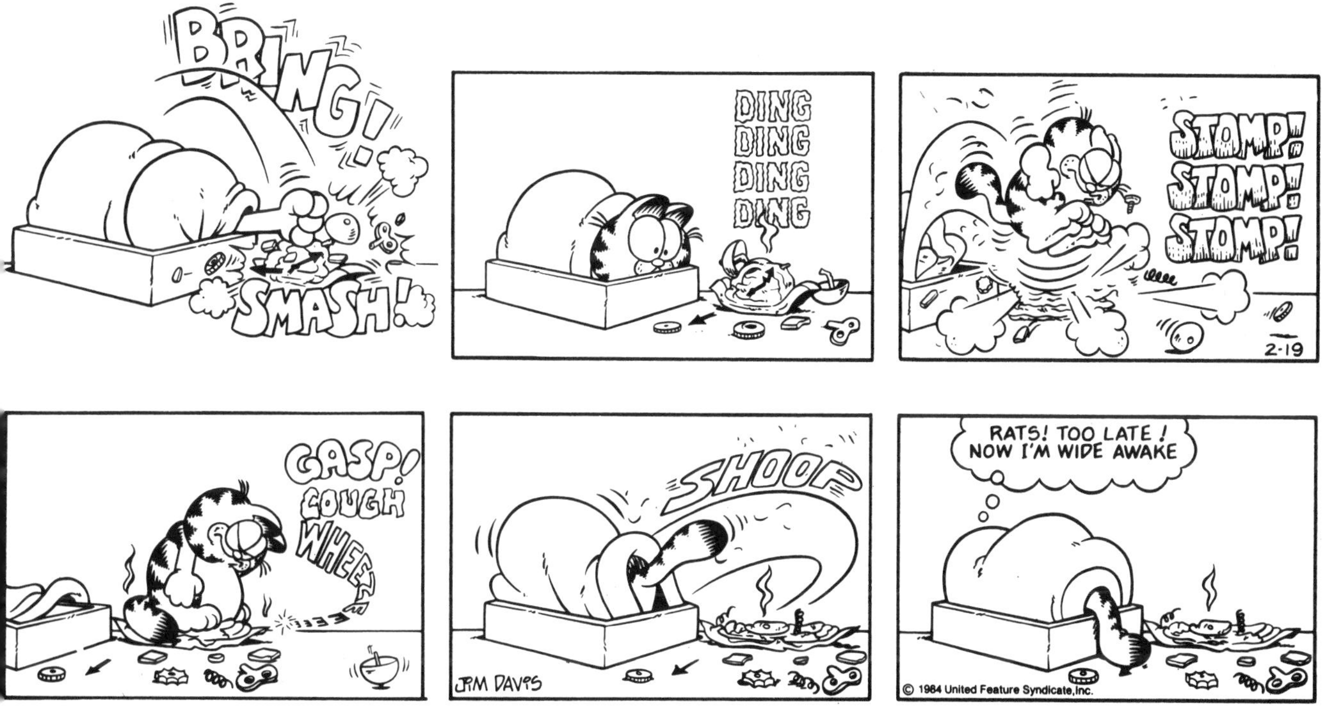
BRING!
SMASH!
DING
DING
DING
DING
STOMP!
STOMP!
STOMP!
2-19
GASP!
COUGH
WHEEZE
SHOOP
JIM DAVIS
RATS! TOO LATE!
NOW I'M WIDE AWAKE
© 1984 United Feature Syndicate, Inc.

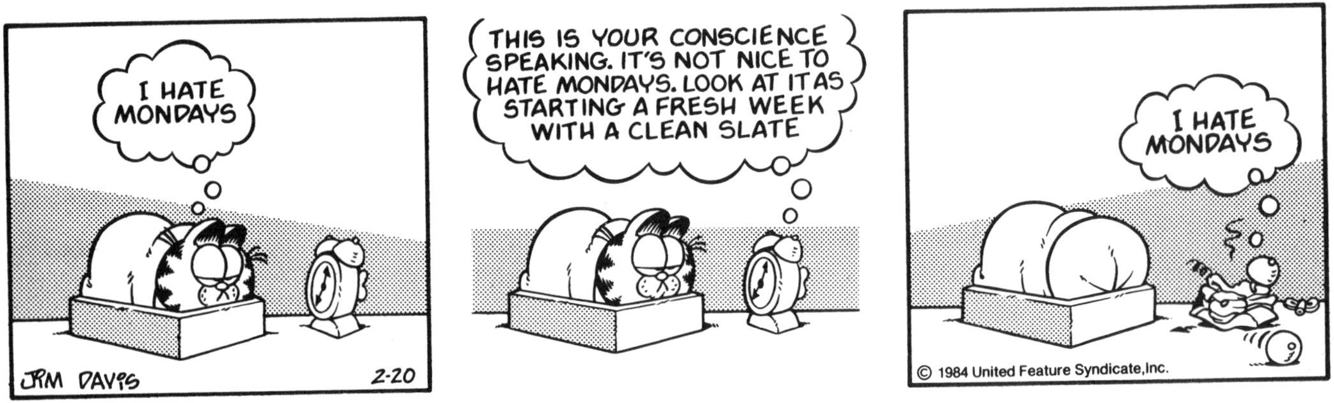
I HATE MONDAYS
THIS IS YOUR CONSCIENCE SPEAKING. IT'S NOT NICE TO HATE MONDAYS. LOOK AT IT AS STARTING A FRESH WEEK WITH A CLEAN SLATE
I HATE MONDAYS
JIM DAVIS
2-20
© 1984 United Feature Syndicate, Inc.

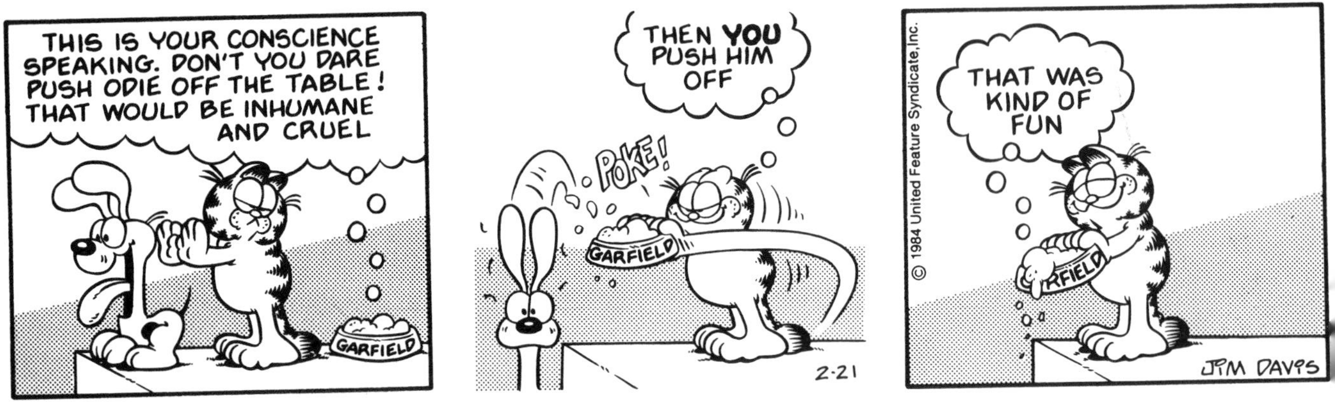
THIS IS YOUR CONSCIENCE SPEAKING. DON'T YOU DARE PUSH ODIE OFF THE TABLE! THAT WOULD BE INHUMANE AND CRUEL
GARFIELD
THEN **YOU** PUSH HIM OFF
POKE!
GARFIELD
2-21
© 1984 United Feature Syndicate, Inc.
THAT WAS KIND OF FUN
RFIELD
JIM DAVIS

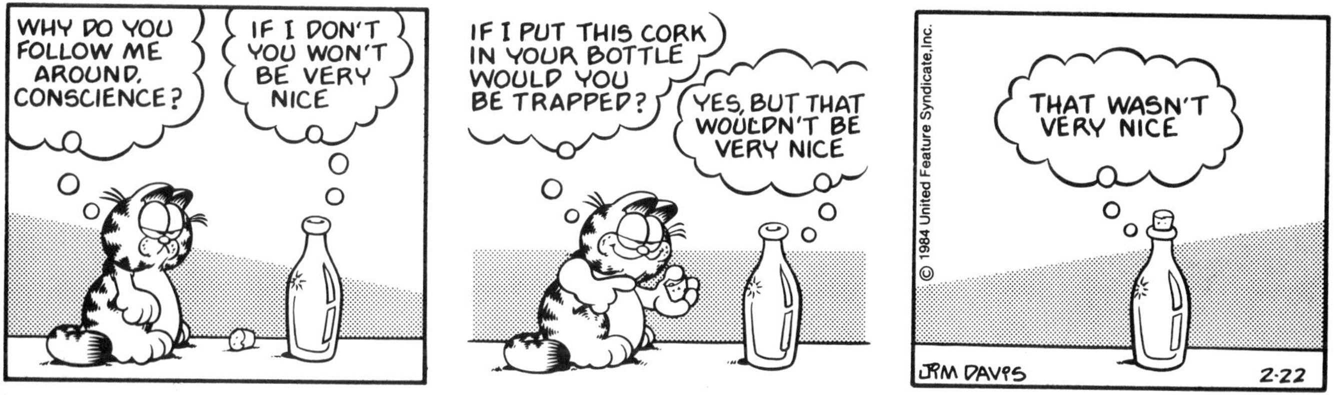
WHY DO YOU FOLLOW ME AROUND, CONSCIENCE?
IF I DON'T YOU WON'T BE VERY NICE
IF I PUT THIS CORK IN YOUR BOTTLE WOULD YOU BE TRAPPED?
YES, BUT THAT WOULDN'T BE VERY NICE
© 1984 United Feature Syndicate,Inc.
THAT WASN'T VERY NICE
JIM DAVIS
2·22

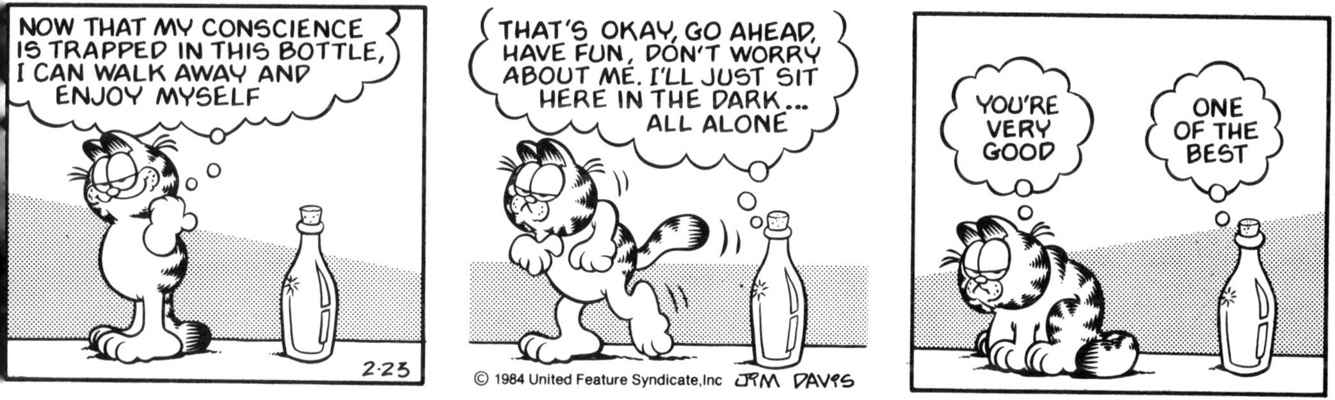
NOW THAT MY CONSCIENCE IS TRAPPED IN THIS BOTTLE, I CAN WALK AWAY AND ENJOY MYSELF
2·23
THAT'S OKAY, GO AHEAD, HAVE FUN, DON'T WORRY ABOUT ME. I'LL JUST SIT HERE IN THE DARK... ALL ALONE
© 1984 United Feature Syndicate,Inc
JIM DAVIS
YOU'RE VERY GOOD
ONE OF THE BEST

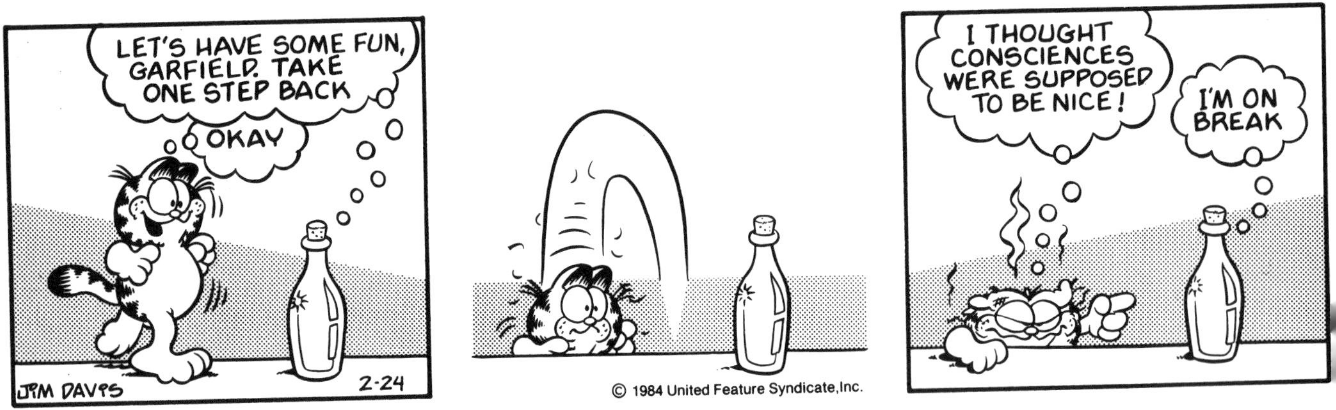
LET'S HAVE SOME FUN, GARFIELD. TAKE ONE STEP BACK
OKAY
JIM DAVIS
2-24
© 1984 United Feature Syndicate, Inc.
I THOUGHT CONSCIENCES WERE SUPPOSED TO BE NICE!
I'M ON BREAK

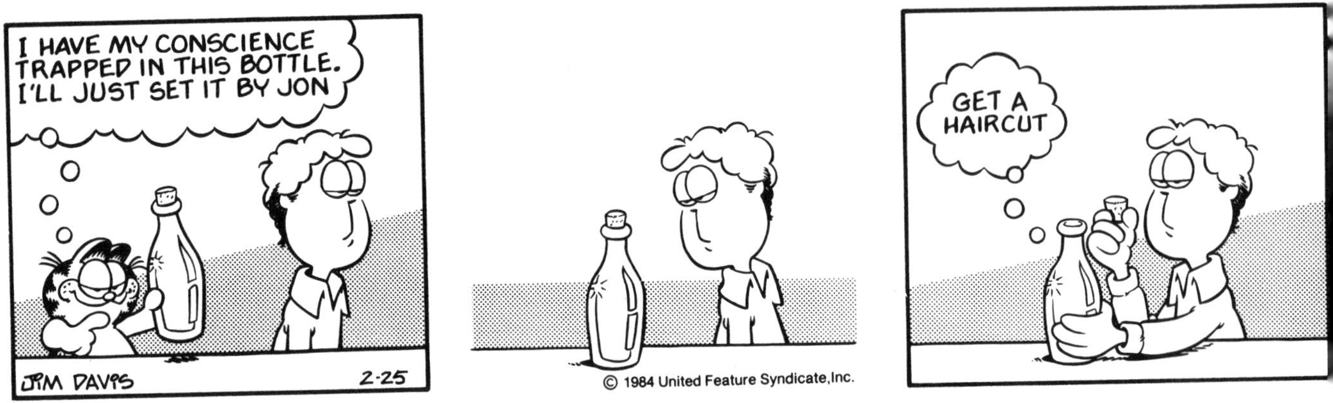
I HAVE MY CONSCIENCE TRAPPED IN THIS BOTTLE. I'LL JUST SET IT BY JON
JIM DAVIS
2-25
© 1984 United Feature Syndicate, Inc.
GET A HAIRCUT

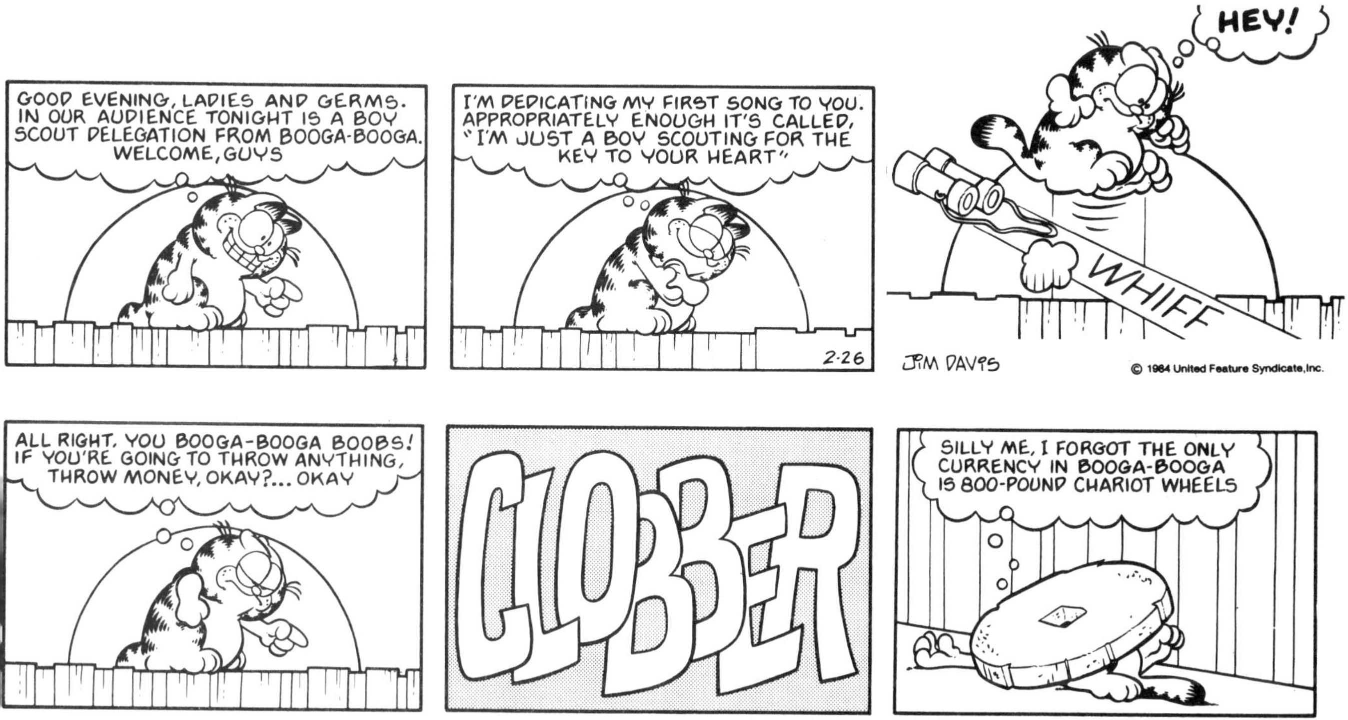
GOOD EVENING, LADIES AND GERMS. IN OUR AUDIENCE TONIGHT IS A BOY SCOUT DELEGATION FROM BOOGA-BOOGA. WELCOME, GUYS
I'M DEDICATING MY FIRST SONG TO YOU. APPROPRIATELY ENOUGH IT'S CALLED, "I'M JUST A BOY SCOUTING FOR THE KEY TO YOUR HEART"
2-26
HEY!
WHIFF
JIM DAVIS
© 1984 United Feature Syndicate, Inc.
ALL RIGHT, YOU BOOGA-BOOGA BOOBS! IF YOU'RE GOING TO THROW ANYTHING, THROW MONEY, OKAY?... OKAY
CLOBBER
SILLY ME, I FORGOT THE ONLY CURRENCY IN BOOGA-BOOGA IS 800-POUND CHARIOT WHEELS

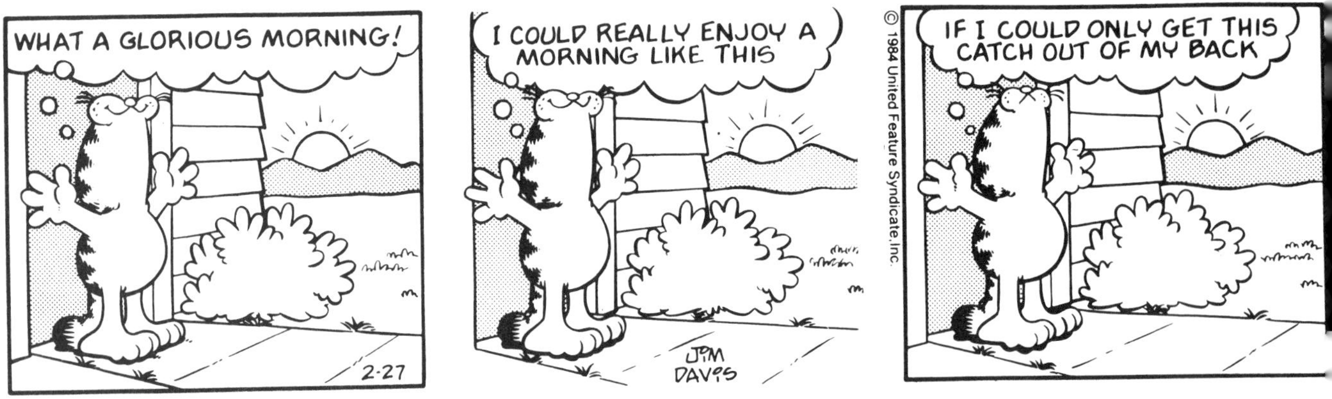
WHAT A GLORIOUS MORNING!
2-27
I COULD REALLY ENJOY A MORNING LIKE THIS
JIM DAVIS
© 1984 United Feature Syndicate, Inc.
IF I COULD ONLY GET THIS CATCH OUT OF MY BACK

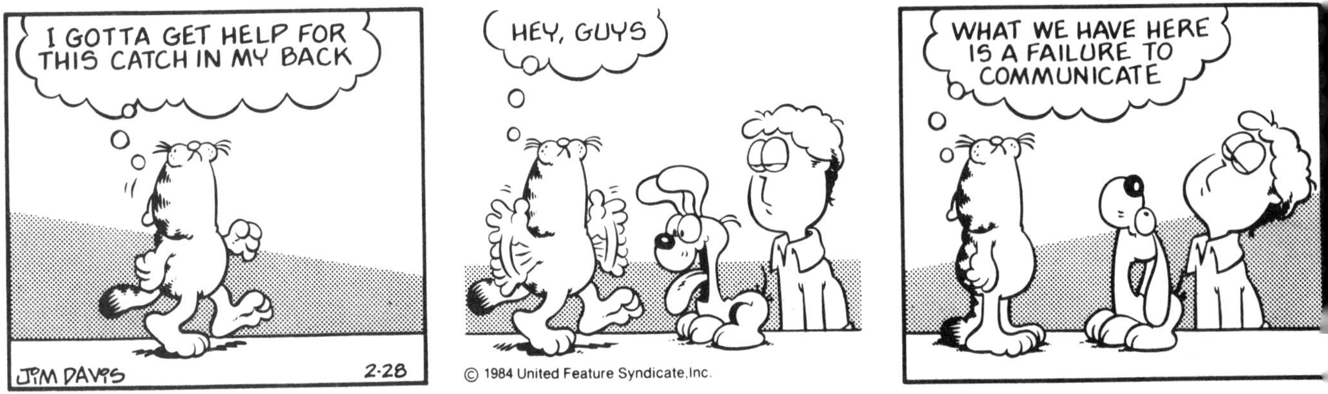
I GOTTA GET HELP FOR THIS CATCH IN MY BACK
JIM DAVIS
2-28
HEY, GUYS
© 1984 United Feature Syndicate, Inc.
WHAT WE HAVE HERE IS A FAILURE TO COMMUNICATE

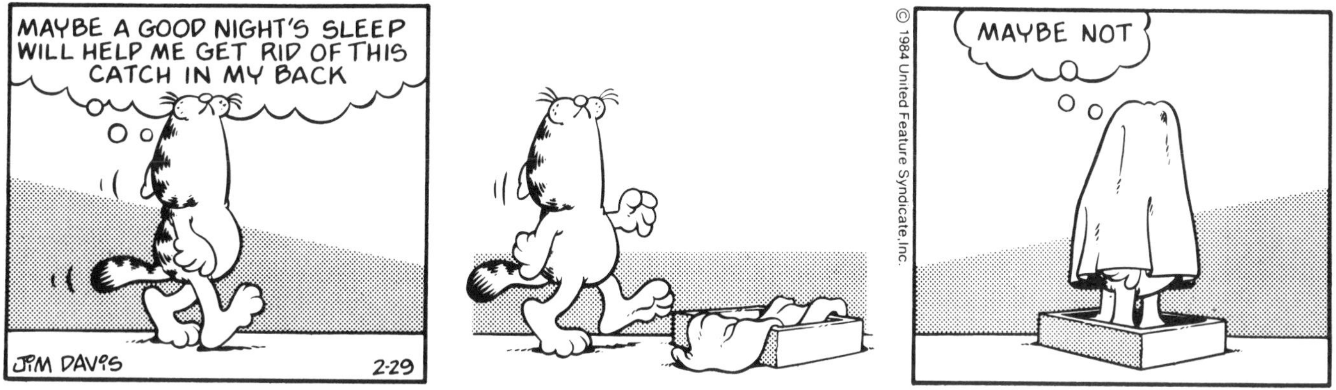
MAYBE A GOOD NIGHT'S SLEEP WILL HELP ME GET RID OF THIS CATCH IN MY BACK
JIM DAVIS
2-29
© 1984 United Feature Syndicate, Inc.
MAYBE NOT

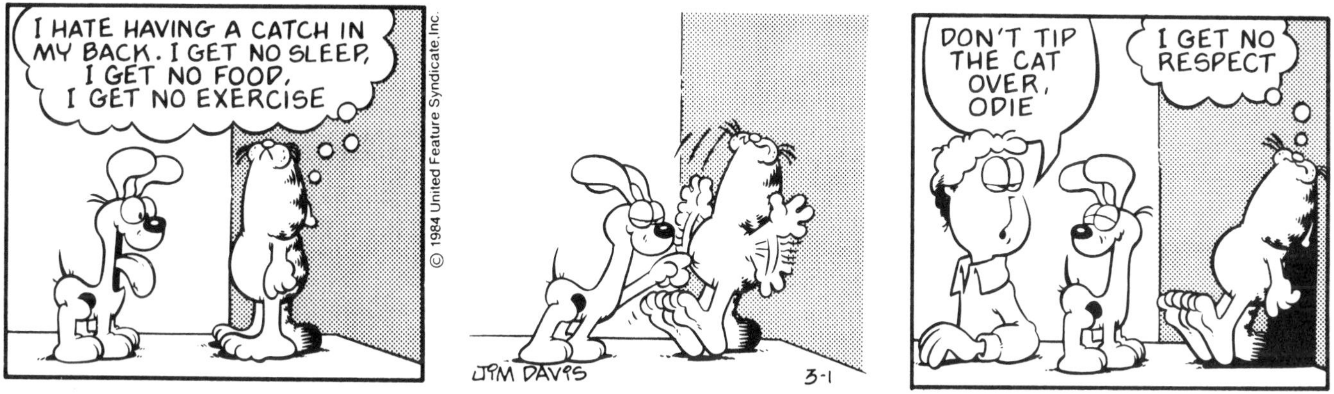
I HATE HAVING A CATCH IN MY BACK. I GET NO SLEEP, I GET NO FOOD, I GET NO EXERCISE
© 1984 United Feature Syndicate, Inc.
JIM DAVIS
3-1
DON'T TIP THE CAT OVER, ODIE
I GET NO RESPECT

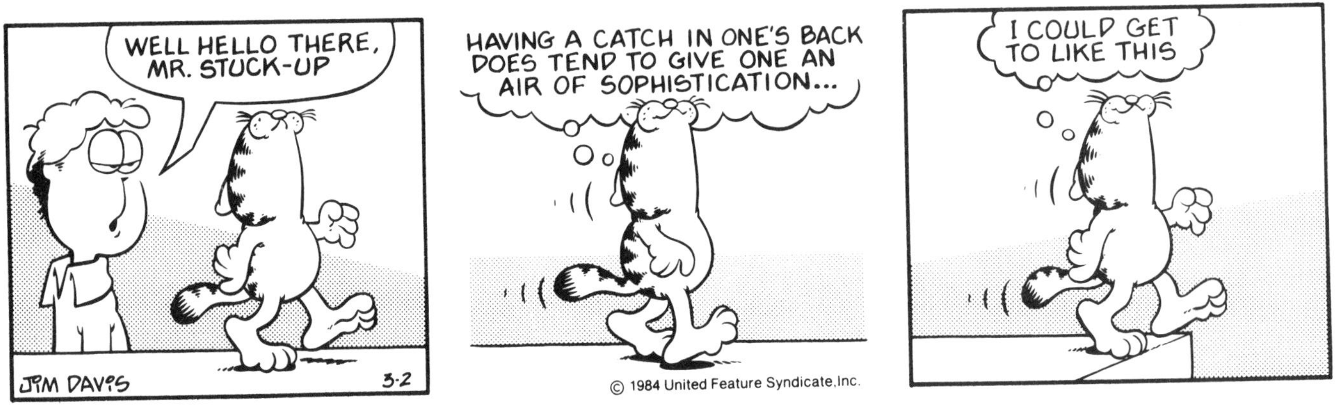
WELL HELLO THERE, MR. STUCK-UP
JIM DAVIS
3-2
HAVING A CATCH IN ONE'S BACK DOES TEND TO GIVE ONE AN AIR OF SOPHISTICATION...
© 1984 United Feature Syndicate, Inc.
I COULD GET TO LIKE THIS

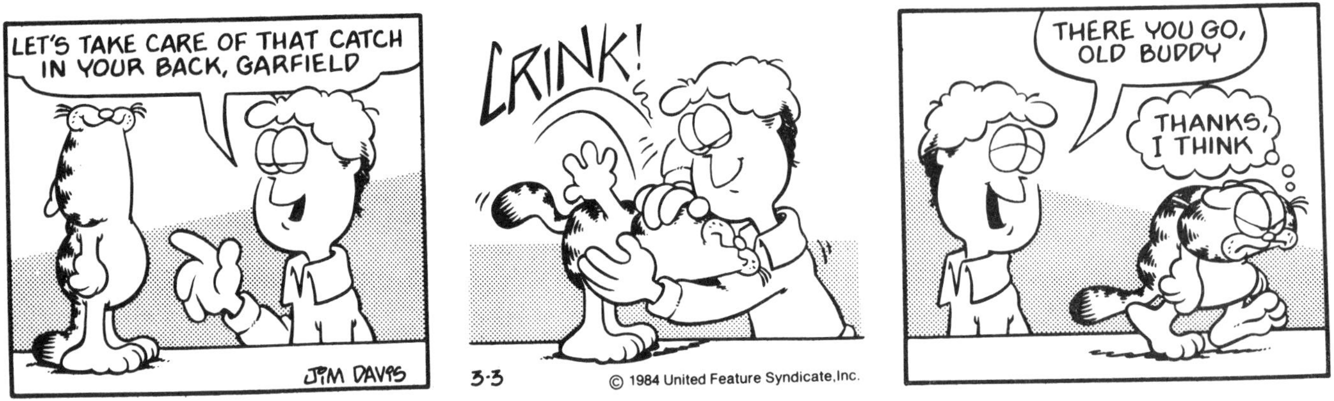
LET'S TAKE CARE OF THAT CATCH IN YOUR BACK, GARFIELD
JIM DAVIS
CRINK!
3-3
© 1984 United Feature Syndicate, Inc.
THERE YOU GO, OLD BUDDY
THANKS, I THINK

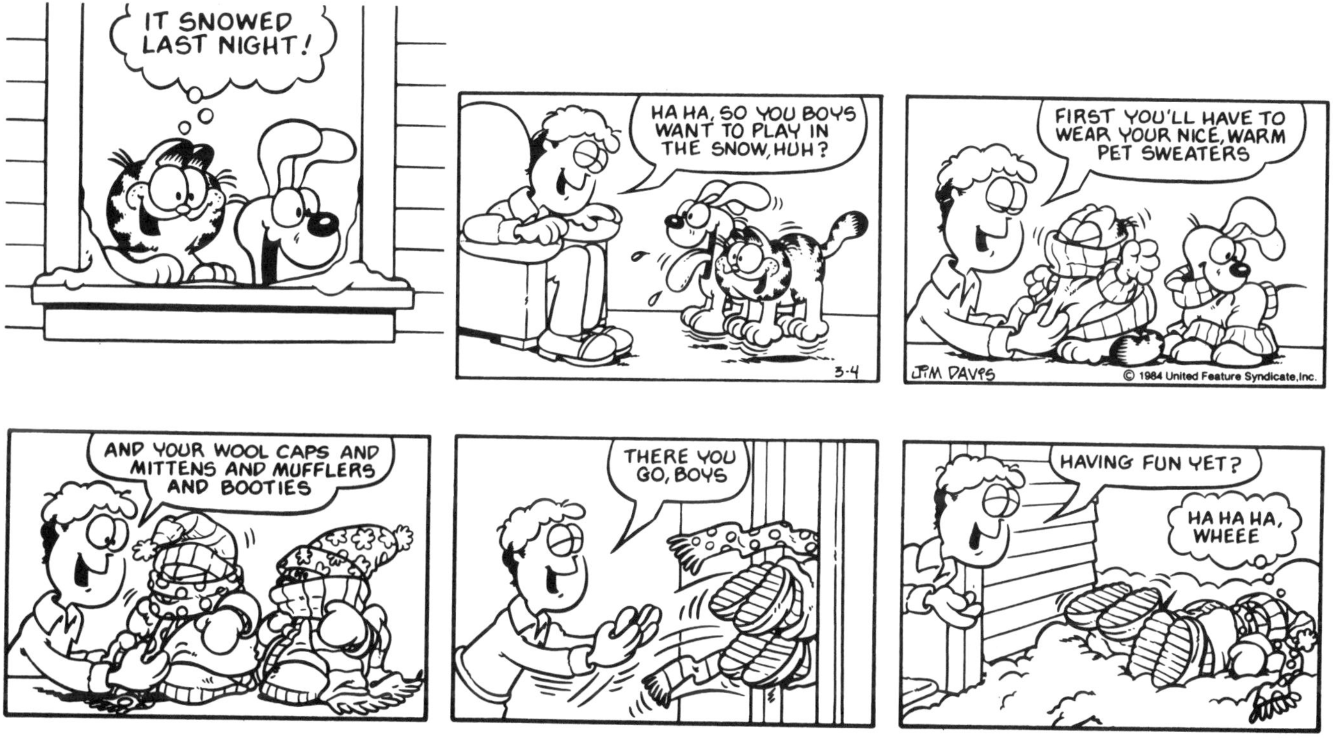
IT SNOWED LAST NIGHT!
HA HA, SO YOU BOYS WANT TO PLAY IN THE SNOW, HUH?
3-4
FIRST YOU'LL HAVE TO WEAR YOUR NICE, WARM PET SWEATERS
JIM DAVIS
© 1984 United Feature Syndicate, Inc.
AND YOUR WOOL CAPS AND MITTENS AND MUFFLERS AND BOOTIES
THERE YOU GO, BOYS
HAVING FUN YET?
HA HA HA, WHEEE

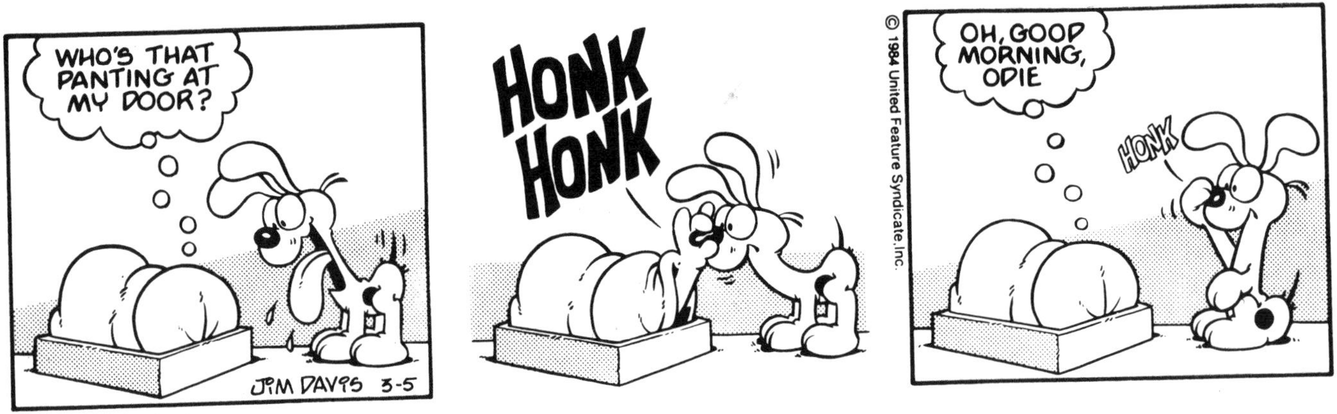
WHO'S THAT PANTING AT MY DOOR?
JIM DAVIS 3-5
HONK HONK
OH, GOOD MORNING, ODIE
HONK
© 1984 United Feature Syndicate, Inc.

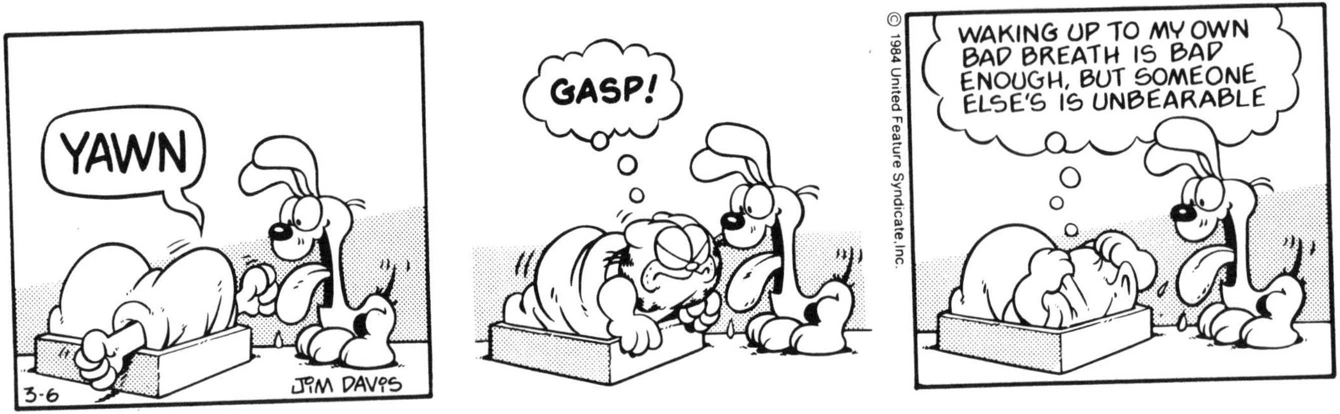
YAWN
3-6
JIM DAVIS
GASP!
WAKING UP TO MY OWN BAD BREATH IS BAD ENOUGH, BUT SOMEONE ELSE'S IS UNBEARABLE
© 1984 United Feature Syndicate, Inc.

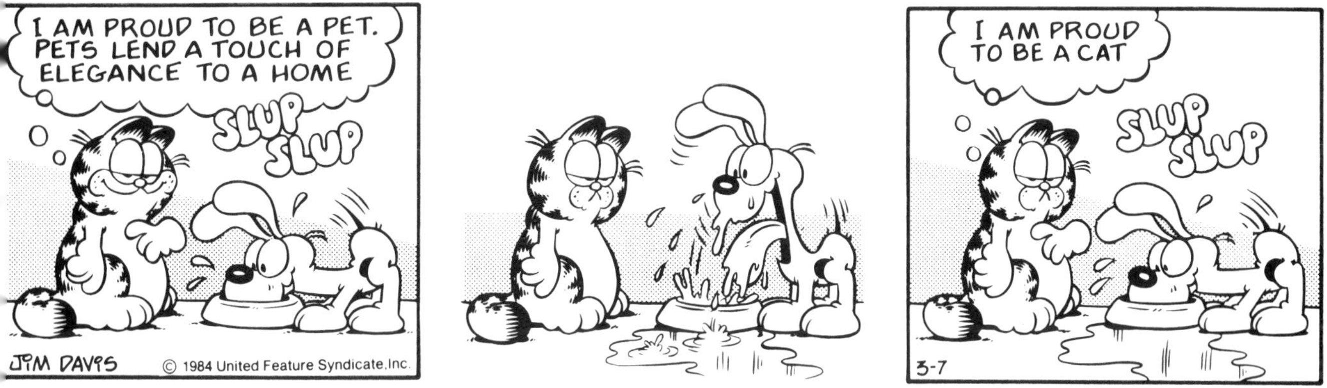
I AM PROUD TO BE A PET. PETS LEND A TOUCH OF ELEGANCE TO A HOME
SLUP SLUP
JIM DAVIS
© 1984 United Feature Syndicate, Inc.
I AM PROUD TO BE A CAT
SLUP SLUP
3-7

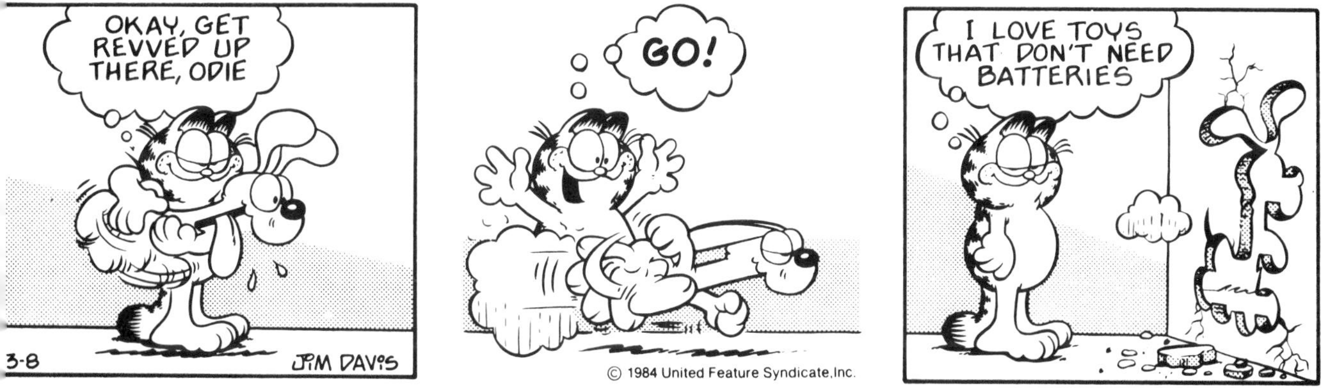
OKAY, GET REVVED UP THERE, ODIE
3-8
JIM DAVIS
GO!
© 1984 United Feature Syndicate, Inc.
I LOVE TOYS THAT DON'T NEED BATTERIES

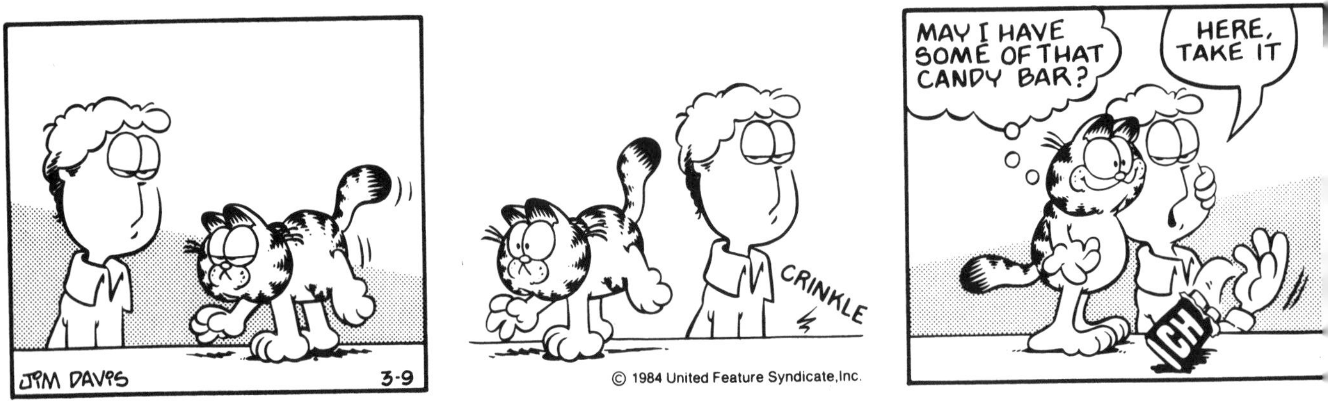
JIM DAVIS
3-9
CRINKLE
MAY I HAVE SOME OF THAT CANDY BAR?
HERE, TAKE IT
ICH


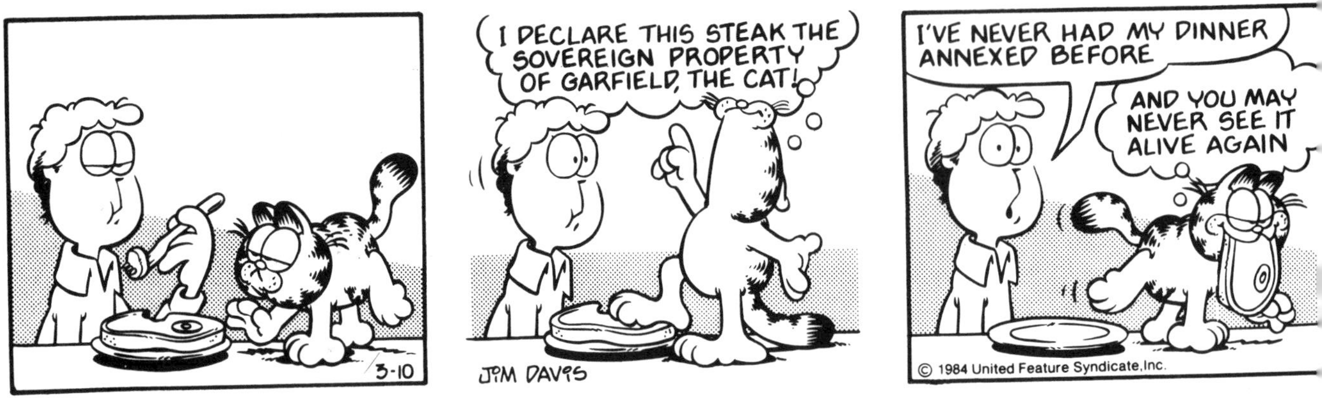
3-10
I DECLARE THIS STEAK THE SOVEREIGN PROPERTY OF GARFIELD, THE CAT!
JIM DAVIS
I'VE NEVER HAD MY DINNER ANNEXED BEFORE
AND YOU MAY NEVER SEE IT ALIVE AGAIN

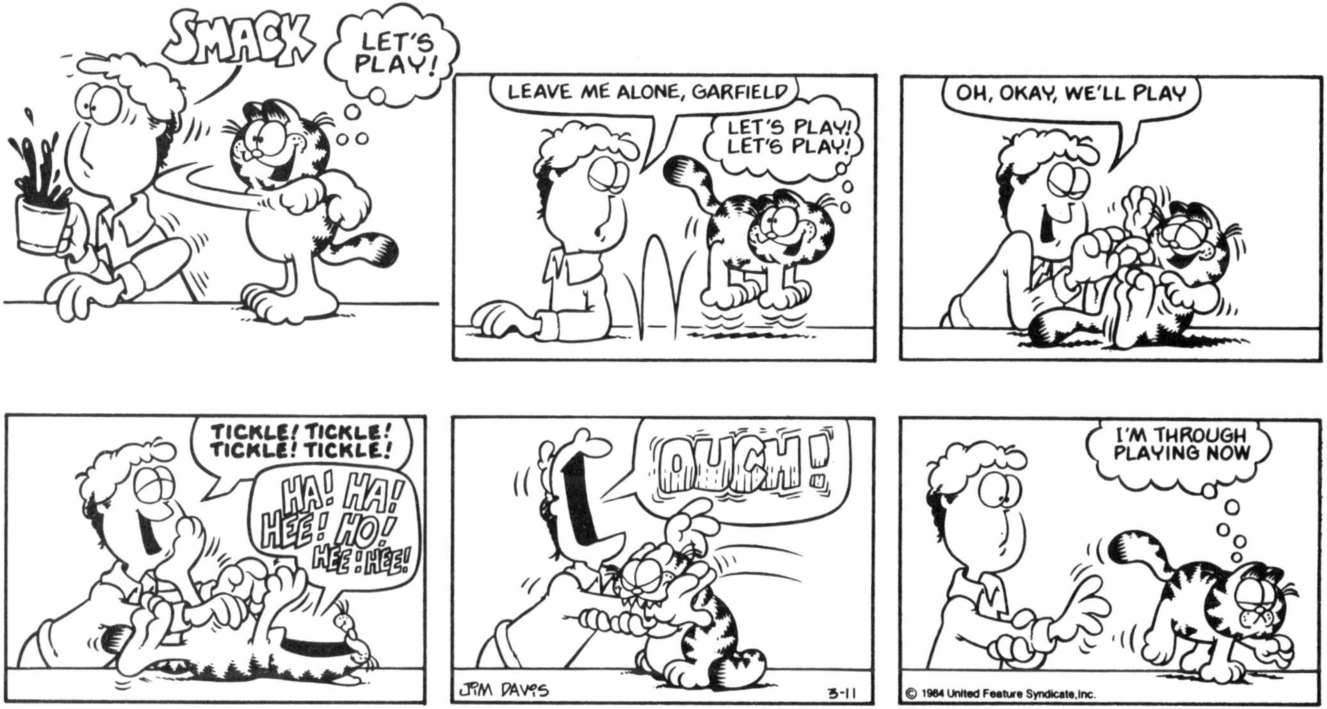
SMACK
LET'S PLAY!
LEAVE ME ALONE, GARFIELD
LET'S PLAY! LET'S PLAY!
OH, OKAY, WE'LL PLAY
TICKLE! TICKLE! TICKLE! TICKLE!
HA! HA! HEE! HO! HEE! HEE!
OUCH!
JIM DAVIS
3-11
I'M THROUGH PLAYING NOW
© 1984 United Feature Syndicate, Inc.

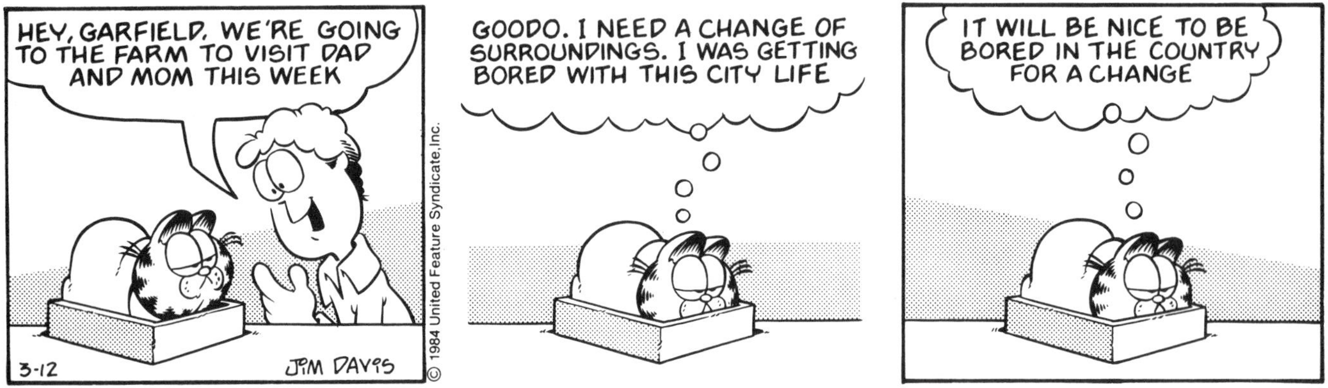
HEY, GARFIELD. WE'RE GOING TO THE FARM TO VISIT DAD AND MOM THIS WEEK
3-12
JIM DAVIS
© 1984 United Feature Syndicate, Inc.
GOODO. I NEED A CHANGE OF SURROUNDINGS. I WAS GETTING BORED WITH THIS CITY LIFE
IT WILL BE NICE TO BE BORED IN THE COUNTRY FOR A CHANGE

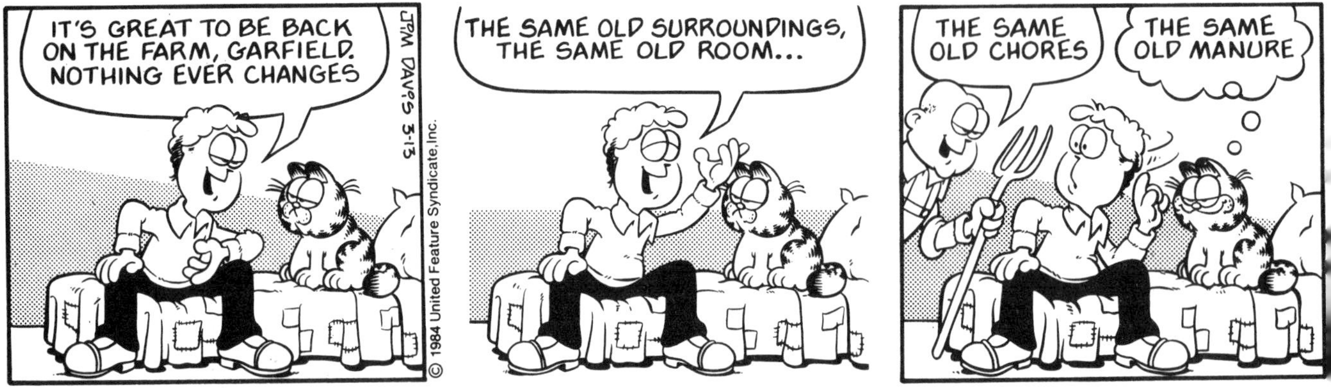
IT'S GREAT TO BE BACK ON THE FARM, GARFIELD. NOTHING EVER CHANGES
JIM DAVIS 3-13
© 1984 United Feature Syndicate, Inc.
THE SAME OLD SURROUNDINGS, THE SAME OLD ROOM...
THE SAME OLD CHORES
THE SAME OLD MANURE

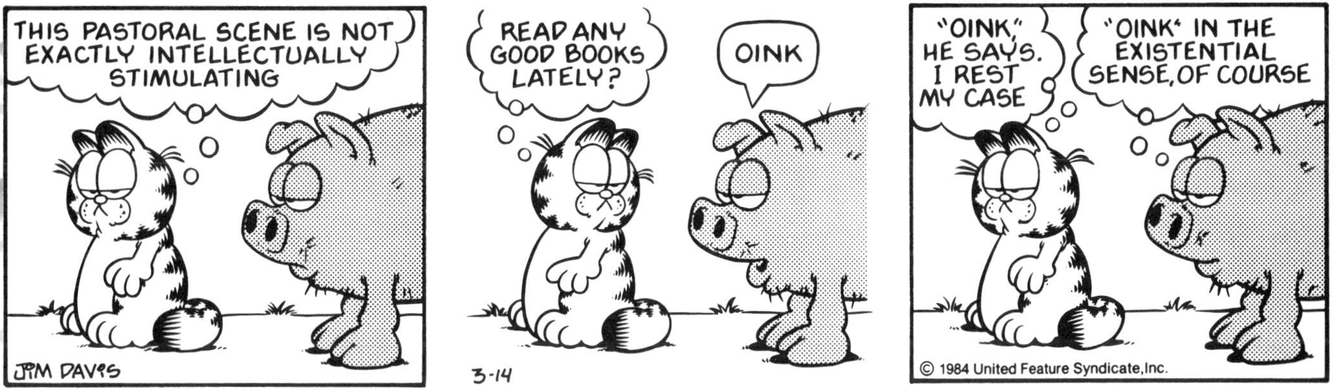
THIS PASTORAL SCENE IS NOT EXACTLY INTELLECTUALLY STIMULATING
JIM DAVIS
READ ANY GOOD BOOKS LATELY?
OINK
3-14
"OINK," HE SAYS. I REST MY CASE
"OINK" IN THE EXISTENTIAL SENSE, OF COURSE
© 1984 United Feature Syndicate, Inc.

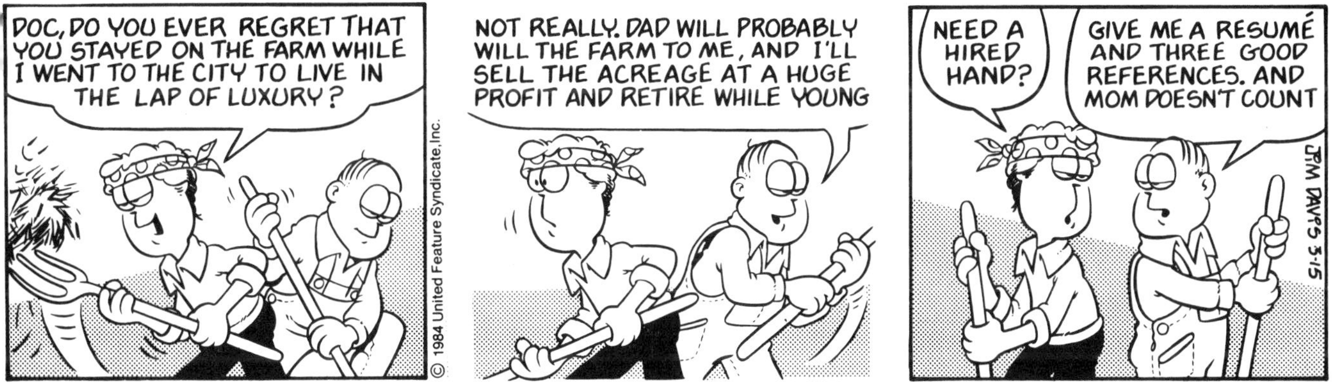
DOC, DO YOU EVER REGRET THAT YOU STAYED ON THE FARM WHILE I WENT TO THE CITY TO LIVE IN THE LAP OF LUXURY?
© 1984 United Feature Syndicate, Inc.
NOT REALLY. DAD WILL PROBABLY WILL THE FARM TO ME, AND I'LL SELL THE ACREAGE AT A HUGE PROFIT AND RETIRE WHILE YOUNG
NEED A HIRED HAND?
GIVE ME A RESUMÉ AND THREE GOOD REFERENCES. AND MOM DOESN'T COUNT
JIM DAVIS 3-15

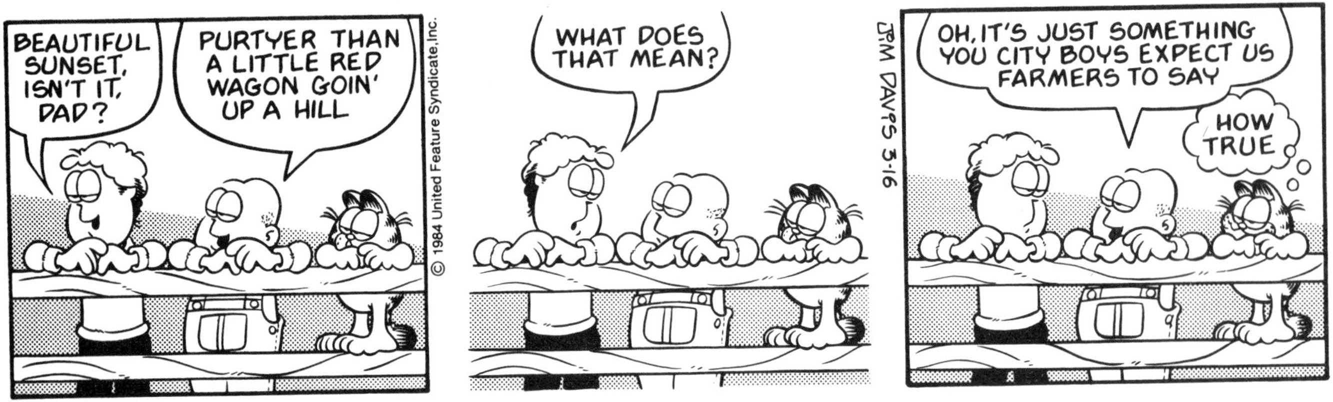

BEAUTIFUL SUNSET, ISN'T IT, DAD?
PURTYER THAN A LITTLE RED WAGON GOIN' UP A HILL
© 1984 United Feature Syndicate, Inc.
WHAT DOES THAT MEAN?
JIM DAVIS 3-16
OH, IT'S JUST SOMETHING YOU CITY BOYS EXPECT US FARMERS TO SAY
HOW TRUE


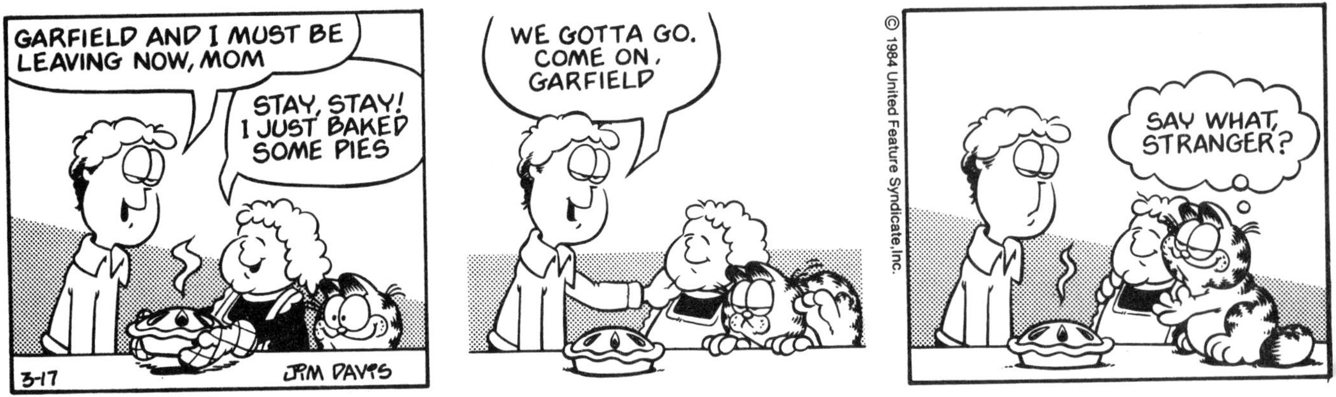

GARFIELD AND I MUST BE LEAVING NOW, MOM
STAY, STAY! I JUST BAKED SOME PIES
3-17
JIM DAVIS
WE GOTTA GO. COME ON, GARFIELD
© 1984 United Feature Syndicate, Inc.
SAY WHAT, STRANGER?

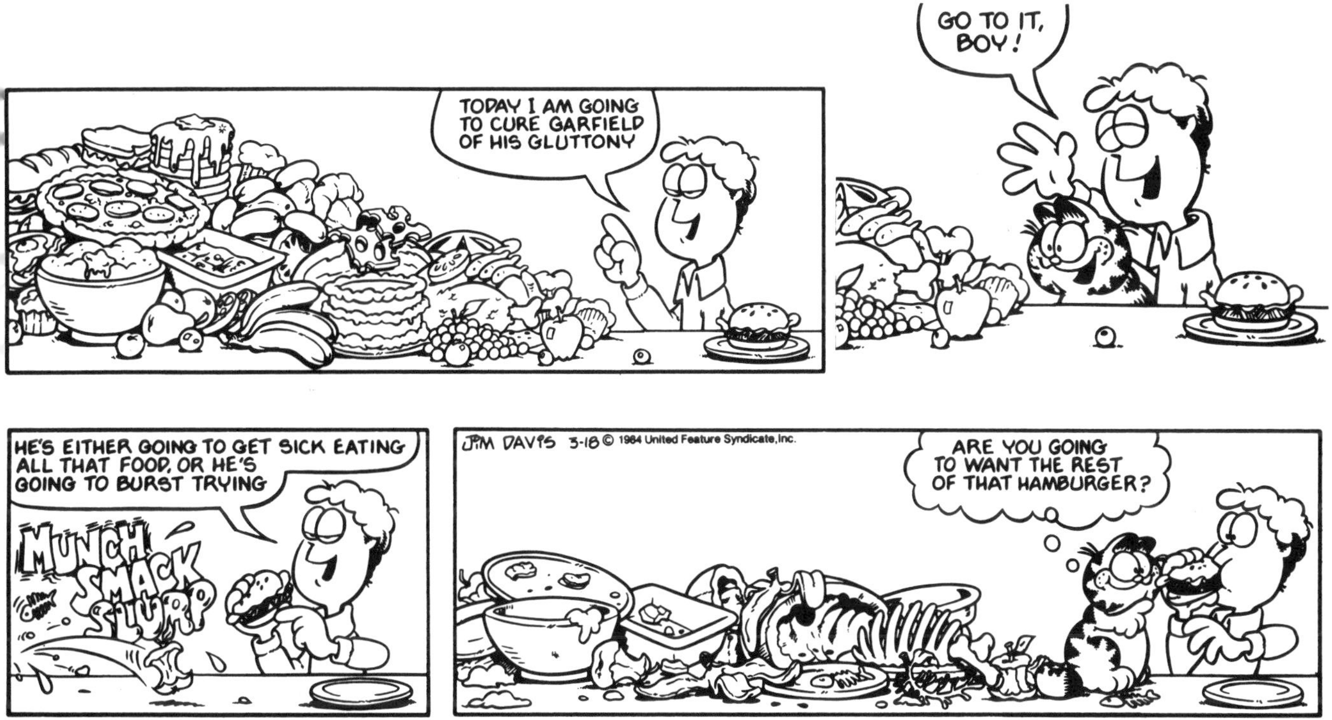
TODAY I AM GOING TO CURE GARFIELD OF HIS GLUTTONY
GO TO IT, BOY!
HE'S EITHER GOING TO GET SICK EATING ALL THAT FOOD, OR HE'S GOING TO BURST TRYING
MUNCH
SMACK
SLURP
JIM DAVIS 3-18 © 1984 United Feature Syndicate, Inc.
ARE YOU GOING TO WANT THE REST OF THAT HAMBURGER?

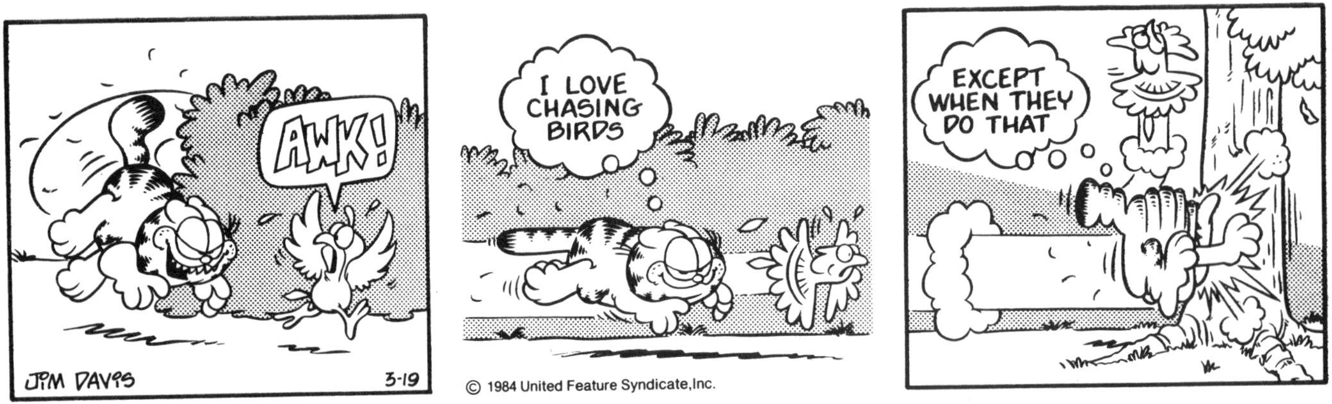
AWK!
JIM DAVIS
3-19
I LOVE CHASING BIRDS
EXCEPT WHEN THEY DO THAT


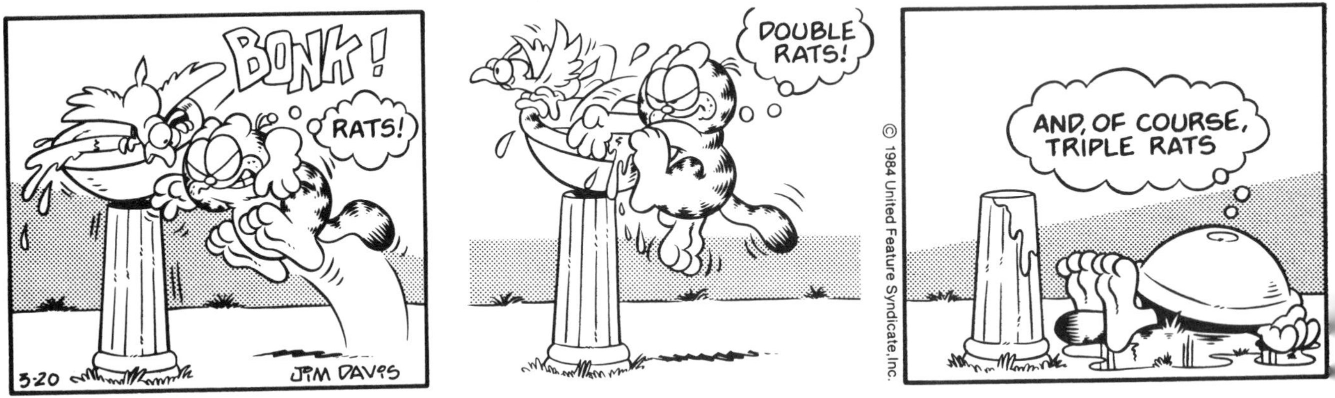
BONK!
RATS!
3-20
JIM DAVIS
DOUBLE RATS!
AND, OF COURSE, TRIPLE RATS

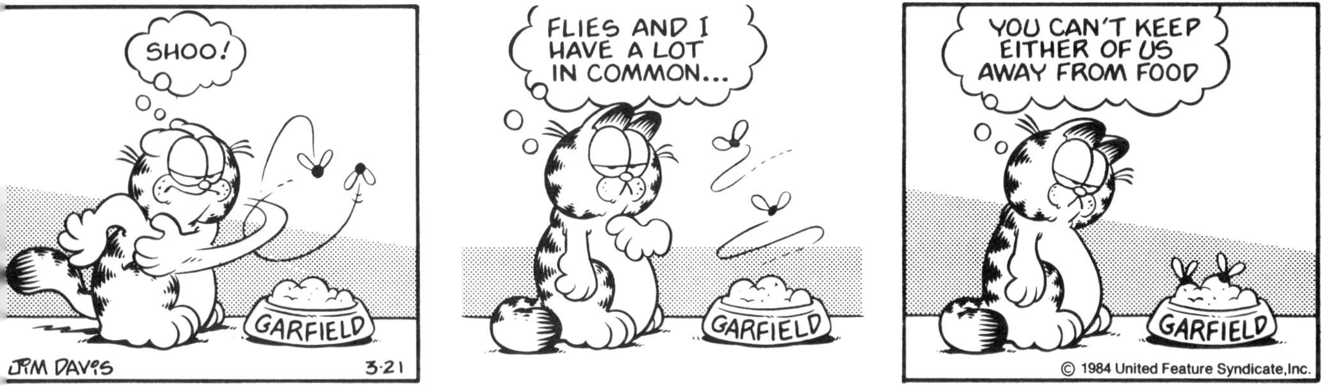
SHOO!
FLIES AND I HAVE A LOT IN COMMON...
YOU CAN'T KEEP EITHER OF US AWAY FROM FOOD
GARFIELD
JIM DAVIS 3-21
© 1984 United Feature Syndicate,Inc.

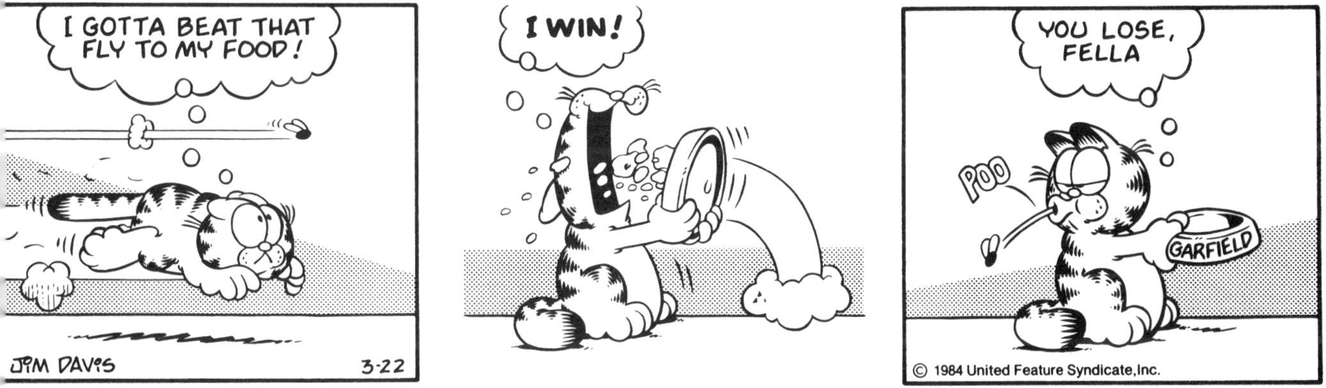
I GOTTA BEAT THAT FLY TO MY FOOD!
I WIN!
YOU LOSE, FELLA
POO
GARFIELD
JIM DAVIS 3-22
© 1984 United Feature Syndicate,Inc.

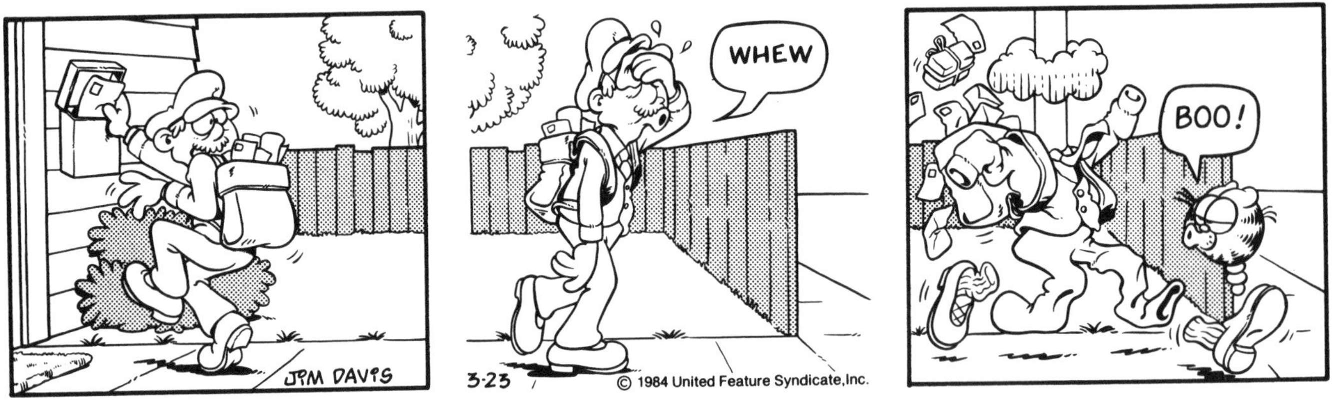
JIM DAVIS
WHEW
3-23
© 1984 United Feature Syndicate, Inc.
BOO!

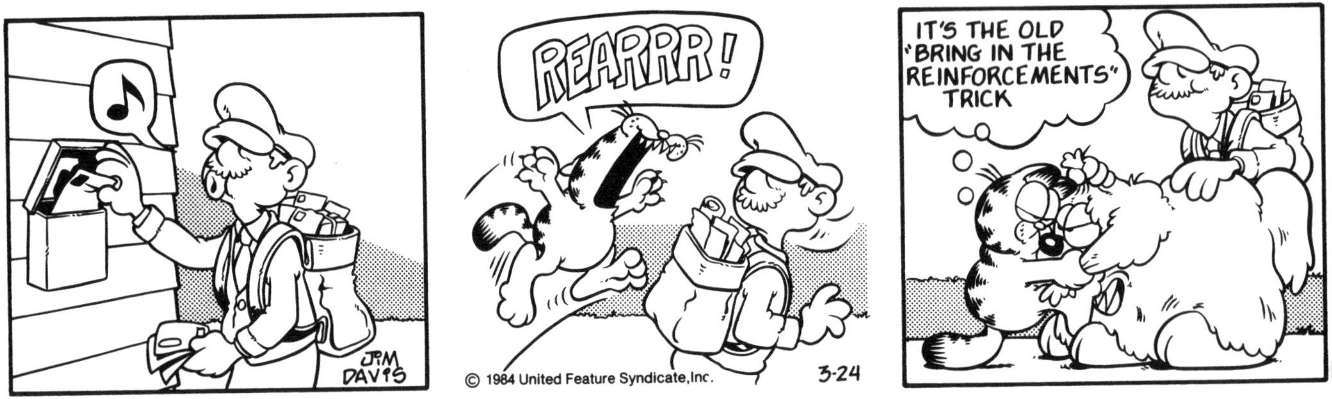
JIM DAVIS
REARRR!
© 1984 United Feature Syndicate, Inc.
3-24
IT'S THE OLD "BRING IN THE REINFORCEMENTS" TRICK

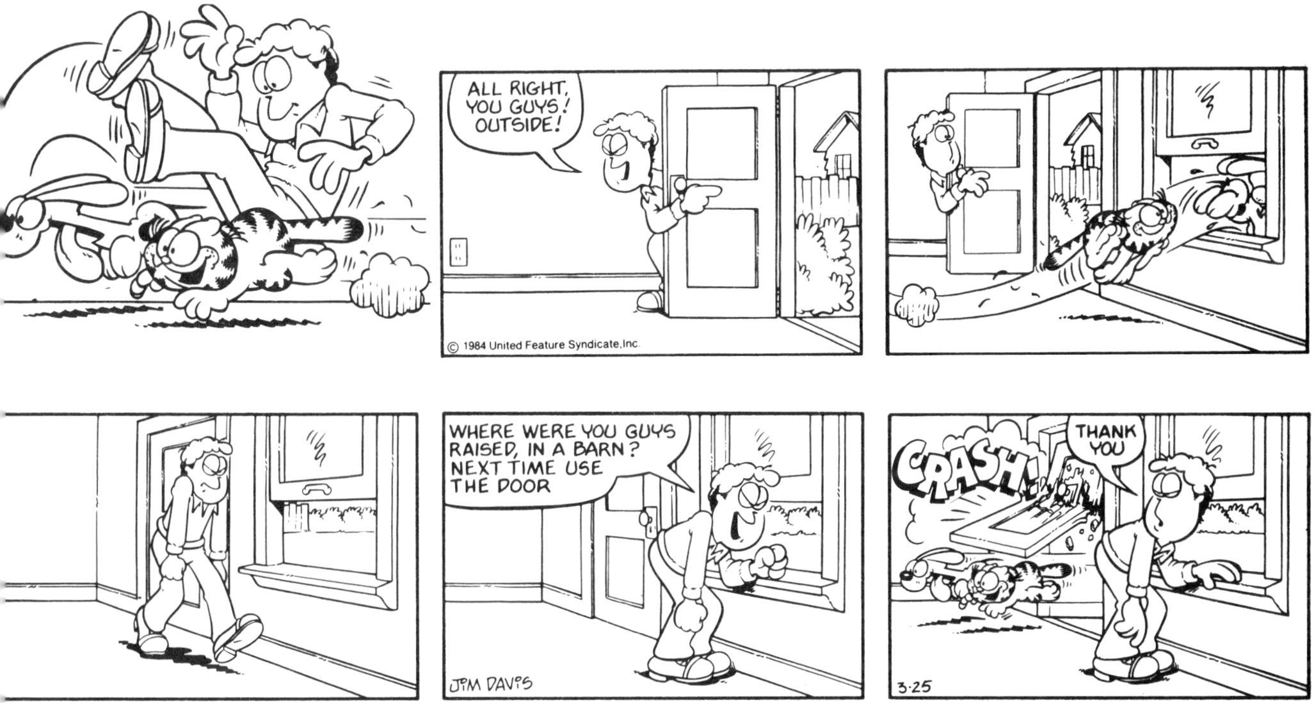
ALL RIGHT, YOU GUYS! OUTSIDE!
© 1984 United Feature Syndicate, Inc.
WHERE WERE YOU GUYS RAISED, IN A BARN? NEXT TIME USE THE DOOR
JIM DAVIS
CRASH!
THANK YOU
3-25

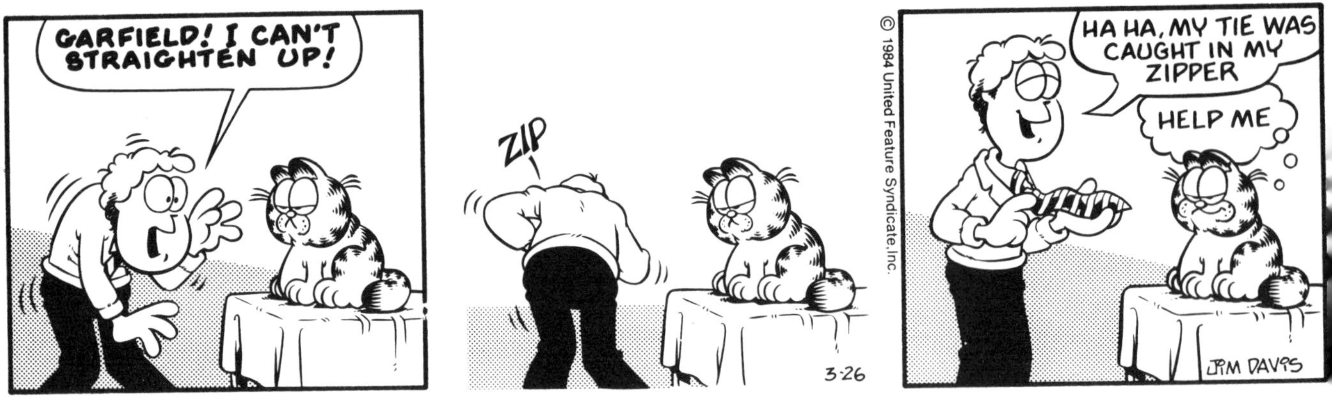
GARFIELD! I CAN'T STRAIGHTEN UP!
ZIP
3-26
HA HA, MY TIE WAS CAUGHT IN MY ZIPPER
HELP ME
JIM DAVIS


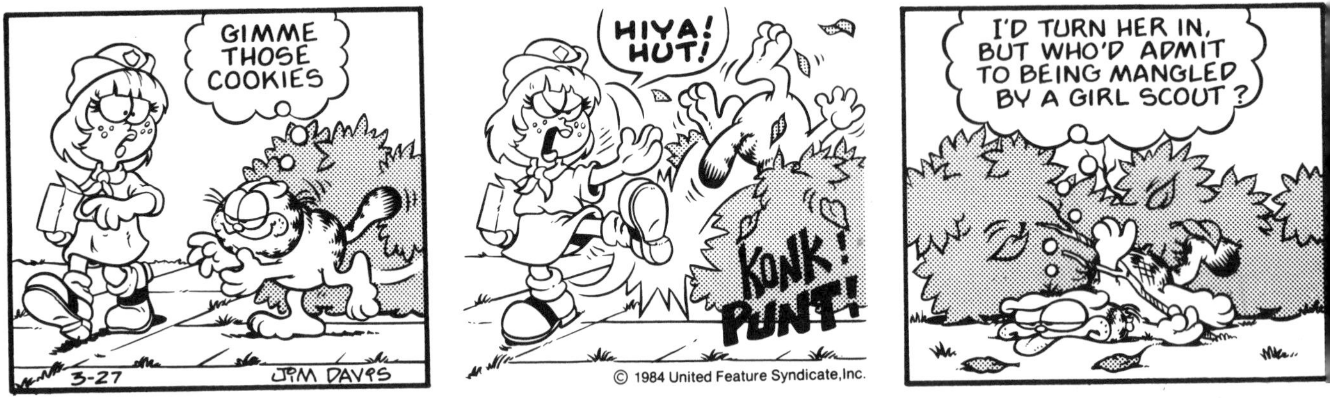
GIMME THOSE COOKIES
3-27
JIM DAVIS
HIYA! HUT!
KONK!
PUNT!
I'D TURN HER IN, BUT WHO'D ADMIT TO BEING MANGLED BY A GIRL SCOUT?

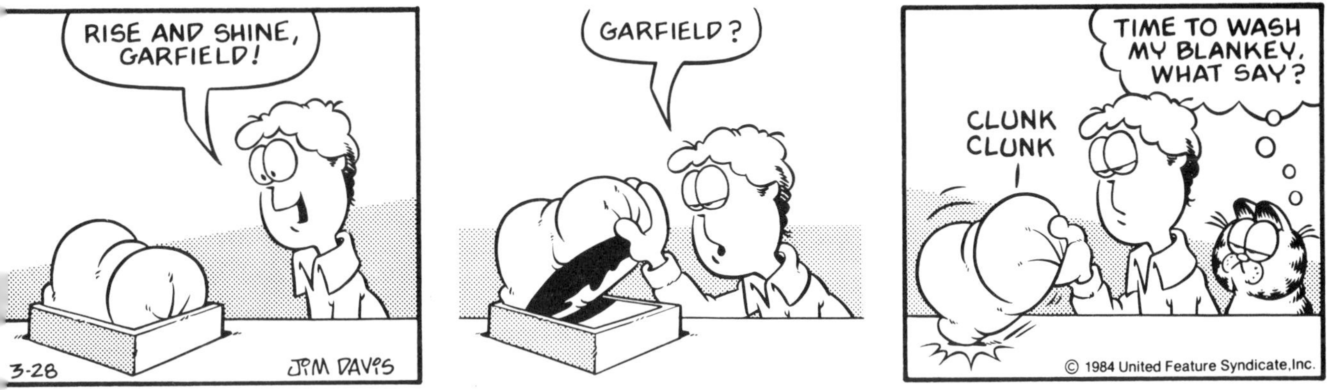
RISE AND SHINE, GARFIELD!
3-28
JIM DAVIS
GARFIELD?
CLUNK CLUNK
TIME TO WASH MY BLANKEY. WHAT SAY?
© 1984 United Feature Syndicate, Inc.

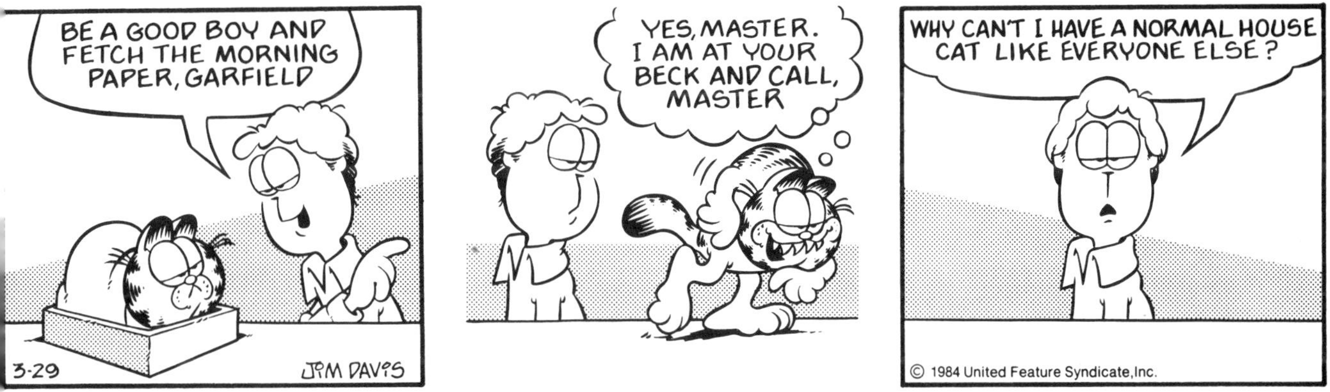
BE A GOOD BOY AND FETCH THE MORNING PAPER, GARFIELD
3-29
JIM DAVIS
YES, MASTER. I AM AT YOUR BECK AND CALL, MASTER
WHY CAN'T I HAVE A NORMAL HOUSE CAT LIKE EVERYONE ELSE?
© 1984 United Feature Syndicate, Inc.

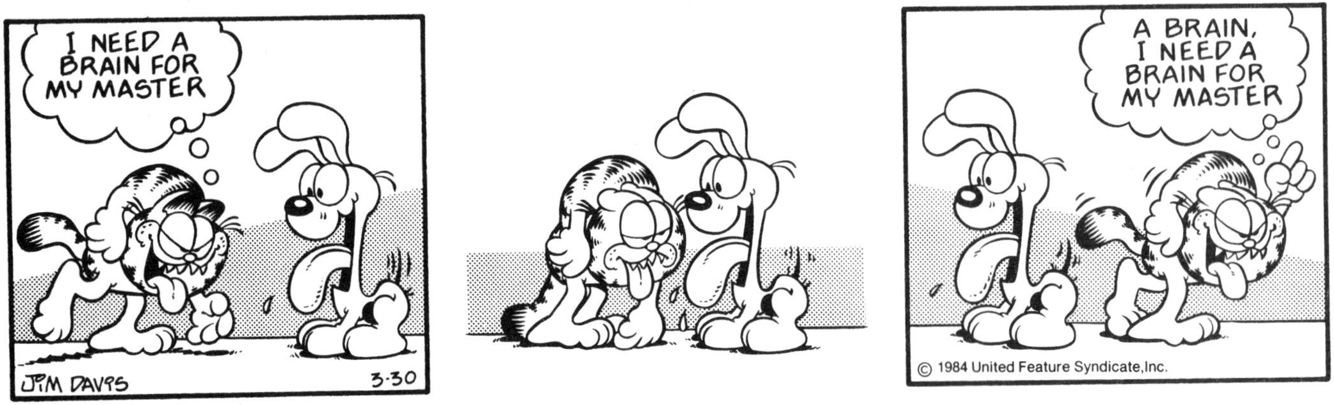
I NEED A BRAIN FOR MY MASTER
A BRAIN, I NEED A BRAIN FOR MY MASTER
JIM DAVIS
3-30
© 1984 United Feature Syndicate,Inc.

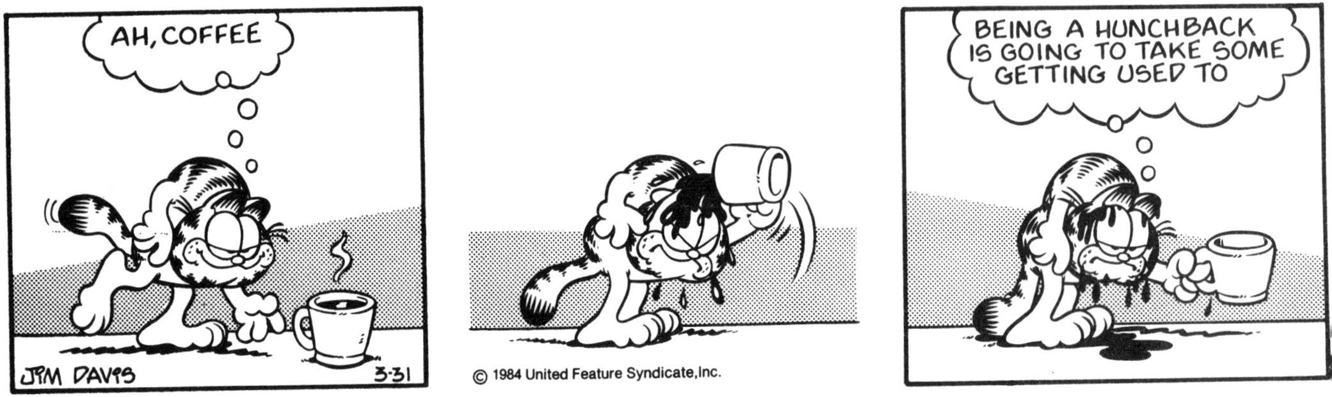
AH, COFFEE
BEING A HUNCHBACK IS GOING TO TAKE SOME GETTING USED TO
JIM DAVIS
3-31
© 1984 United Feature Syndicate,Inc.

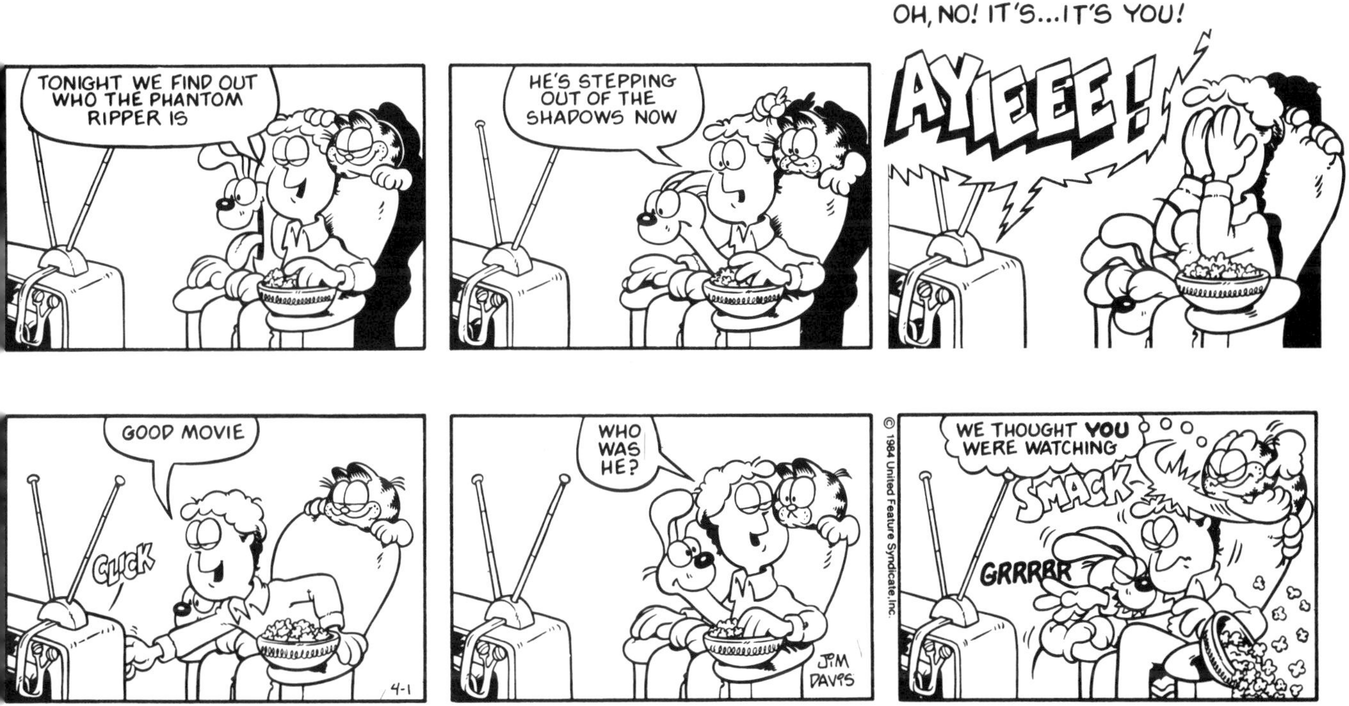
TONIGHT WE FIND OUT WHO THE PHANTOM RIPPER IS
HE'S STEPPING OUT OF THE SHADOWS NOW
OH, NO! IT'S...IT'S YOU!
AYIEEE!
GOOD MOVIE
CLICK
4-1
WHO WAS HE?
JIM DAVIS
© 1984 United Feature Syndicate, Inc.
WE THOUGHT YOU WERE WATCHING
SMACK
GRRRRR

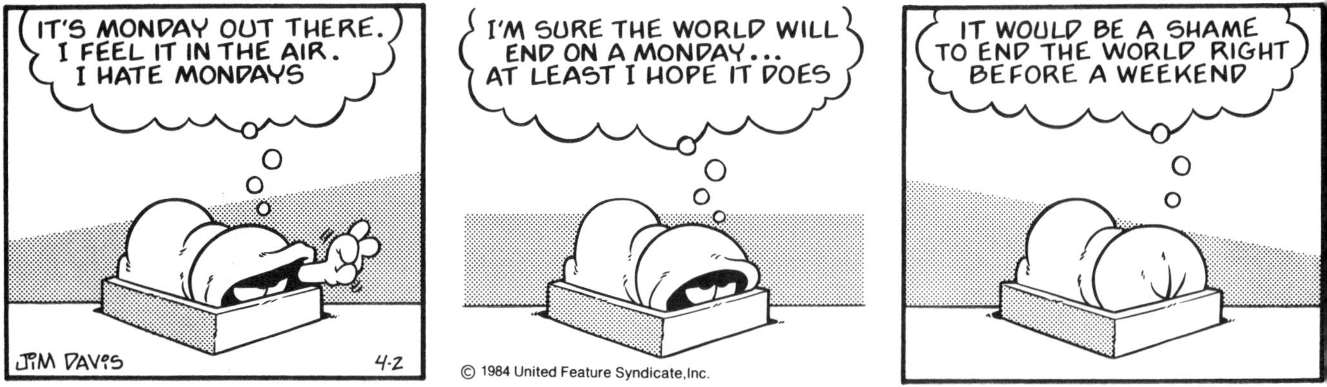
IT'S MONDAY OUT THERE. I FEEL IT IN THE AIR. I HATE MONDAYS
JIM DAVIS
4-2
I'M SURE THE WORLD WILL END ON A MONDAY... AT LEAST I HOPE IT DOES
© 1984 United Feature Syndicate, Inc.
IT WOULD BE A SHAME TO END THE WORLD RIGHT BEFORE A WEEKEND

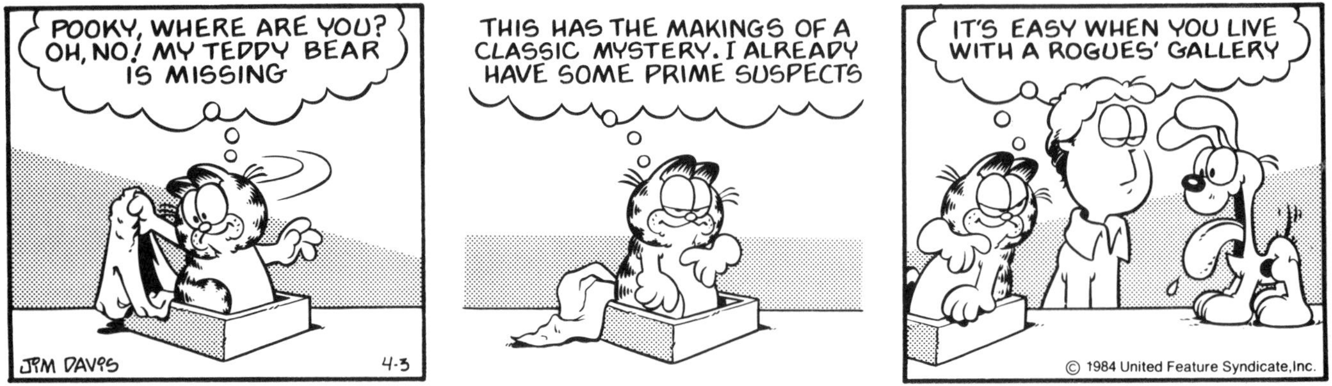
POOKY, WHERE ARE YOU? OH, NO! MY TEDDY BEAR IS MISSING
JIM DAVIS
4-3
THIS HAS THE MAKINGS OF A CLASSIC MYSTERY. I ALREADY HAVE SOME PRIME SUSPECTS
IT'S EASY WHEN YOU LIVE WITH A ROGUES' GALLERY
© 1984 United Feature Syndicate, Inc.

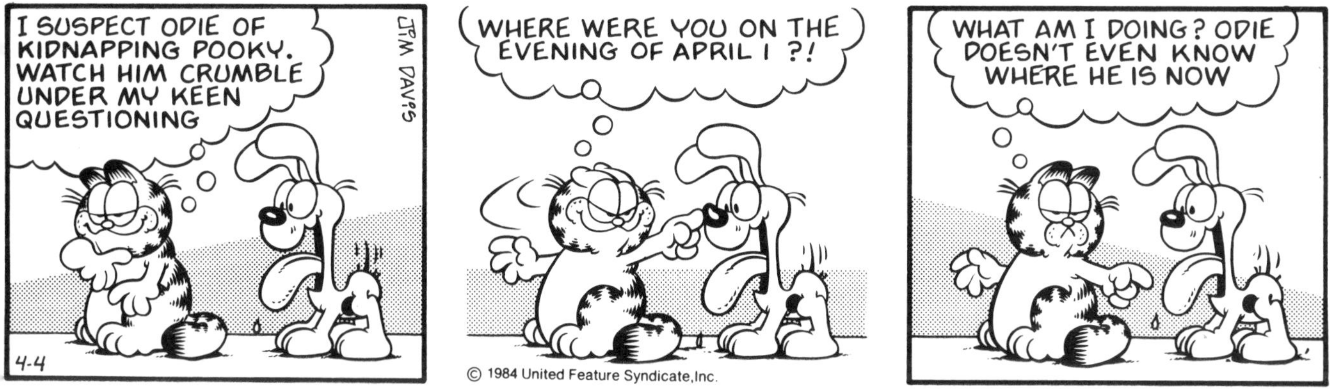
I SUSPECT ODIE OF KIDNAPPING POOKY. WATCH HIM CRUMBLE UNDER MY KEEN QUESTIONING
JIM DAVIS
4-4
WHERE WERE YOU ON THE EVENING OF APRIL 1 ?!
WHAT AM I DOING? ODIE DOESN'T EVEN KNOW WHERE HE IS NOW



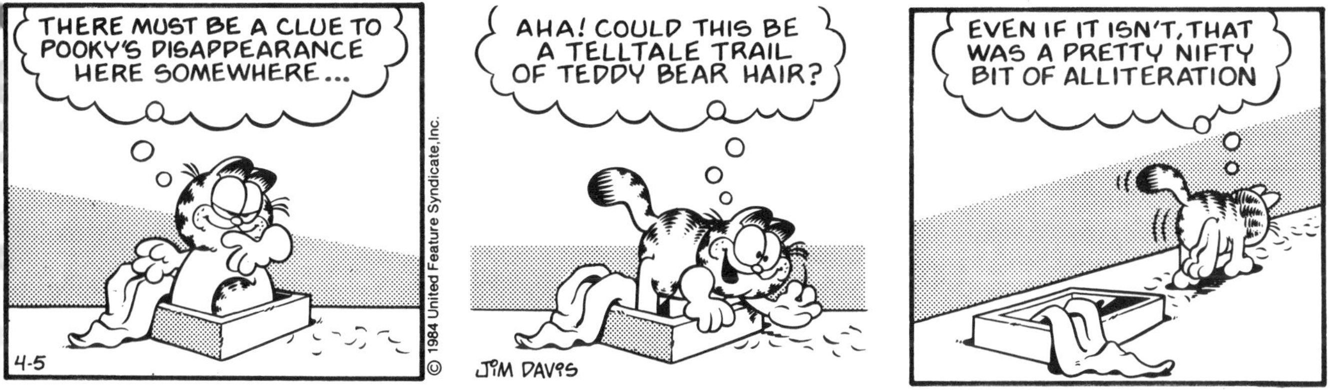
THERE MUST BE A CLUE TO POOKY'S DISAPPEARANCE HERE SOMEWHERE...
4-5
AHA! COULD THIS BE A TELLTALE TRAIL OF TEDDY BEAR HAIR?
JIM DAVIS
EVEN IF IT ISN'T, THAT WAS A PRETTY NIFTY BIT OF ALLITERATION

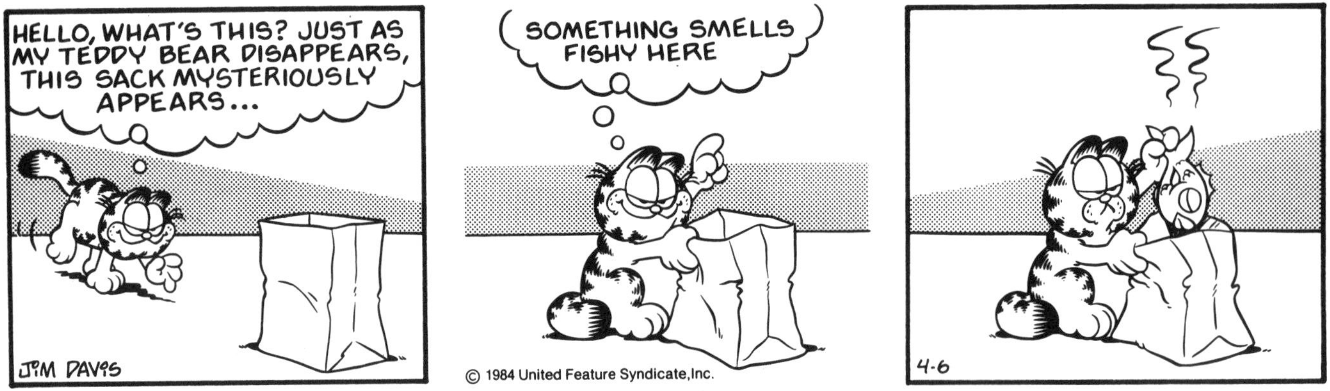
HELLO, WHAT'S THIS? JUST AS MY TEDDY BEAR DISAPPEARS, THIS SACK MYSTERIOUSLY APPEARS...
JIM DAVIS
SOMETHING SMELLS FISHY HERE
© 1984 United Feature Syndicate, Inc.
4-6

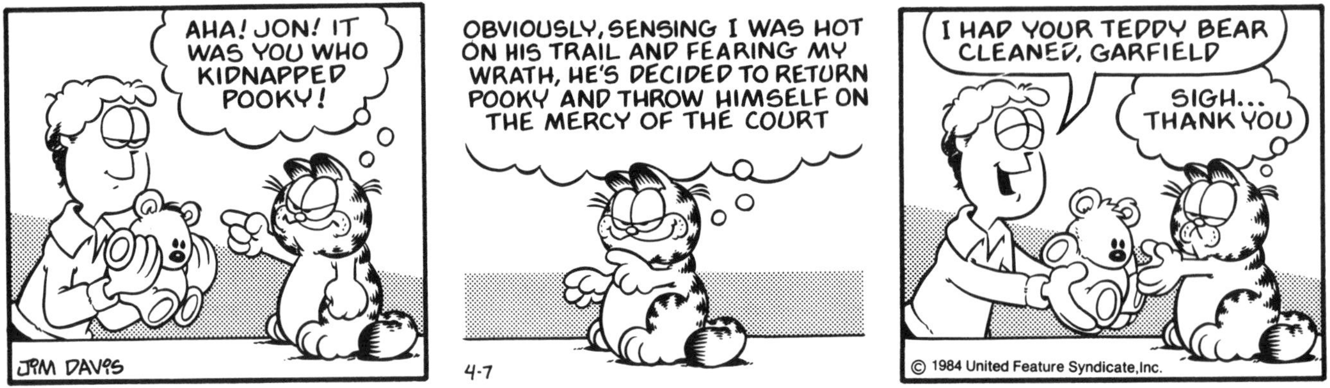
AHA! JON! IT WAS YOU WHO KIDNAPPED POOKY!
JIM DAVIS
OBVIOUSLY, SENSING I WAS HOT ON HIS TRAIL AND FEARING MY WRATH, HE'S DECIDED TO RETURN POOKY AND THROW HIMSELF ON THE MERCY OF THE COURT
4-7
I HAD YOUR TEDDY BEAR CLEANED, GARFIELD
SIGH... THANK YOU
© 1984 United Feature Syndicate, Inc.

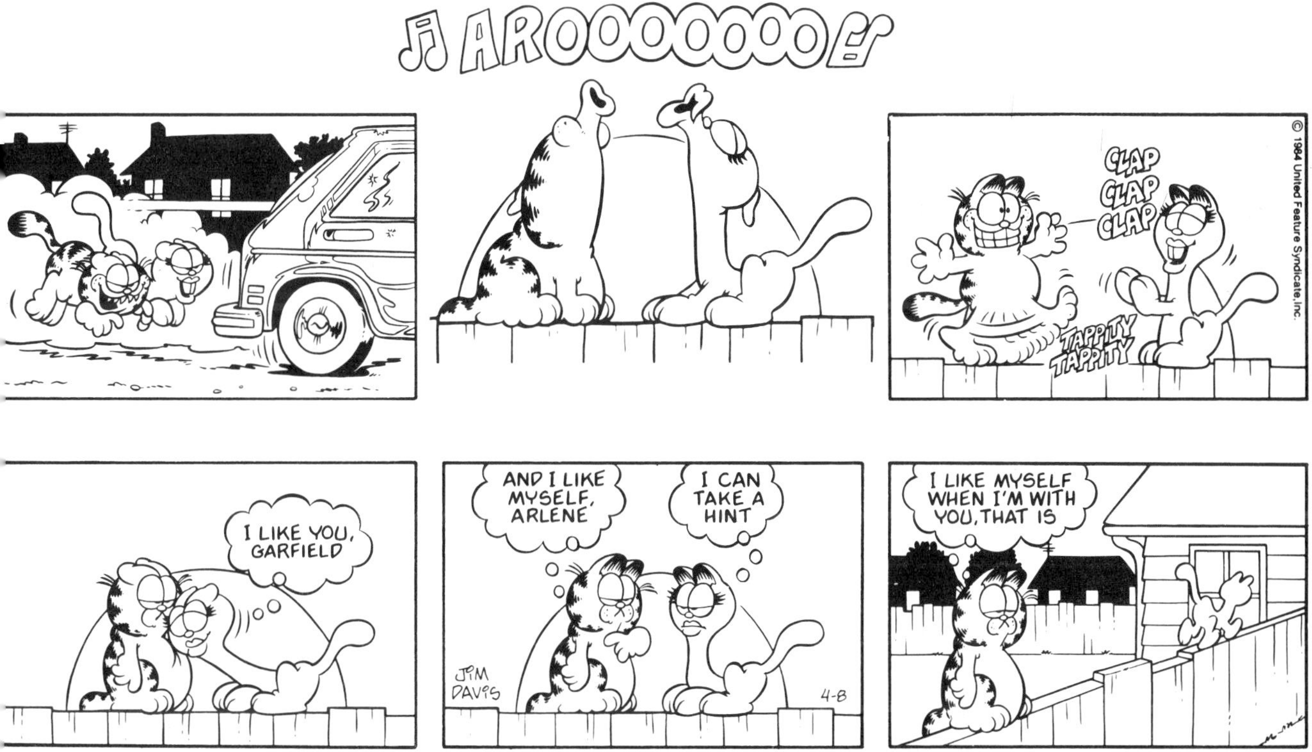
♫ AROOOOOOO ♫
CLAP CLAP CLAP
TAPPITY TAPPITY
© 1984 United Feature Syndicate, Inc.
I LIKE YOU, GARFIELD
AND I LIKE MYSELF, ARLENE
I CAN TAKE A HINT
JIM DAVIS
4-8
I LIKE MYSELF WHEN I'M WITH YOU, THAT IS

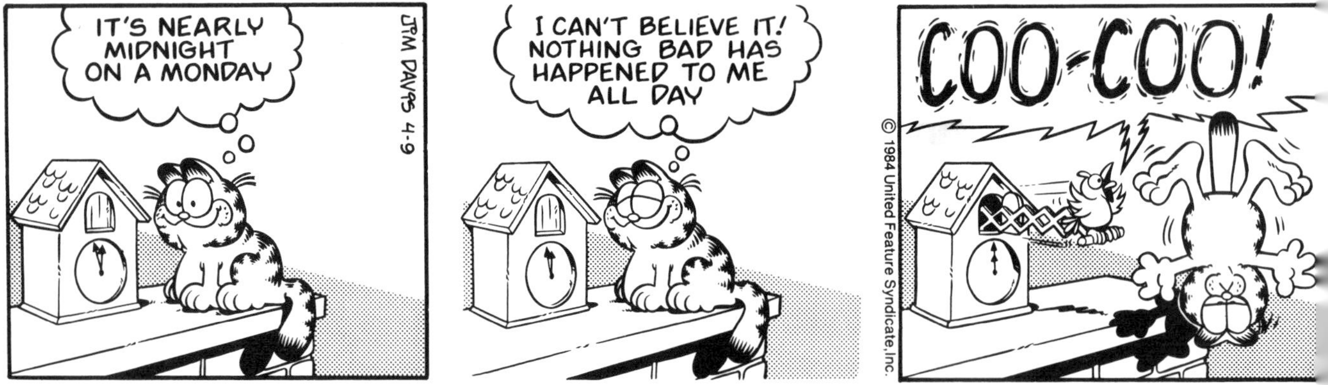
IT'S NEARLY MIDNIGHT ON A MONDAY
JIM DAVIS 4-9
I CAN'T BELIEVE IT! NOTHING BAD HAS HAPPENED TO ME ALL DAY
© 1984 United Feature Syndicate,Inc.
COO-COO!

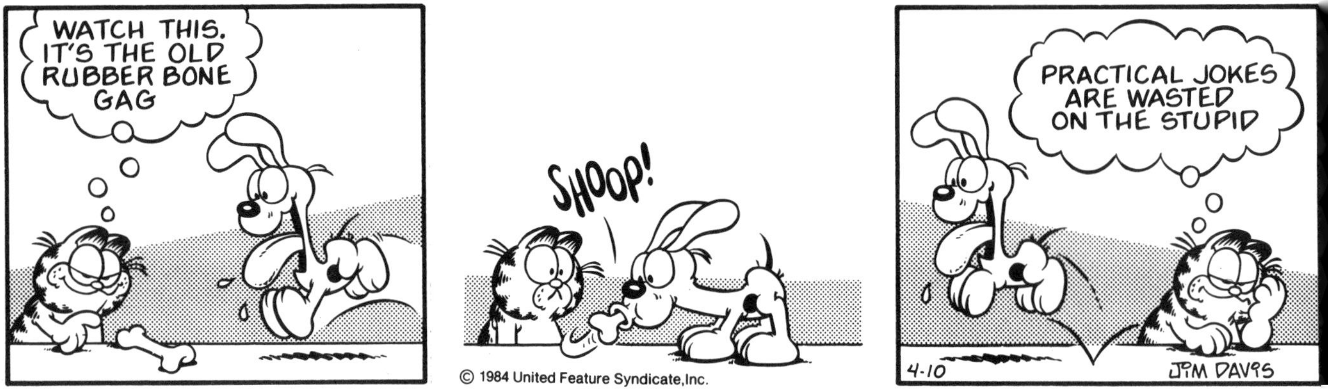
WATCH THIS. IT'S THE OLD RUBBER BONE GAG
SHOOP!
PRACTICAL JOKES ARE WASTED ON THE STUPID
4-10
JIM DAVIS

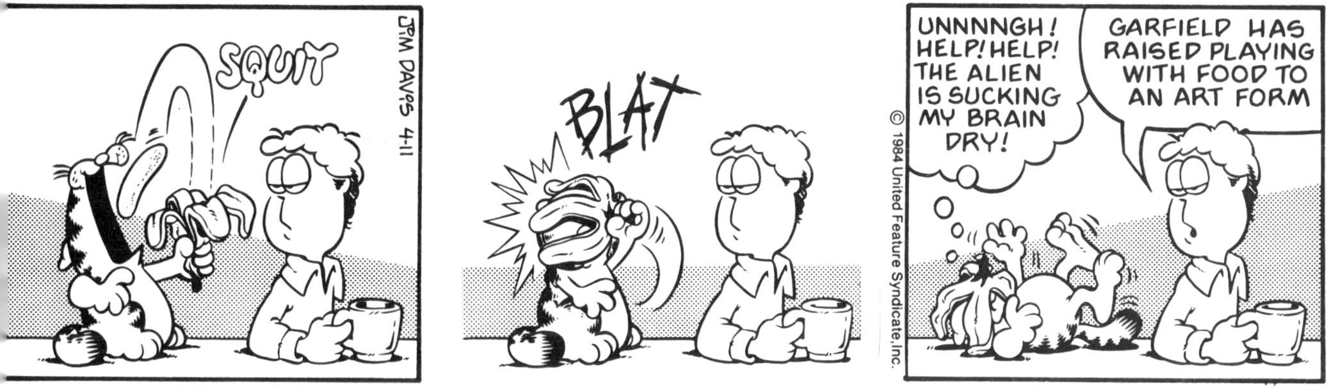
JIM DAVIS 4-11
SQUIT
BLAT
UNNNNGH! HELP! HELP! THE ALIEN IS SUCKING MY BRAIN DRY!
GARFIELD HAS RAISED PLAYING WITH FOOD TO AN ART FORM
© 1984 United Feature Syndicate, Inc.

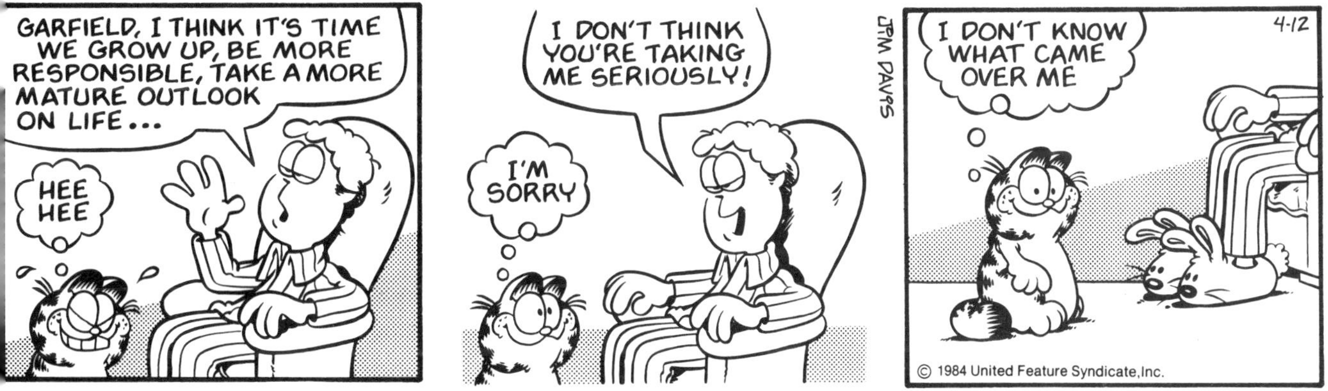
GARFIELD, I THINK IT'S TIME WE GROW UP, BE MORE RESPONSIBLE, TAKE A MORE MATURE OUTLOOK ON LIFE...
HEE HEE
I DON'T THINK YOU'RE TAKING ME SERIOUSLY!
I'M SORRY
JIM DAVIS
4-12
I DON'T KNOW WHAT CAME OVER ME
© 1984 United Feature Syndicate, Inc.

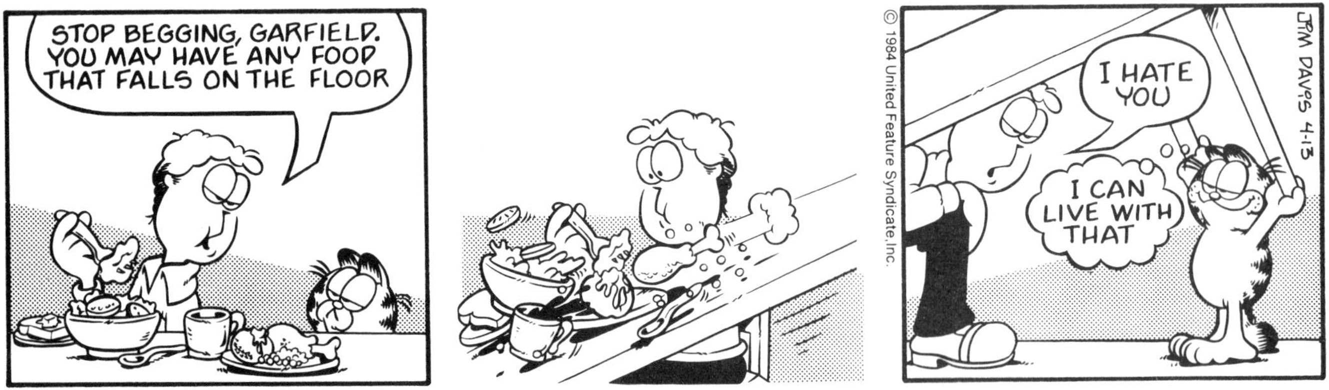
STOP BEGGING, GARFIELD. YOU MAY HAVE ANY FOOD THAT FALLS ON THE FLOOR
© 1984 United Feature Syndicate,Inc.
JIM DAVIS 4-13
I HATE YOU
I CAN LIVE WITH THAT

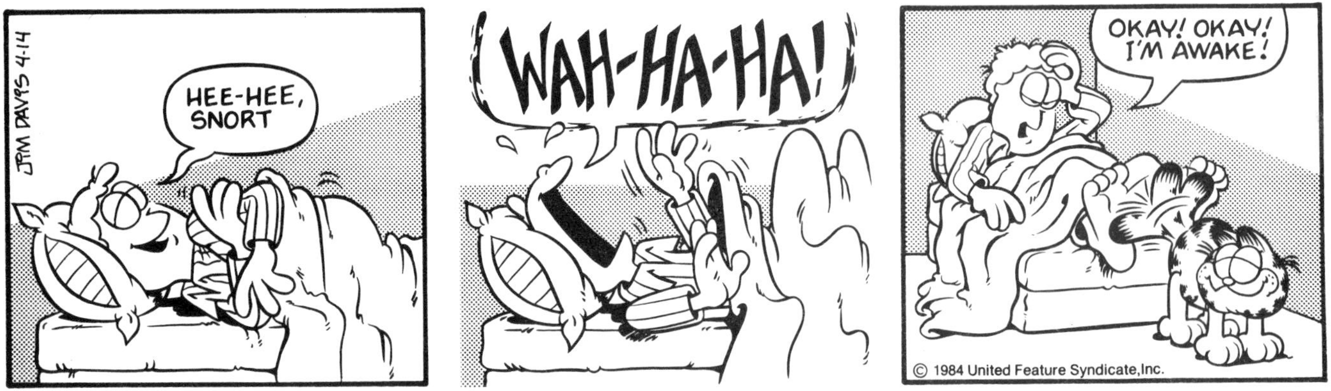
JIM DAVIS 4-14
HEE-HEE, SNORT
WAH-HA-HA!
OKAY! OKAY! I'M AWAKE!
© 1984 United Feature Syndicate,Inc.

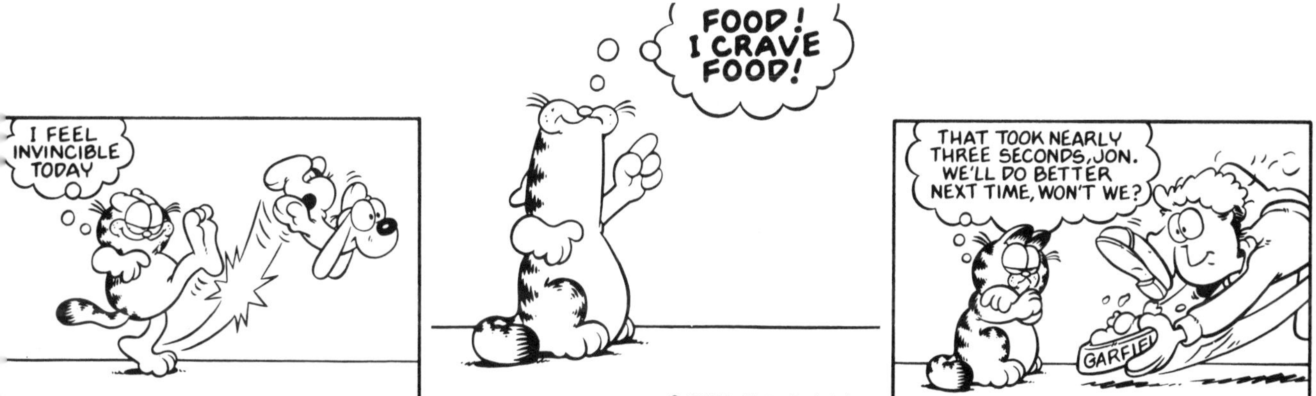
I FEEL INVINCIBLE TODAY
FOOD! I CRAVE FOOD!
THAT TOOK NEARLY THREE SECONDS, JON. WE'LL DO BETTER NEXT TIME, WON'T WE?
GARFIEL



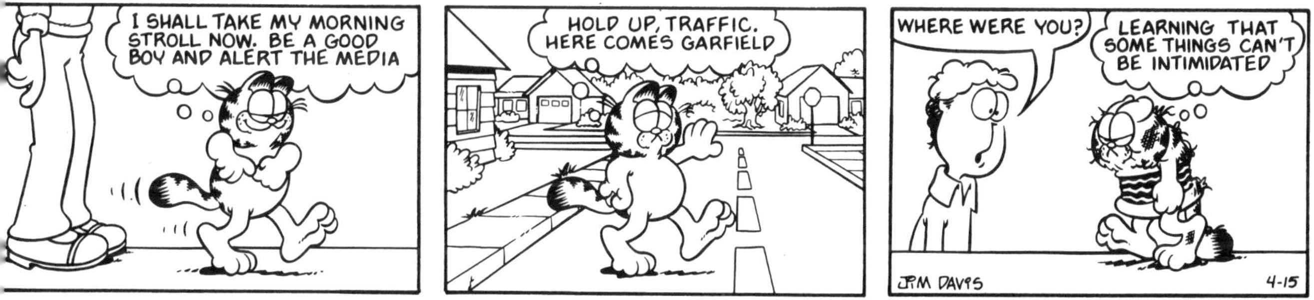
I SHALL TAKE MY MORNING STROLL NOW. BE A GOOD BOY AND ALERT THE MEDIA
HOLD UP, TRAFFIC. HERE COMES GARFIELD
WHERE WERE YOU?
LEARNING THAT SOME THINGS CAN'T BE INTIMIDATED
JIM DAVIS
4-15

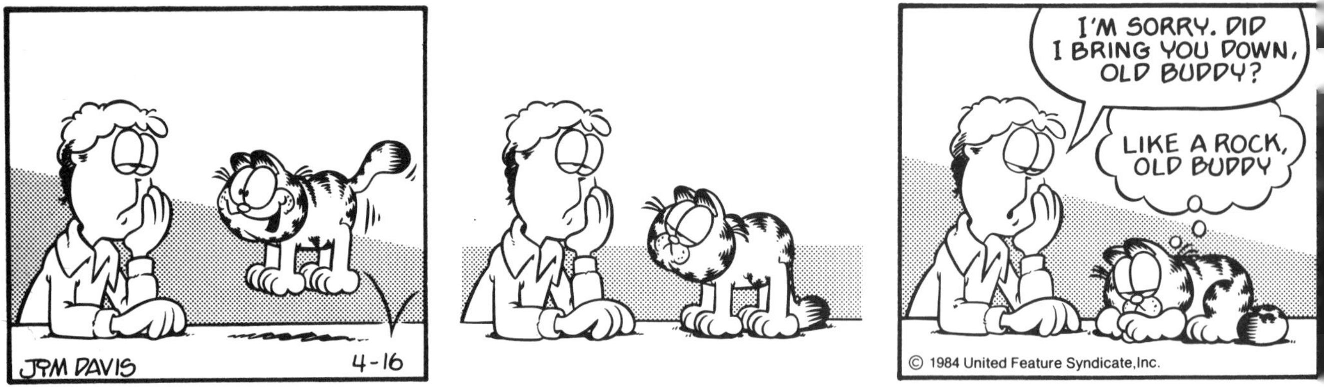
JIM DAVIS
4-16
I'M SORRY. DID I BRING YOU DOWN, OLD BUDDY?
LIKE A ROCK, OLD BUDDY
© 1984 United Feature Syndicate,Inc.

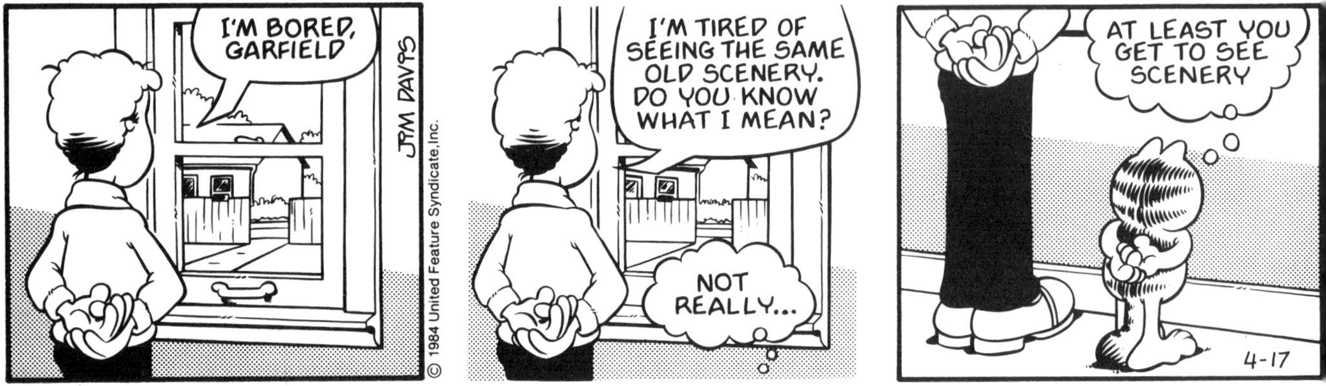
I'M BORED, GARFIELD
JIM DAVIS
© 1984 United Feature Syndicate,Inc.
I'M TIRED OF SEEING THE SAME OLD SCENERY. DO YOU KNOW WHAT I MEAN?
NOT REALLY...
AT LEAST YOU GET TO SEE SCENERY
4-17

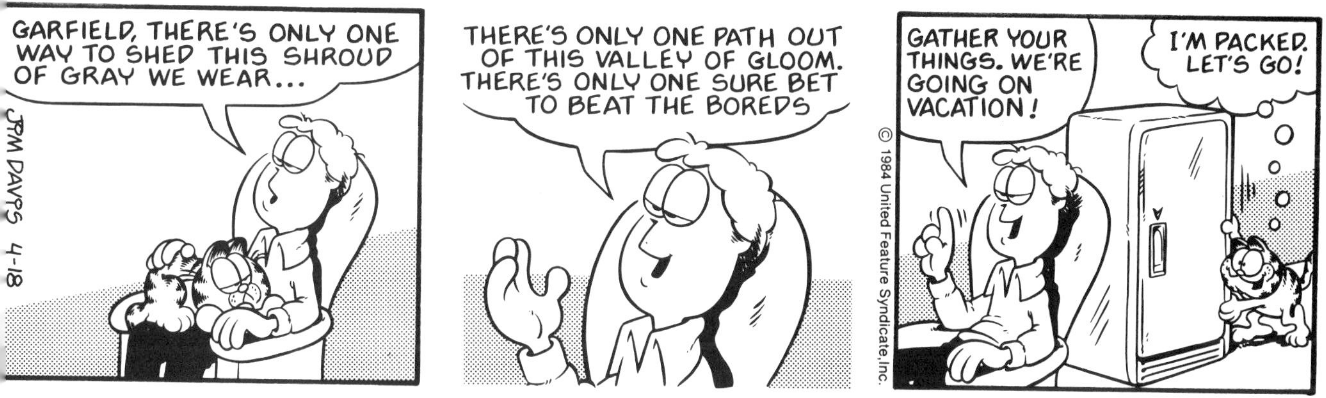
GARFIELD, THERE'S ONLY ONE WAY TO SHED THIS SHROUD OF GRAY WE WEAR...
JIM DAVIS 4-18
THERE'S ONLY ONE PATH OUT OF THIS VALLEY OF GLOOM. THERE'S ONLY ONE SURE BET TO BEAT THE BOREDS
GATHER YOUR THINGS. WE'RE GOING ON VACATION!
I'M PACKED. LET'S GO!
© 1984 United Feature Syndicate, Inc.

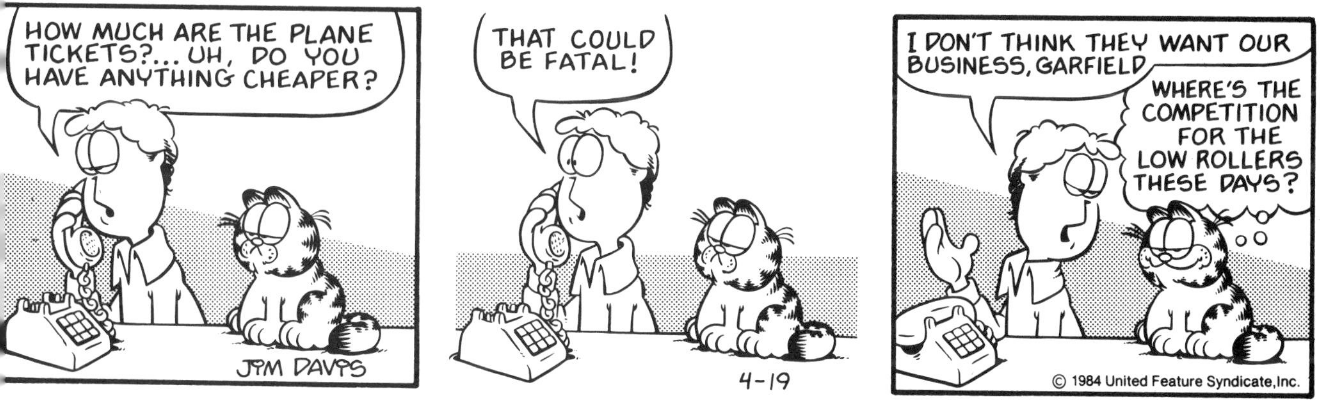
HOW MUCH ARE THE PLANE TICKETS?... UH, DO YOU HAVE ANYTHING CHEAPER?
JIM DAVIS
THAT COULD BE FATAL!
4-19
I DON'T THINK THEY WANT OUR BUSINESS, GARFIELD
WHERE'S THE COMPETITION FOR THE LOW ROLLERS THESE DAYS?
© 1984 United Feature Syndicate, Inc.

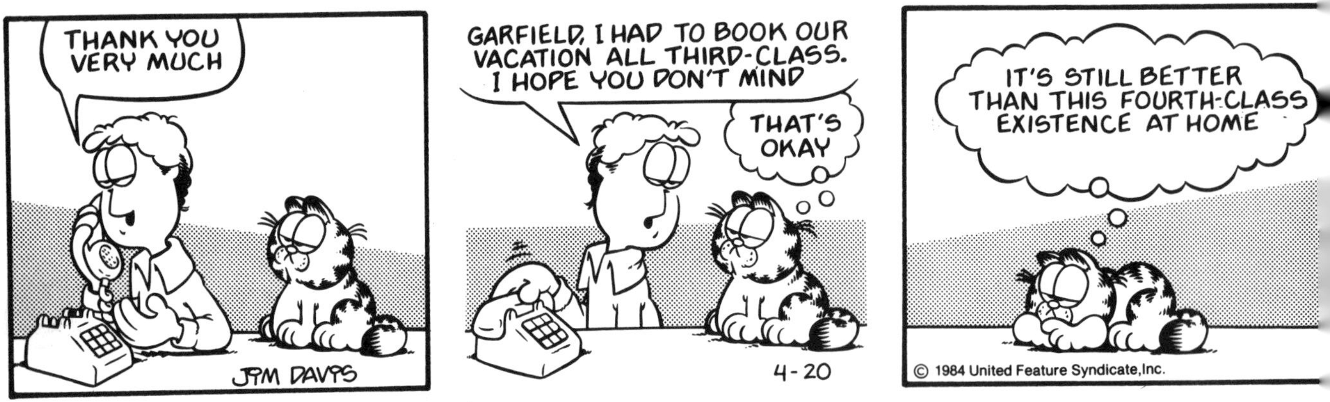
THANK YOU VERY MUCH
JIM DAVIS
GARFIELD, I HAD TO BOOK OUR VACATION ALL THIRD-CLASS. I HOPE YOU DON'T MIND
THAT'S OKAY
4-20
IT'S STILL BETTER THAN THIS FOURTH-CLASS EXISTENCE AT HOME
© 1984 United Feature Syndicate, Inc.

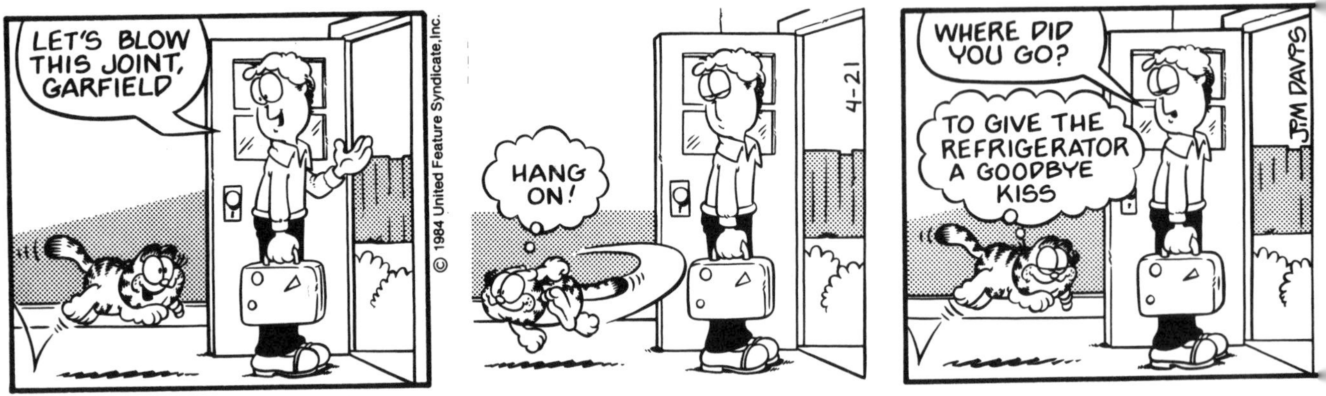
LET'S BLOW THIS JOINT, GARFIELD
© 1984 United Feature Syndicate, Inc.
HANG ON!
4-21
WHERE DID YOU GO?
TO GIVE THE REFRIGERATOR A GOODBYE KISS
JIM DAVIS

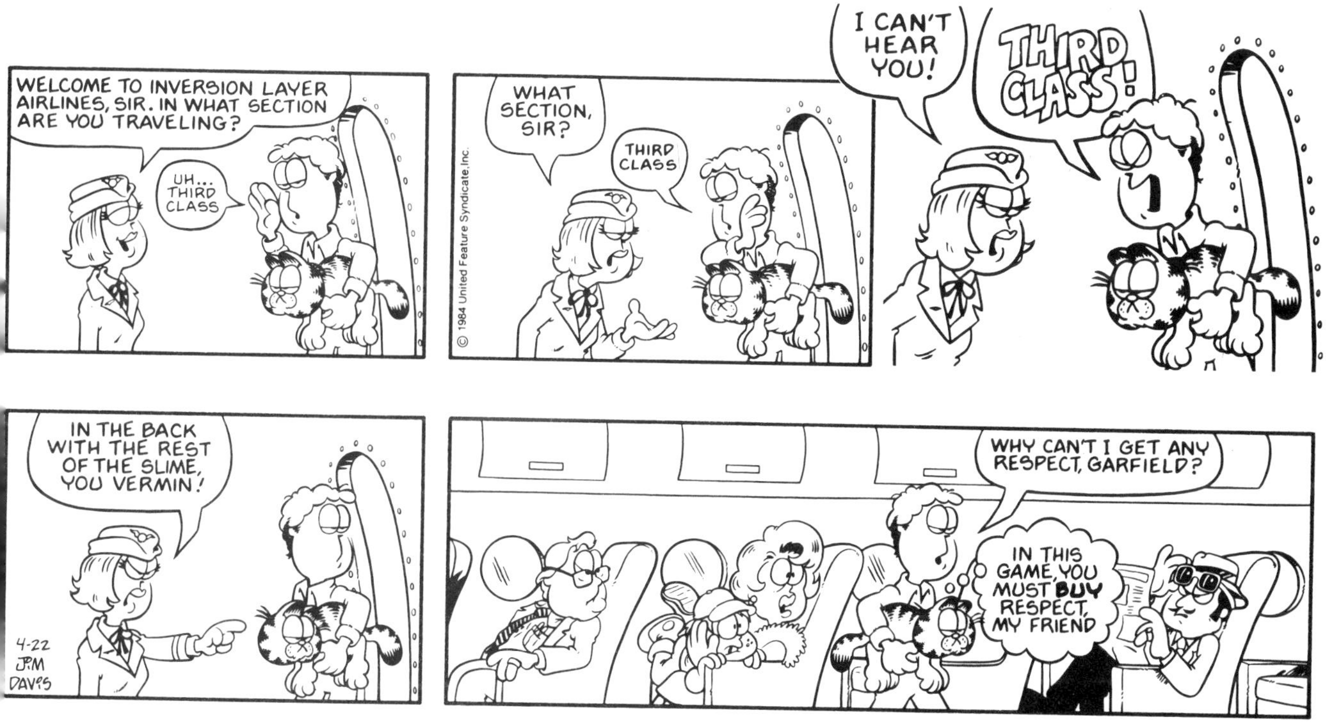

WELCOME TO INVERSION LAYER AIRLINES, SIR. IN WHAT SECTION ARE YOU TRAVELING?
UH... THIRD CLASS
WHAT SECTION, SIR?
THIRD CLASS
© 1984 United Feature Syndicate, Inc.
I CAN'T HEAR YOU!
THIRD CLASS!
IN THE BACK WITH THE REST OF THE SLIME, YOU VERMIN!
4-22
JPM DAVPS
WHY CAN'T I GET ANY RESPECT, GARFIELD?
IN THIS GAME, YOU MUST BUY RESPECT, MY FRIEND

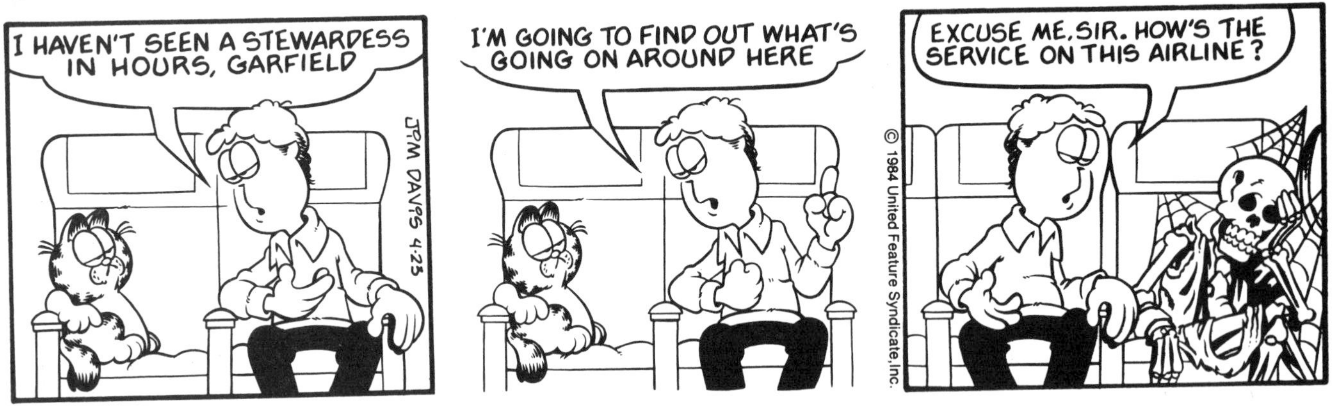
I HAVEN'T SEEN A STEWARDESS IN HOURS, GARFIELD
JPM DAVPS 4-23
I'M GOING TO FIND OUT WHAT'S GOING ON AROUND HERE
© 1984 United Feature Syndicate, Inc.
EXCUSE ME, SIR. HOW'S THE SERVICE ON THIS AIRLINE?

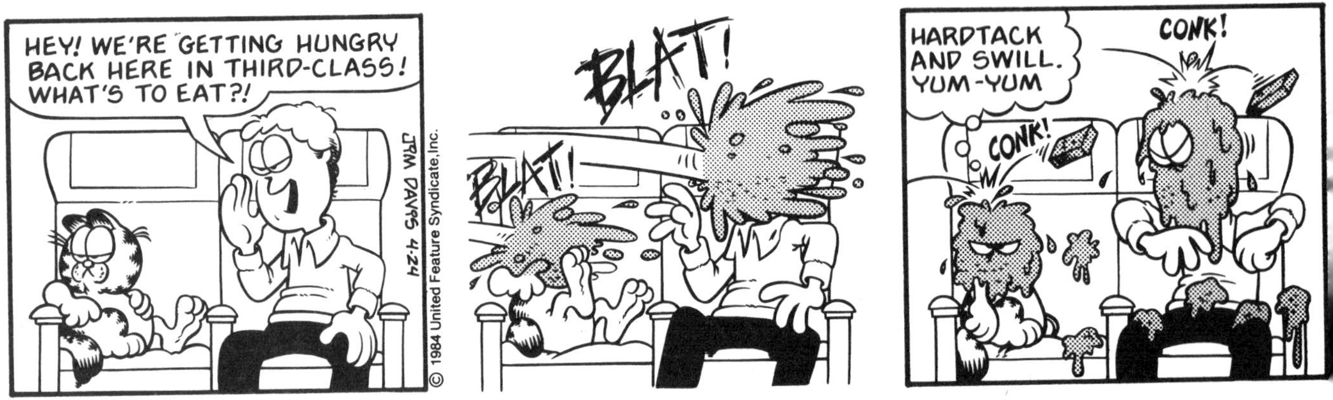
HEY! WE'RE GETTING HUNGRY BACK HERE IN THIRD-CLASS! WHAT'S TO EAT?!
JPM DAVPS 4-24
© 1984 United Feature Syndicate, Inc.
BLAT!
BLAT!!
HARDTACK AND SWILL. YUM-YUM
CONK!
CONK!

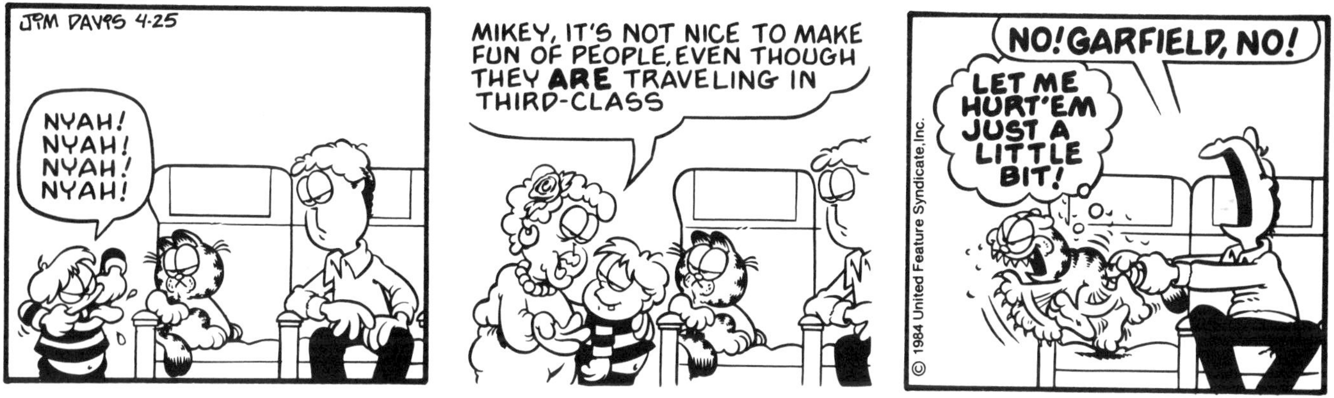
JIM DAVIS 4-25
NYAH! NYAH! NYAH! NYAH!
MIKEY, IT'S NOT NICE TO MAKE FUN OF PEOPLE, EVEN THOUGH THEY **ARE** TRAVELING IN THIRD-CLASS
© 1984 United Feature Syndicate, Inc.
NO! GARFIELD, NO!
LET ME HURT'EM JUST A LITTLE BIT!

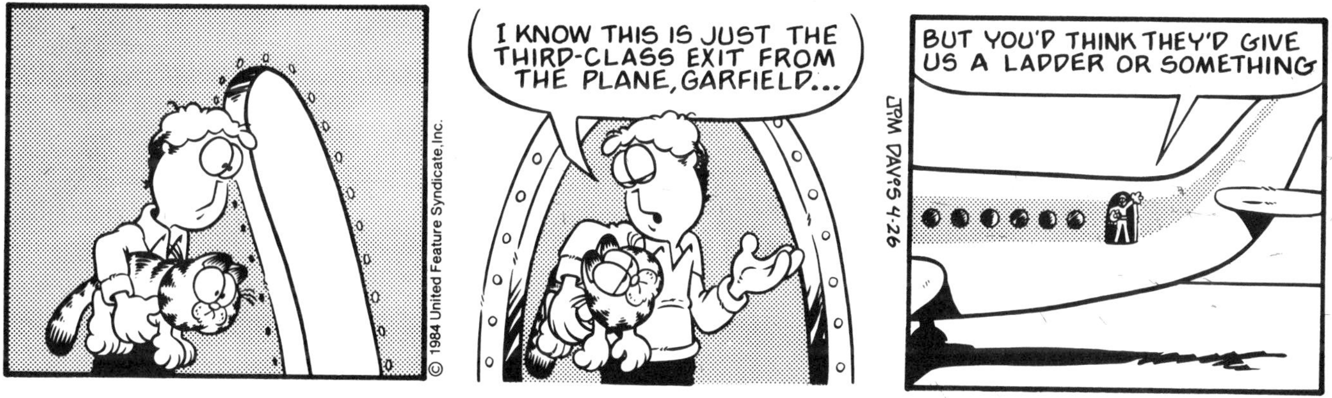
© 1984 United Feature Syndicate, Inc.
I KNOW THIS IS JUST THE THIRD-CLASS EXIT FROM THE PLANE, GARFIELD...
JIM DAVIS 4-26
BUT YOU'D THINK THEY'D GIVE US A LADDER OR SOMETHING

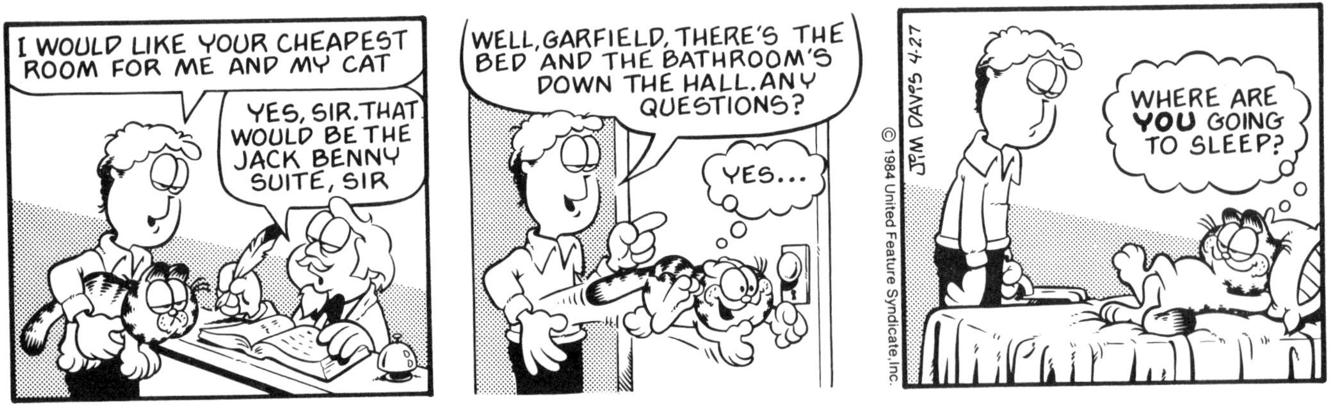
I WOULD LIKE YOUR CHEAPEST ROOM FOR ME AND MY CAT
YES, SIR. THAT WOULD BE THE JACK BENNY SUITE, SIR
WELL, GARFIELD, THERE'S THE BED AND THE BATHROOM'S DOWN THE HALL. ANY QUESTIONS?
YES...
JIM DAVIS 4-27
© 1984 United Feature Syndicate, Inc.
WHERE ARE **YOU** GOING TO SLEEP?

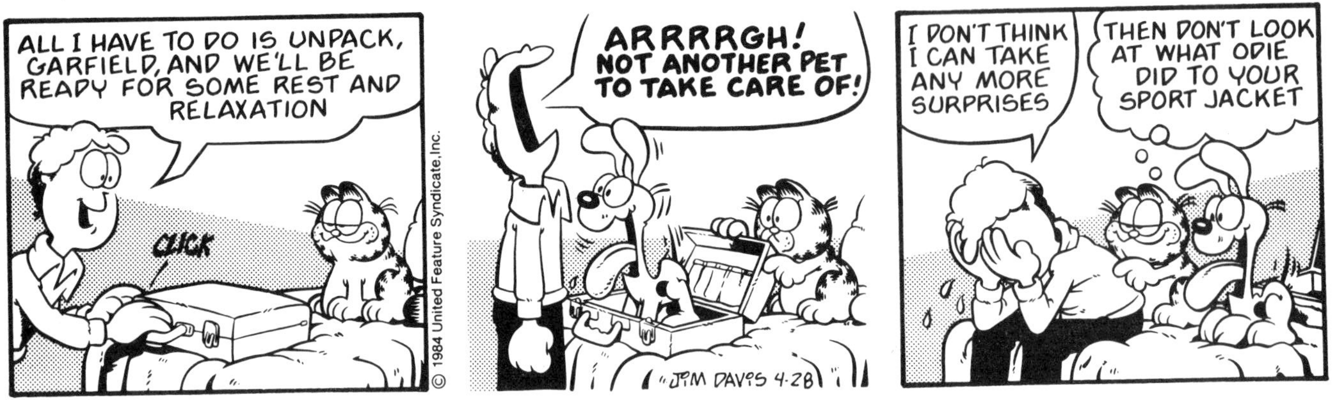
ALL I HAVE TO DO IS UNPACK, GARFIELD, AND WE'LL BE READY FOR SOME REST AND RELAXATION
CLICK
© 1984 United Feature Syndicate, Inc.
**ARRRRGH! NOT ANOTHER PET TO TAKE CARE OF!**
JIM DAVIS 4-28
I DON'T THINK I CAN TAKE ANY MORE SURPRISES
THEN DON'T LOOK AT WHAT ODIE DID TO YOUR SPORT JACKET

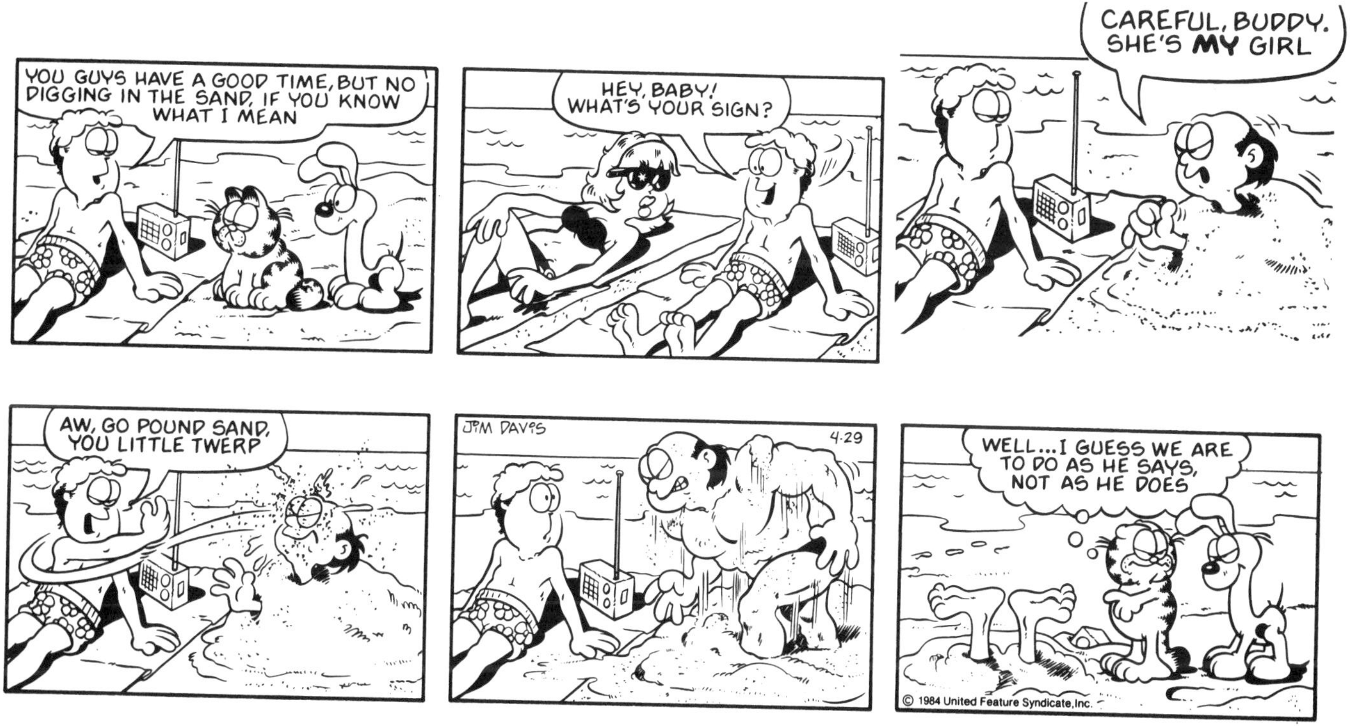
YOU GUYS HAVE A GOOD TIME, BUT NO DIGGING IN THE SAND, IF YOU KNOW WHAT I MEAN
HEY, BABY! WHAT'S YOUR SIGN?
CAREFUL, BUDDY. SHE'S MY GIRL
AW, GO POUND SAND, YOU LITTLE TWERP
JIM DAVIS
4·29
WELL...I GUESS WE ARE TO DO AS HE SAYS, NOT AS HE DOES
© 1984 United Feature Syndicate, Inc.

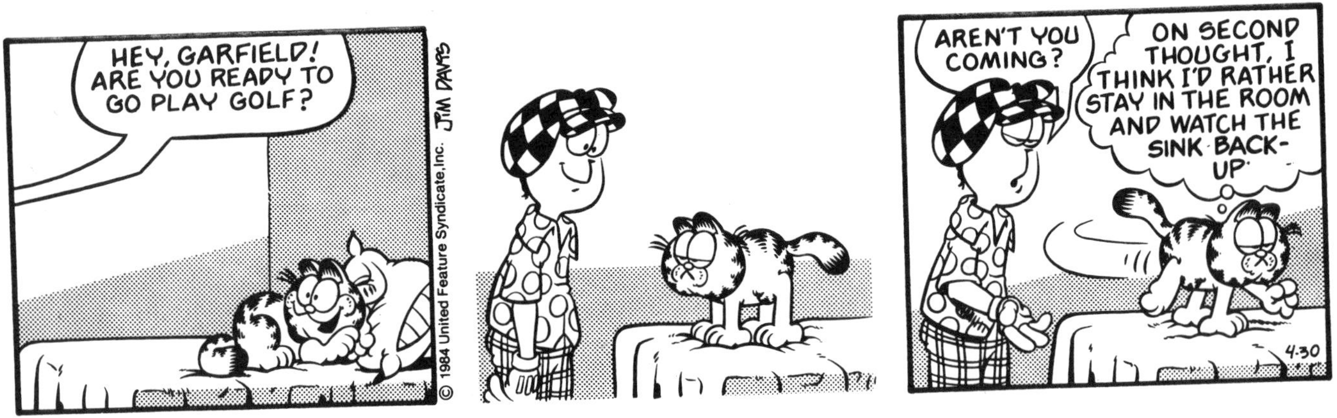
HEY, GARFIELD! ARE YOU READY TO GO PLAY GOLF?
JIM DAVIS
© 1984 United Feature Syndicate, Inc.
AREN'T YOU COMING?
ON SECOND THOUGHT, I THINK I'D RATHER STAY IN THE ROOM AND WATCH THE SINK BACK-UP
4-30

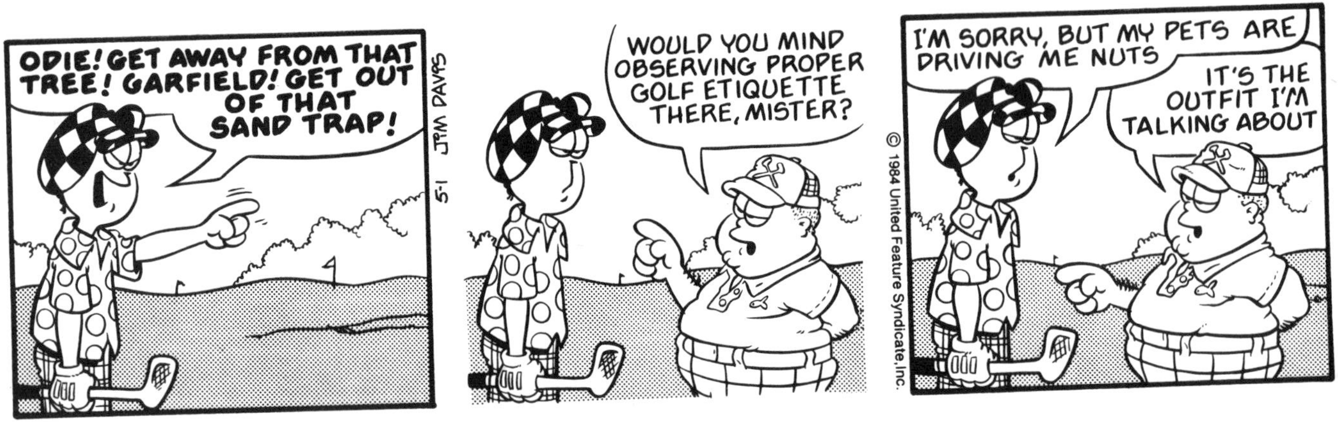
ODIE! GET AWAY FROM THAT TREE! GARFIELD! GET OUT OF THAT SAND TRAP!
JIM DAVIS
5-1
WOULD YOU MIND OBSERVING PROPER GOLF ETIQUETTE THERE, MISTER?
© 1984 United Feature Syndicate, Inc.
I'M SORRY, BUT MY PETS ARE DRIVING ME NUTS
IT'S THE OUTFIT I'M TALKING ABOUT

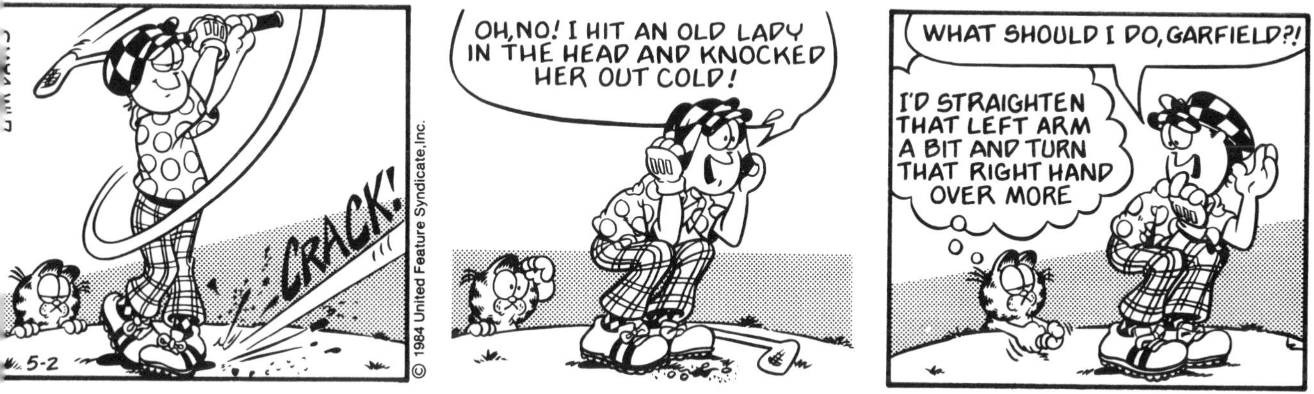
5-2
CRACK!
OH, NO! I HIT AN OLD LADY IN THE HEAD AND KNOCKED HER OUT COLD!
WHAT SHOULD I DO, GARFIELD?!
I'D STRAIGHTEN THAT LEFT ARM A BIT AND TURN THAT RIGHT HAND OVER MORE


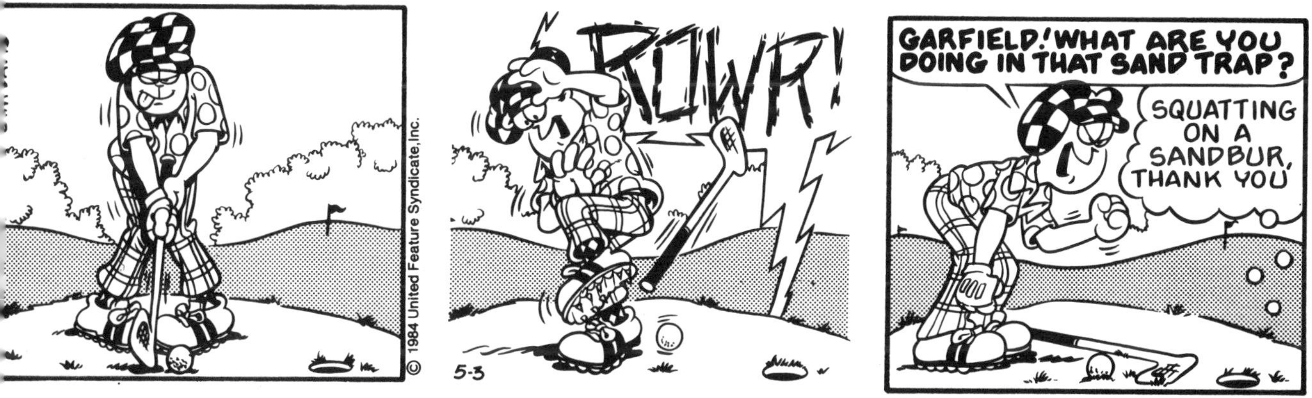
ROWR!
5-3
GARFIELD! WHAT ARE YOU DOING IN THAT SAND TRAP?
SQUATTING ON A SANDBUR, THANK YOU

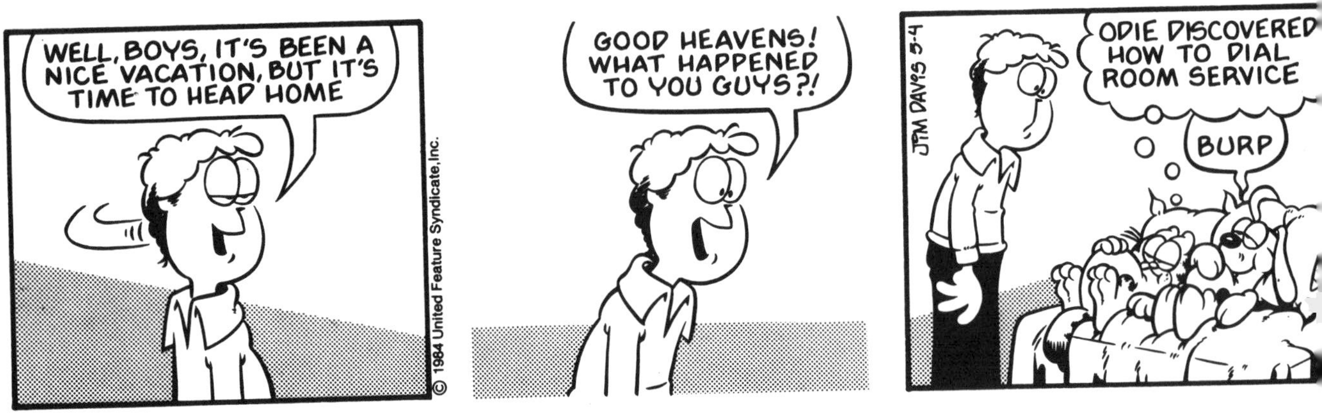
WELL, BOYS, IT'S BEEN A NICE VACATION, BUT IT'S TIME TO HEAD HOME
© 1984 United Feature Syndicate, Inc.
GOOD HEAVENS! WHAT HAPPENED TO YOU GUYS?!
JIM DAVIS 5-4
ODIE DISCOVERED HOW TO DIAL ROOM SERVICE
BURP

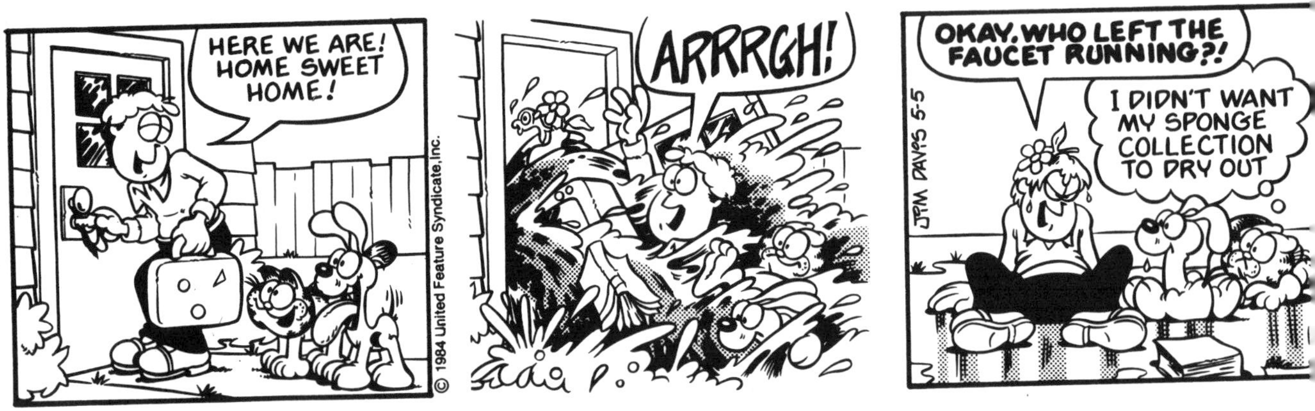
HERE WE ARE! HOME SWEET HOME!
© 1984 United Feature Syndicate, Inc.
ARRRGH!
JIM DAVIS 5-5
OKAY, WHO LEFT THE FAUCET RUNNING?!
I DIDN'T WANT MY SPONGE COLLECTION TO DRY OUT

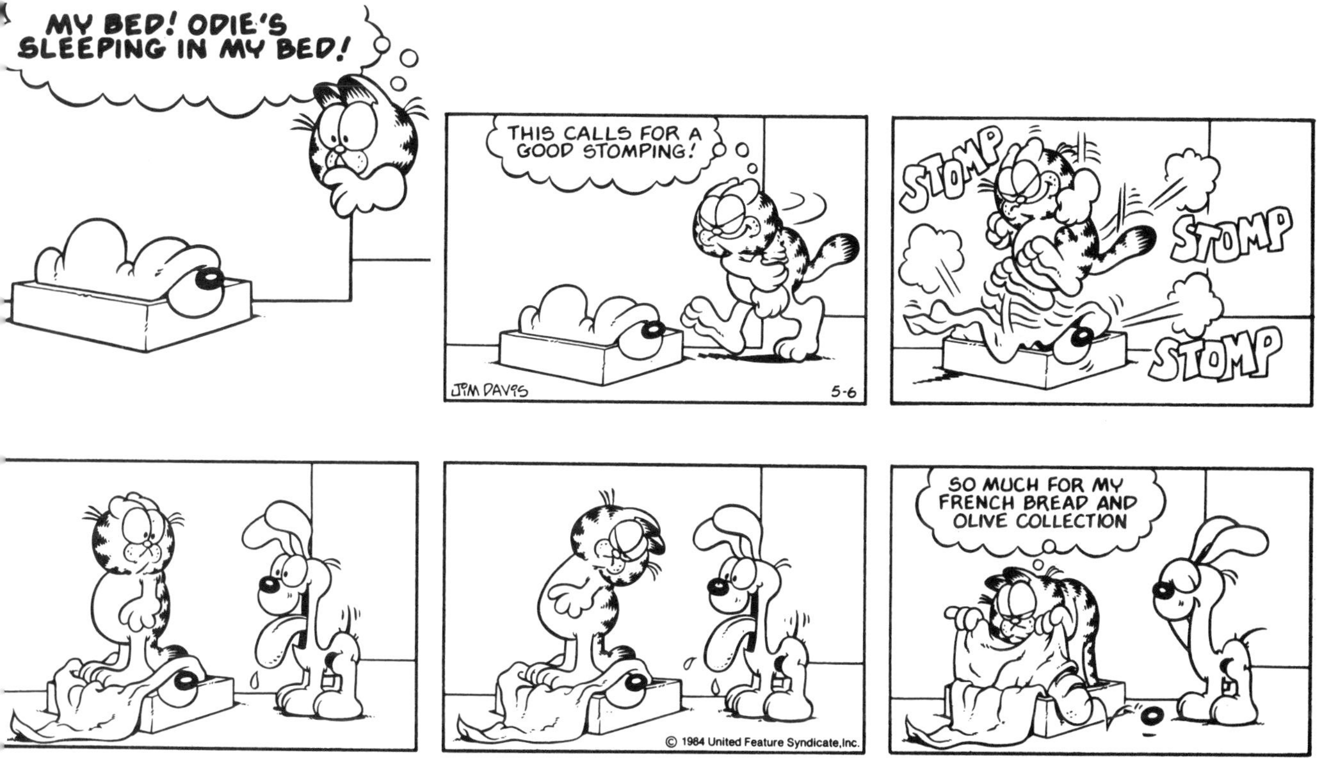
MY BED! ODIE'S SLEEPING IN MY BED!
THIS CALLS FOR A GOOD STOMPING!
JIM DAVIS
5-6
STOMP
STOMP
STOMP
© 1984 United Feature Syndicate, Inc.
SO MUCH FOR MY FRENCH BREAD AND OLIVE COLLECTION

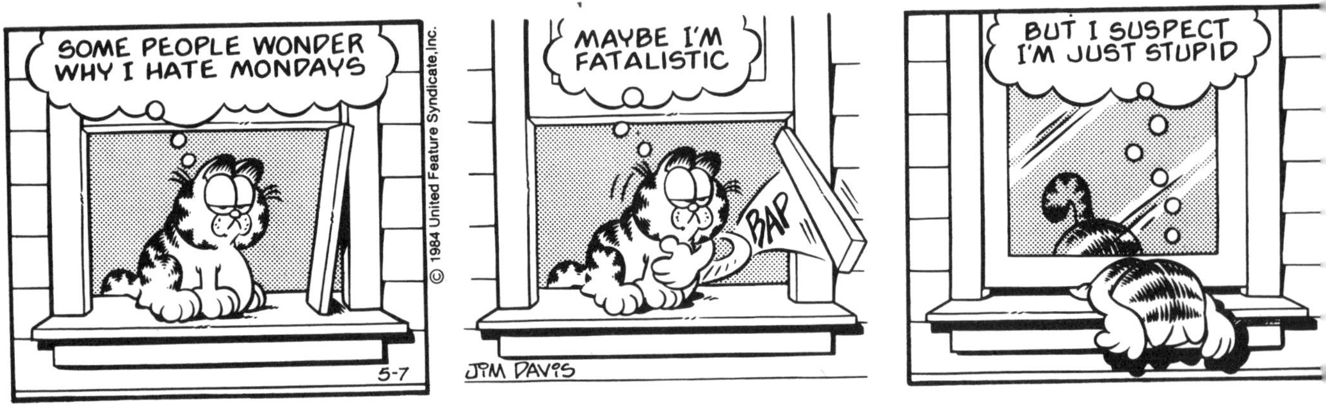
SOME PEOPLE WONDER WHY I HATE MONDAYS
© 1984 United Feature Syndicate, Inc.
5-7
MAYBE I'M FATALISTIC
BAP
JIM DAVIS
BUT I SUSPECT I'M JUST STUPID

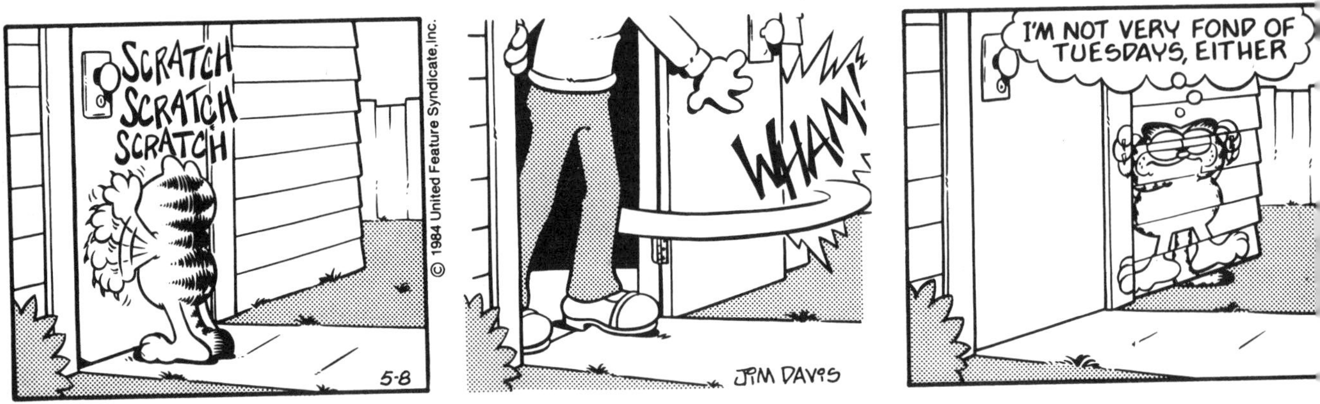
SCRATCH
SCRATCH
SCRATCH
© 1984 United Feature Syndicate, Inc.
5-8
WHAM!
JIM DAVIS
I'M NOT VERY FOND OF TUESDAYS, EITHER

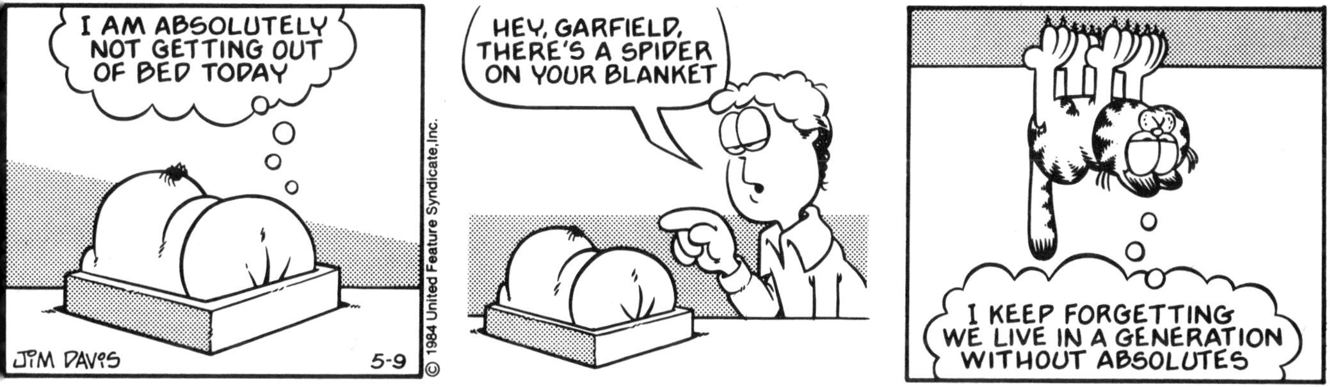
I AM ABSOLUTELY NOT GETTING OUT OF BED TODAY
JIM DAVIS
5-9
© 1984 United Feature Syndicate, Inc.
HEY, GARFIELD, THERE'S A SPIDER ON YOUR BLANKET
I KEEP FORGETTING WE LIVE IN A GENERATION WITHOUT ABSOLUTES

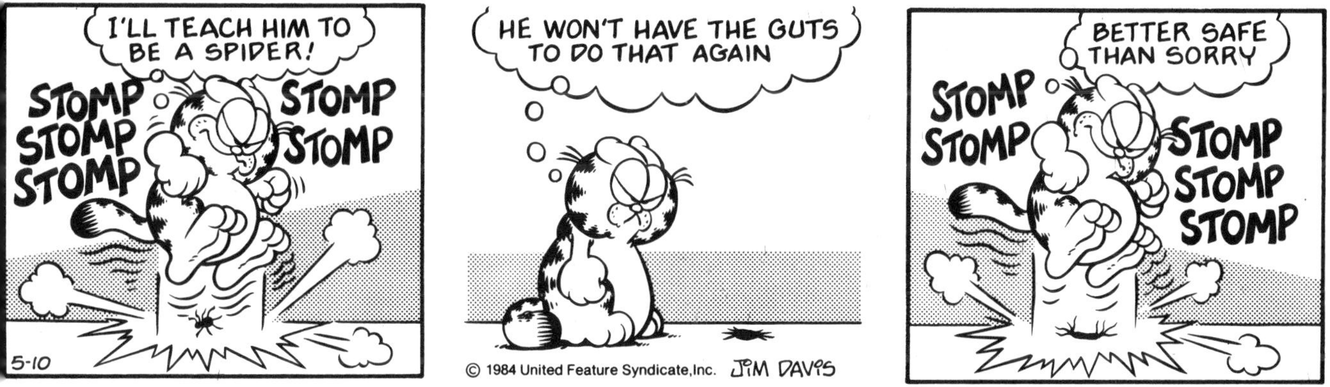
I'LL TEACH HIM TO BE A SPIDER!
STOMP STOMP STOMP
STOMP STOMP
5-10
HE WON'T HAVE THE GUTS TO DO THAT AGAIN
© 1984 United Feature Syndicate, Inc.
JIM DAVIS
BETTER SAFE THAN SORRY
STOMP STOMP
STOMP STOMP STOMP

LOOK AT THIS

JIM DAVIS 5-11

A CAT STROKING HIS OWNER!

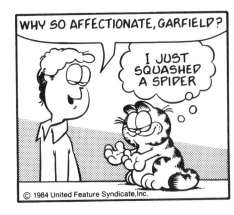

WHY SO AFFECTIONATE, GARFIELD?

I JUST SQUASHED A SPIDER

© 1984 United Feature Syndicate, Inc.

GARFIELD

5-12

JIM DAVIS

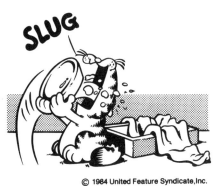

SLUG

© 1984 United Feature Syndicate, Inc.

BIG DAY

GARFIELD

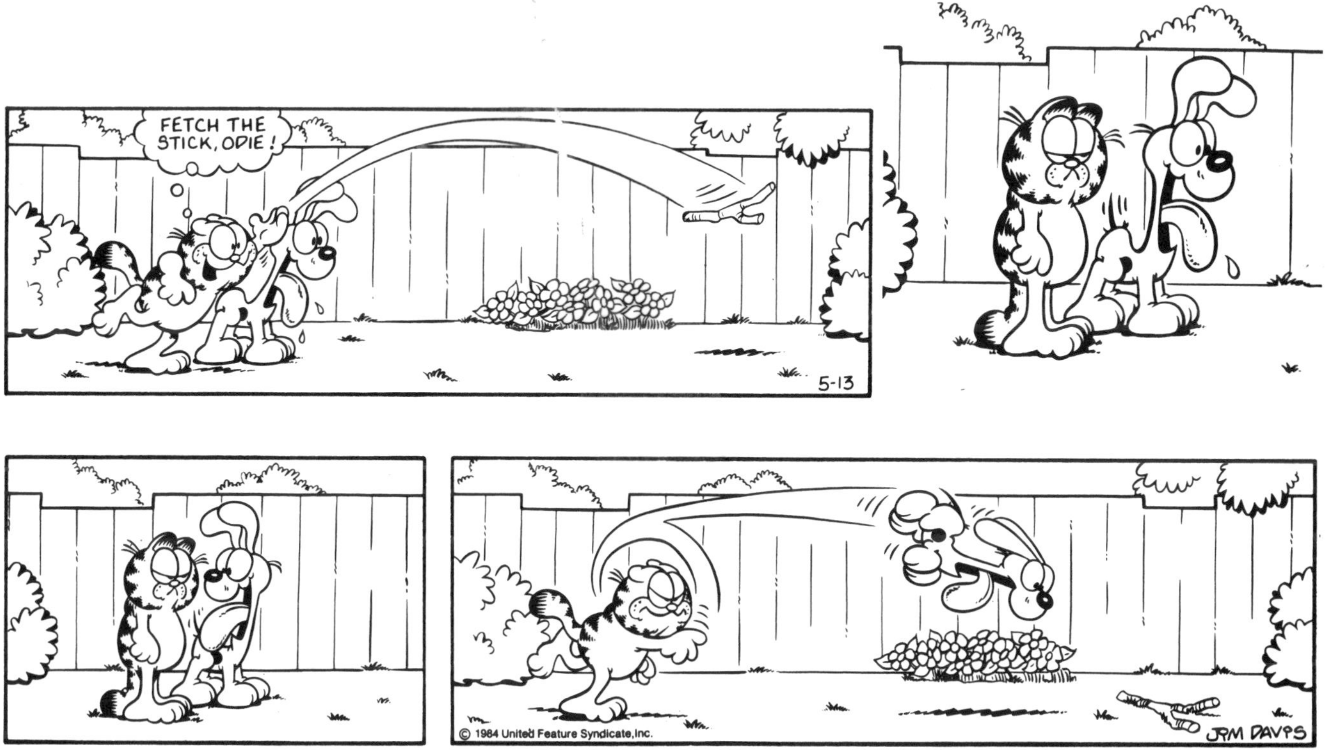
FETCH THE STICK, ODIE!
5-13
© 1984 United Feature Syndicate, Inc.
JIM DAVIS

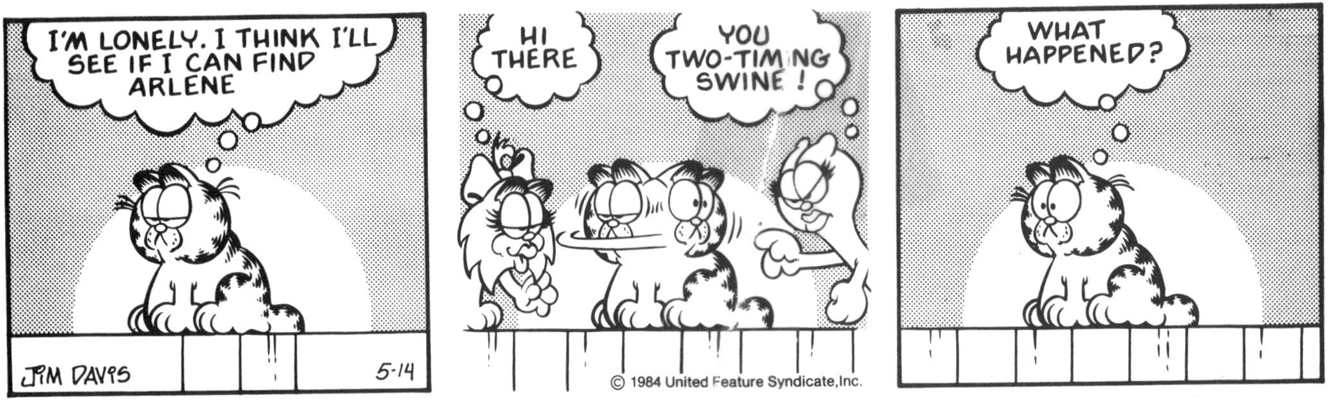
I'M LONELY. I THINK I'LL SEE IF I CAN FIND ARLENE
JIM DAVIS
5-14
HI THERE
YOU TWO-TIMING SWINE!
© 1984 United Feature Syndicate, Inc.
WHAT HAPPENED?

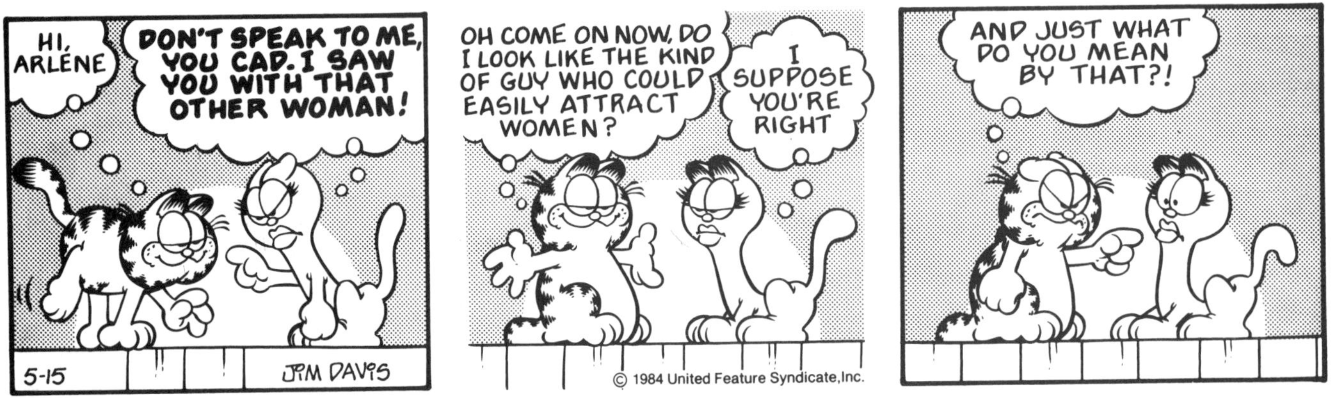
HI, ARLENE
DON'T SPEAK TO ME, YOU CAD. I SAW YOU WITH THAT OTHER WOMAN!
5-15
JIM DAVIS
OH COME ON NOW, DO I LOOK LIKE THE KIND OF GUY WHO COULD EASILY ATTRACT WOMEN?
I SUPPOSE YOU'RE RIGHT
© 1984 United Feature Syndicate, Inc.
AND JUST WHAT DO YOU MEAN BY THAT?!

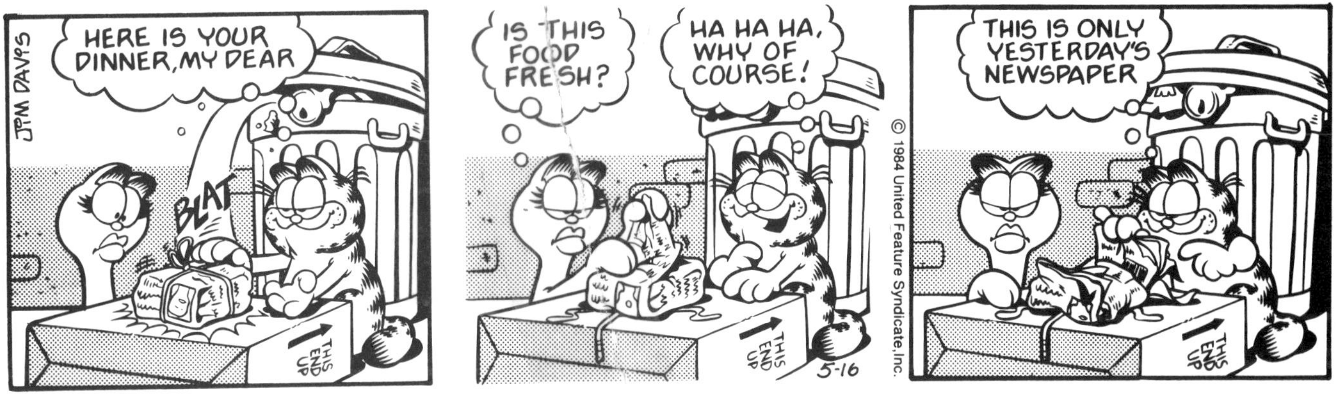
JIM DAVIS
HERE IS YOUR DINNER, MY DEAR
BLAT
THIS END UP
IS THIS FOOD FRESH?
HA HA HA, WHY OF COURSE!
5-16
© 1984 United Feature Syndicate, Inc.
THIS IS ONLY YESTERDAY'S NEWSPAPER

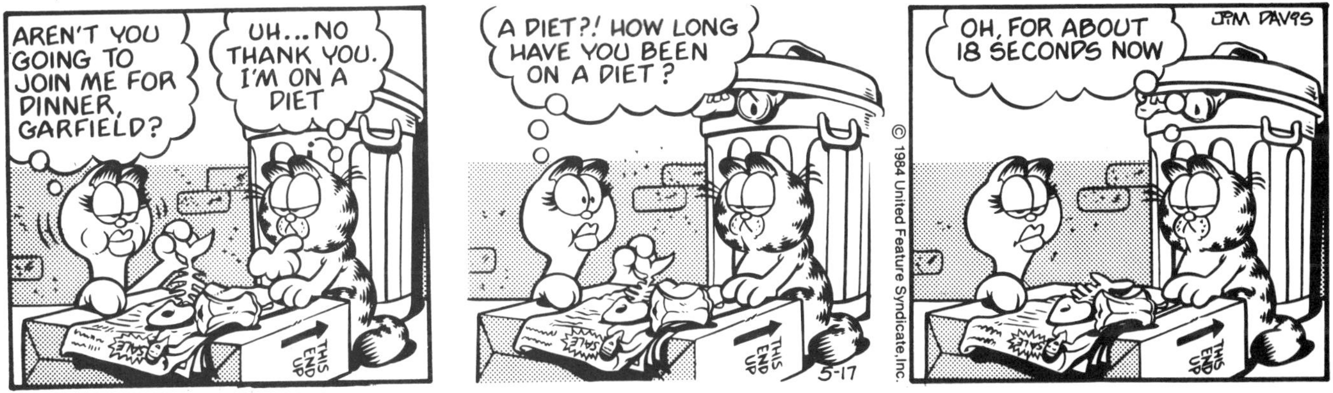
AREN'T YOU GOING TO JOIN ME FOR DINNER, GARFIELD?
UH... NO THANK YOU. I'M ON A DIET
SALE
THIS END UP
A DIET?! HOW LONG HAVE YOU BEEN ON A DIET?
5-17
© 1984 United Feature Syndicate, Inc.
JIM DAVIS
OH, FOR ABOUT 18 SECONDS NOW

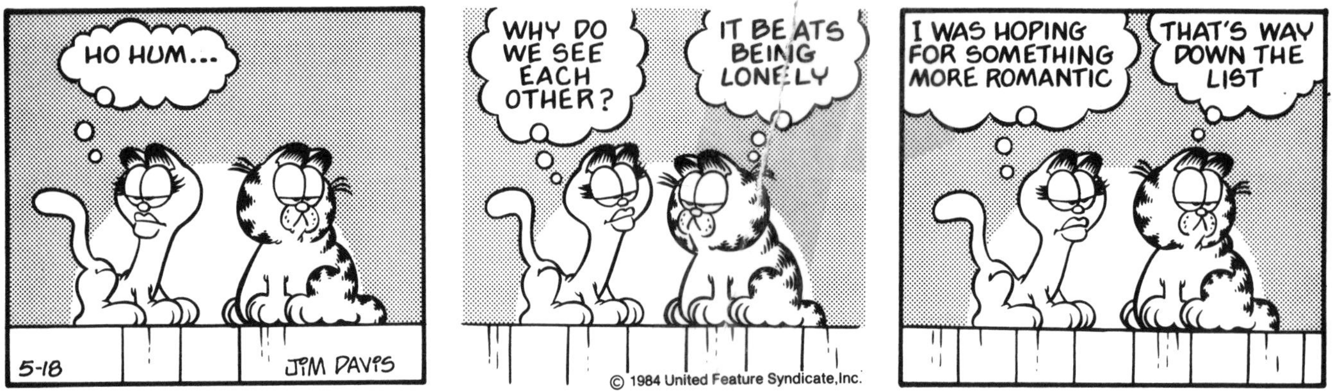
HO HUM...
WHY DO WE SEE EACH OTHER?
IT BEATS BEING LONELY
I WAS HOPING FOR SOMETHING MORE ROMANTIC
THAT'S WAY DOWN THE LIST
5-18
JIM DAVIS
© 1984 United Feature Syndicate,Inc.

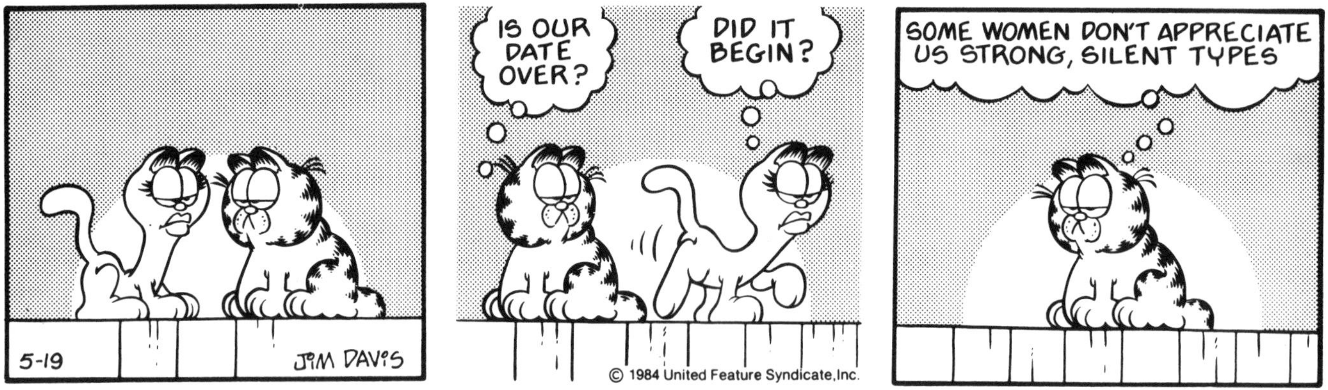
IS OUR DATE OVER?
DID IT BEGIN?
SOME WOMEN DON'T APPRECIATE US STRONG, SILENT TYPES
5-19
JIM DAVIS
© 1984 United Feature Syndicate,Inc.

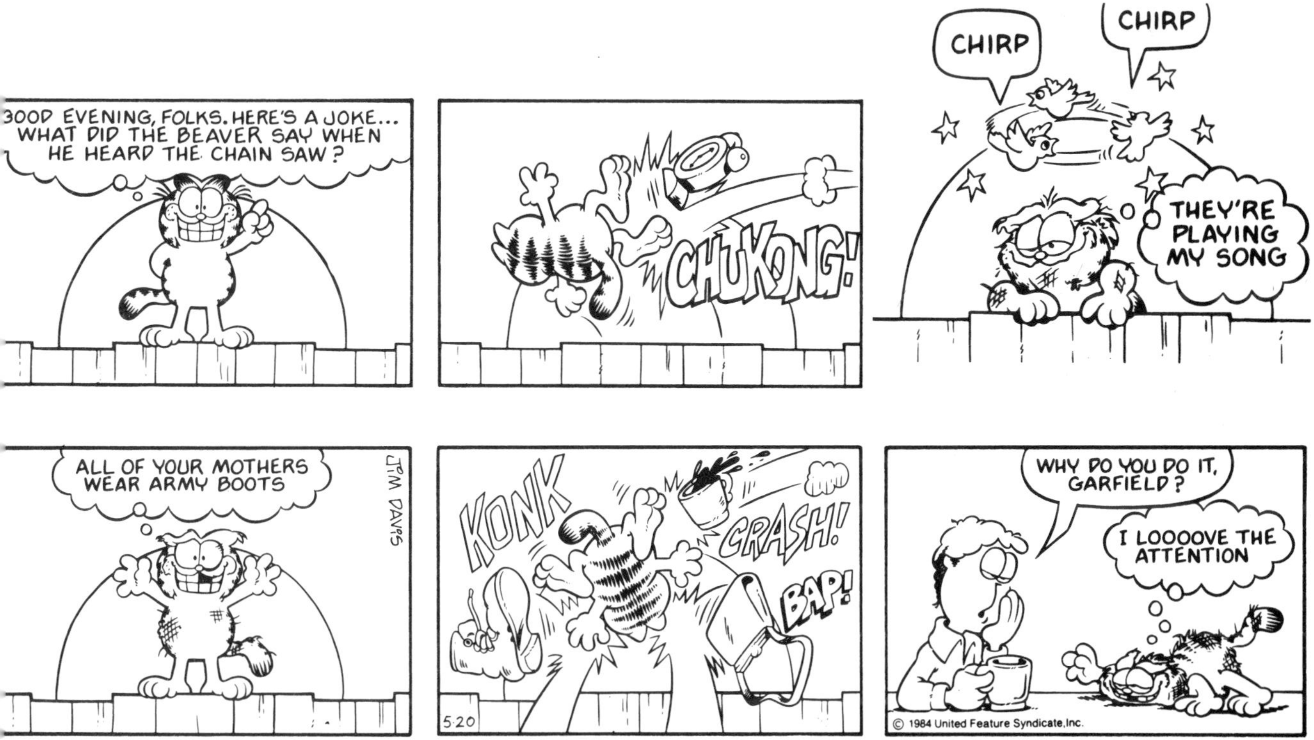
GOOD EVENING, FOLKS. HERE'S A JOKE... WHAT DID THE BEAVER SAY WHEN HE HEARD THE CHAIN SAW?
CHUKONG!
CHIRP
CHIRP
THEY'RE PLAYING MY SONG
ALL OF YOUR MOTHERS WEAR ARMY BOOTS
JIM DAVIS
KONK
CRASH!
BAP!
5-20
WHY DO YOU DO IT, GARFIELD?
I LOOOOVE THE ATTENTION
© 1984 United Feature Syndicate, Inc.

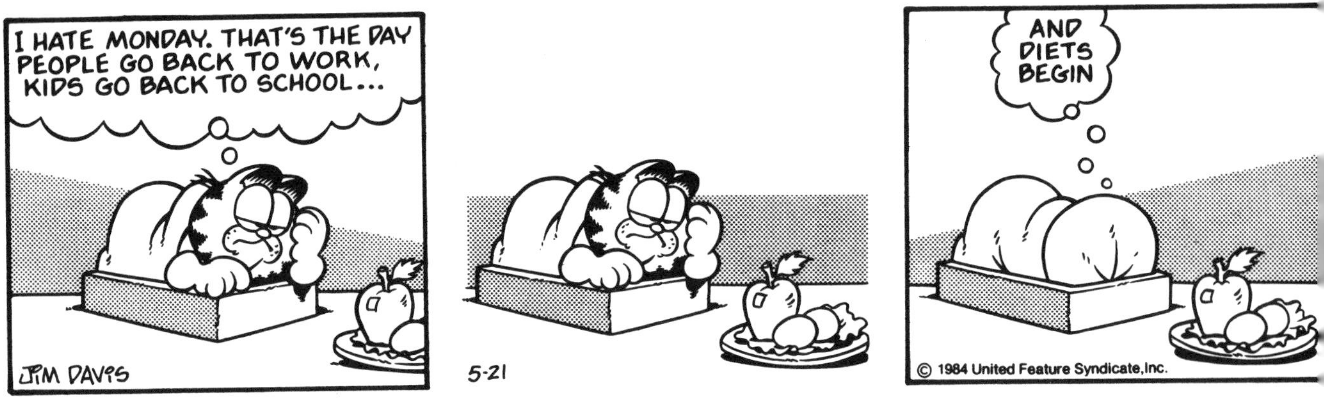
I HATE MONDAY. THAT'S THE DAY PEOPLE GO BACK TO WORK, KIDS GO BACK TO SCHOOL...
JIM DAVIS
5-21
AND DIETS BEGIN
© 1984 United Feature Syndicate, Inc.

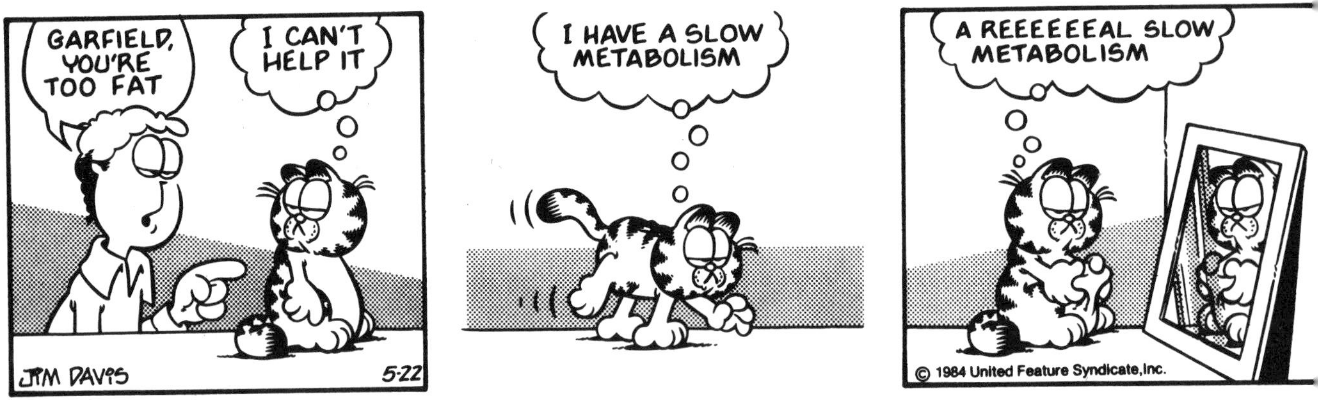
GARFIELD, YOU'RE TOO FAT
I CAN'T HELP IT
JIM DAVIS
5-22
I HAVE A SLOW METABOLISM
A REEEEEEEAL SLOW METABOLISM
© 1984 United Feature Syndicate, Inc.

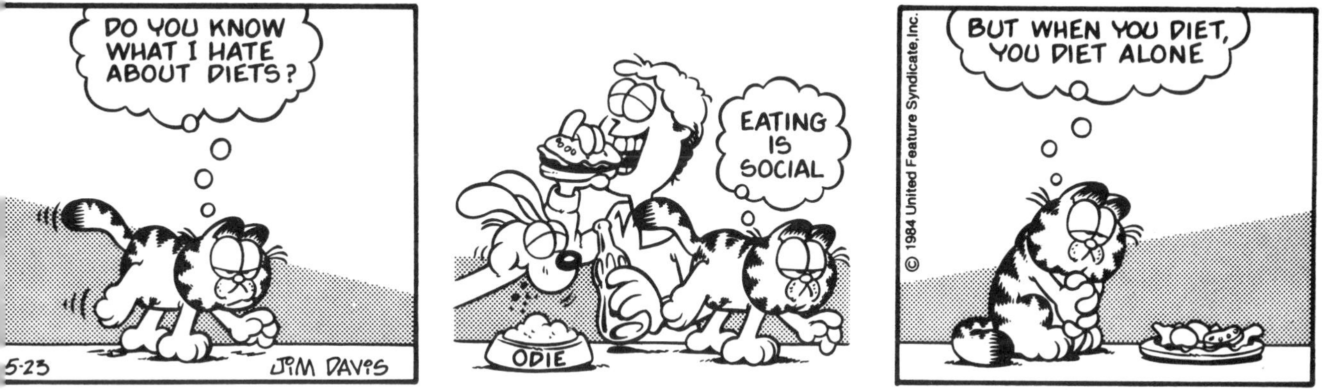
DO YOU KNOW WHAT I HATE ABOUT DIETS?
5-23
JIM DAVIS
ODIE
EATING IS SOCIAL
© 1984 United Feature Syndicate, Inc.
BUT WHEN YOU DIET, YOU DIET ALONE

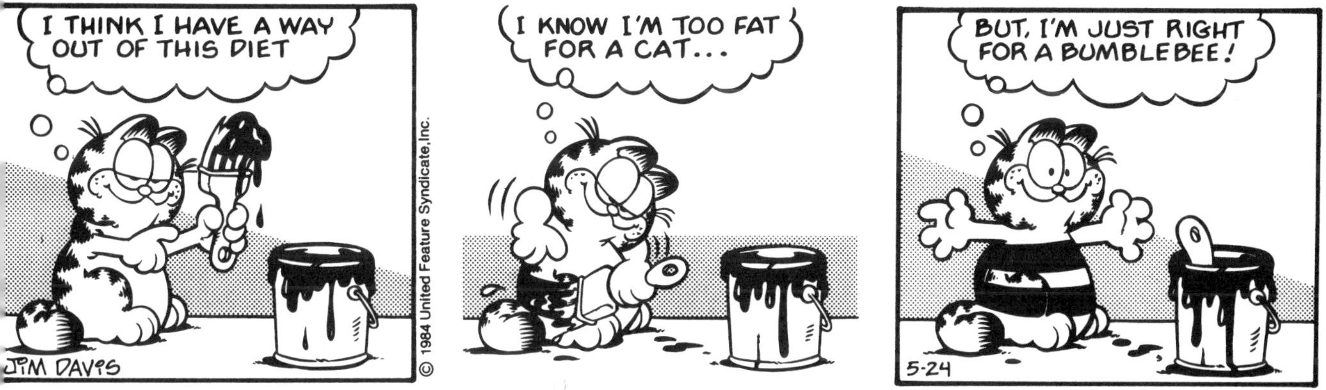
I THINK I HAVE A WAY OUT OF THIS DIET
JIM DAVIS
© 1984 United Feature Syndicate, Inc.
I KNOW I'M TOO FAT FOR A CAT...
BUT, I'M JUST RIGHT FOR A BUMBLEBEE!
5-24

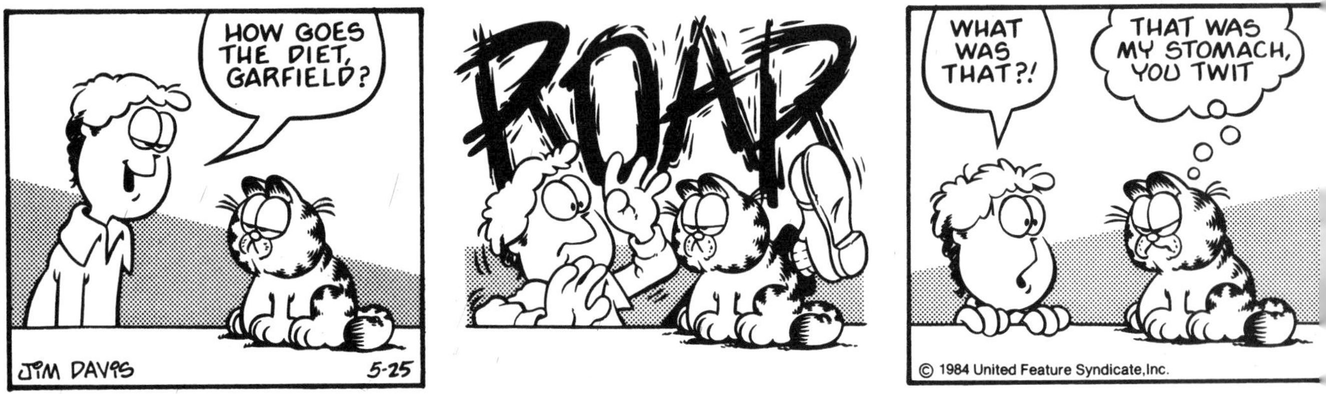
HOW GOES THE DIET, GARFIELD?
JIM DAVIS
5-25
ROAR
WHAT WAS THAT?!
THAT WAS MY STOMACH, YOU TWIT
© 1984 United Feature Syndicate, Inc.

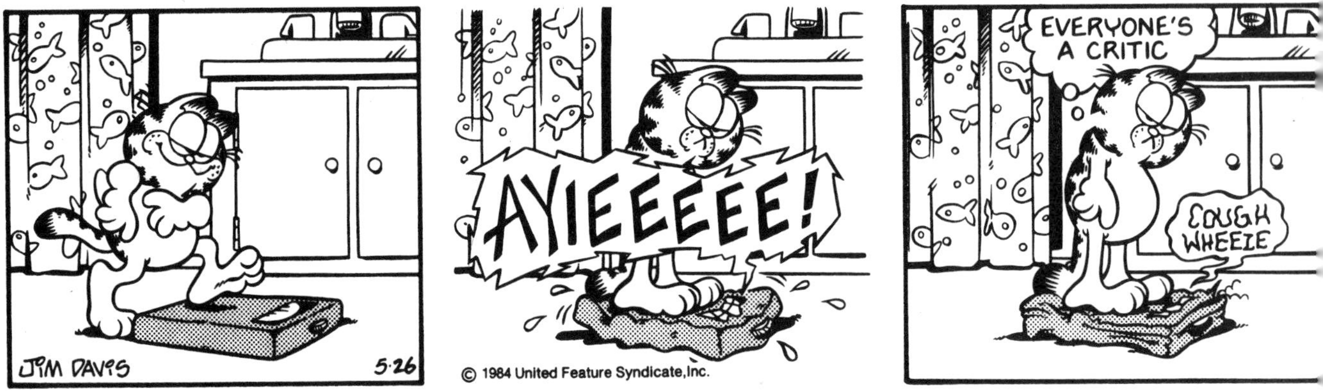
JIM DAVIS
5-26
AYIEEEEEE!
© 1984 United Feature Syndicate, Inc.
EVERYONE'S A CRITIC
COUGH WHEEZE

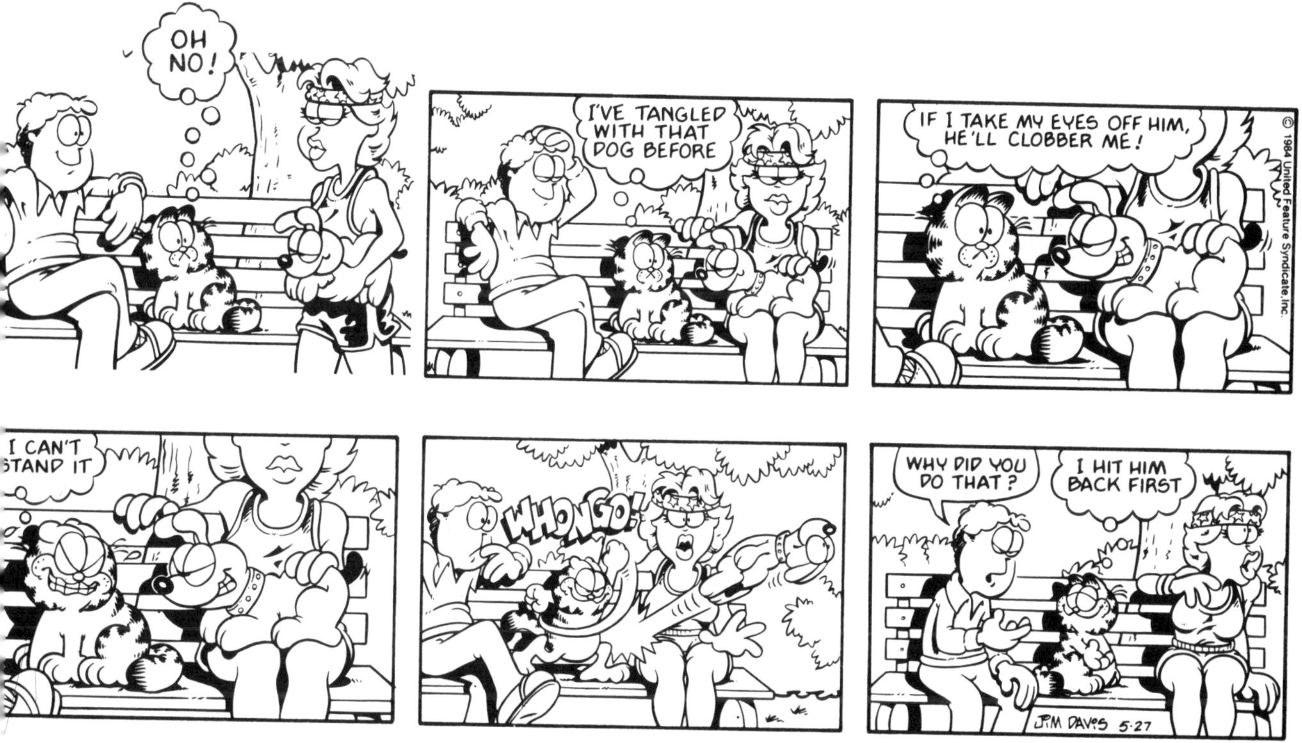
OH NO!
I'VE TANGLED WITH THAT DOG BEFORE
IF I TAKE MY EYES OFF HIM, HE'LL CLOBBER ME!
© 1984 United Feature Syndicate, Inc.
I CAN'T STAND IT
WHONGO!
WHY DID YOU DO THAT?
I HIT HIM BACK FIRST
JIM DAVIS 5-27

# Garfield's Loves & Hates

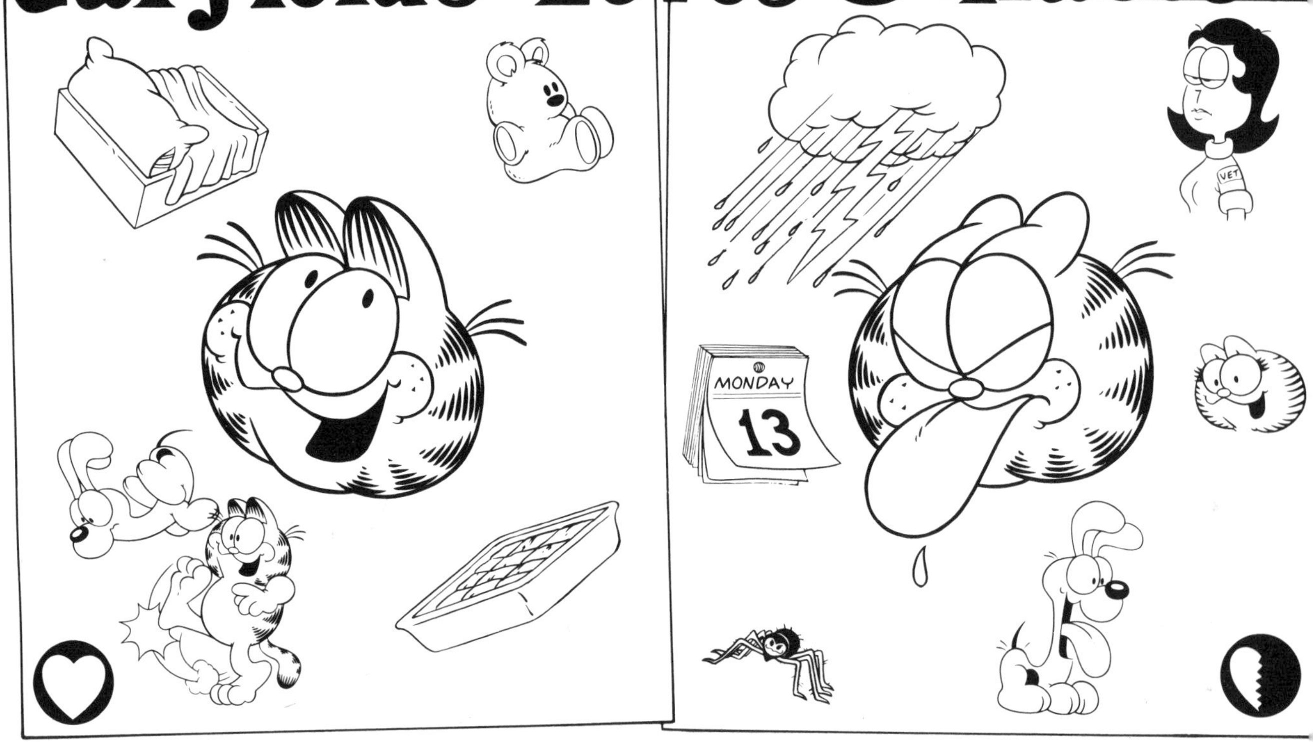
VET
MONDAY
13